D1159863

1-24-55

The University of Kentucky
Origins & Early Years

JOHN B. BOWMAN
Regent of Kentucky University

The University of Kentucky

Origins and Early Years

By

JAMES F. HOPKINS

University of Kentucky Press

LEXINGTON

PRINTED AT THE
UNIVERSITY OF KENTUCKY BY
THE KERNEL PRESS AND BOUND BY
THE KINGSPORT PRESS, INC.

To Bernice

Preface

THE UNIVERSITY OF KENTUCKY IS A YOUNG INSTITUTION in comparison with most of the state universities east of the Mississippi River. It is young, moreover, in comparison with Kentucky herself, the second state to join the original thirteen in the Federal Union. Founded at the end of the Civil War under provisions of the Morrill Land Grant Act, it represents the second effort on the part of Kentucky to launch a public institution of higher learning. The first state university was Transylvania, which was not properly supported by the commonwealth and eventually was allowed to pass from public control. The story of the present university is not a continuation of the history of Transylvania, although there is a connection between the two. Believing that an understanding of the struggles and frustrations of the Agricultural and Mechanical College (forerunner of the University of Kentucky) cannot be gained without some knowledge of the reasons for the failure of the first university, I have included by way of introducing the main story a review of the history of Transylvania.

In undertaking to give an account of the origins and early development of the University of Kentucky, this volume covers the most trying period in the history of the institution. The story is largely one of disappointment, of denominational bickering, and of poverty; but it is also a story of devotion to an ideal, of determination, of slow progress, and of eventual success. The account is carried through the Patterson administration, past the transformation of the Agricultural and Mechanical College into the State University. Patterson was connected with the school from its beginning, and his resignation marks the end of an era in its history.

The modern period, which began soon afterward, is properly the subject of another volume.

The present volume can claim to be noteworthy in at least one respect: it is the first published history of the university. Manuscript accounts by Professor George Roberts and the late Professor Merry L. Pence are valuable to the historian largely because both men wrote with knowledge and understanding based on long association with the institution. Professor Ezra L Gillis' pamphlet, *The University of Kentucky: Its History and Development . . .* (rev. ed., Lexington, 1950), presents the history of the school in a series of statistical charts. It is indispensable to the researcher and helpful to anyone who seeks knowledge of the university's past. Mabel Hardy Pollitt, *A Biography of James Kennedy Patterson . . .* (Louisville, 1925) and an unpublished biography of the same subject by William B. Smith also give much information on the history of the university. Briefer accounts are included in various histories of the state and histories of education in Kentucky.

In the preparation of this volume I have become indebted to a large number of people. The work was begun by researchers employed by the Writers' Project of the W.P.A. I wish to express my appreciation especially to Mrs. Ruth Smith, Mrs. Minnie Merritt, Mrs. Mary Scully, Miss Virgalene Snedegar, and Miss Sarah Chorn for their careful labors in gathering, typing, and filing a vast quantity of source material on the history of the university.

I am most grateful to Professor Ezra L Gillis and Miss Mary Hester Cooper of the Bureau of Source Materials in Higher Education, without whose help and inexhaustible files this book could hardly have been written. Professor Gillis has given freely of his profound knowledge of the university, and Miss Cooper has proven many times that she has a tremendous amount of information at her fingertips.

To President Herman Lee Donovan, President Emeritus

Frank L. McVey, and Professor Thomas D. Clark I wish to express my thanks for their interest and encouragement. Professor J. Merton England has given freely of his time and has been most helpful in reading the manuscript and offering suggestions for improvement The staffs of the Lexington Public Library and the libraries of Transylvania College and the University of Kentucky were unfailingly courteous and generous in their assistance. I am grateful to the University of Kentucky Press Committee for its approval of this work for publication.

I am especially indebted to Messrs. Bruce F. Denbo and Kenneth W. Elliott of the University of Kentucky Press for their invaluable work in transforming my manuscript into the finished product.

It is my hope that this volume will contribute in some measure to an appreciation of the founders of the University of Kentucky and to a better understanding of the school and the history of the state.

James F. Hopkins

Lexington
April 3, 1951

Contents

Illustrations

Chapter One

The First University's Struggle for Existence

THE UNIVERSITY OF KENTUCKY TRACES ITS BEGINNING to 1865, to the Agricultural and Mechanical College founded in that year under the terms of the Morrill Act. By that time Kentucky had been a member of the Union for nearly three quarters of a century and had already established, early in her history, a quasi-state university which was permitted to languish for want of support. Early Kentuckians were not indifferent to educational needs, although even in the face of the democratizing influence of the frontier they did not see that publicly supported schools should be available to children of all classes on an equal basis. Instead, they relied upon private academies to provide an education for those who were able to pay for it, expecting that from the ranks of the wealthier and more cultured families would come the future leaders of the state. Later they built schools which were more like public institutions but which depended for their existence upon the income from land endowments rather than upon taxes. Beginning in 1849, on four occasions the people themselves voted approval of tax levies for the support of schools, but the General Assembly was reluctant to follow the initiative in this regard. Not until 1904 did the legislature without a specific mandate levy a general tax to support a public school system, although the constitution of 1891 had provided for such legislation.

Primitive schools were established in the pioneer forts in Kentucky almost from the beginning of settlement, the first being taught at Fort Harrod by Mrs. William Coomes as early as 1775 or 1776. Less crude than the fort or neighborhood schools were the private academies, the earliest of which was established in Lexington by John Filson, the first Kentucky historian, in the early 1780's. Easterners and Europeans came to Kentucky to open various seminaries, academies, dancing schools, fencing schools, "female academies," and other institutions where one might learn a smattering of languages, bookkeeping, surveying, or even navigation. Kentuckians of that day accepted the fact that their schools were privately owned and operated and came to believe that education was not a matter of concern for the state. Neither the constitution of 1792, adopted when Kentucky became a state, nor that of 1799 made mention of public education.[1]

Grants of land by Virginia to a seminary of learning in Kentucky as early as 1780 established a precedent for a type of state support of education, a precedent which the Kentucky legislature did not follow until eighteen years later. Beginning in 1798 land grants were made to several academies, and a scheme was worked out whereby a school in each county would prepare students for further work in the state university. No provision was made for elementary education, and no consideration was given to the needs of students who would not continue their education at an institution of higher learning. The plan was not completely carried out, for some of the counties did not establish academies. In 1815 the state gave up responsibility for these schools, and by 1821 it was recognized that the whole plan had failed.

Governor Gabriel Slaughter in 1816 stressed the need for

[1] Accounts of the progress of education in Kentucky may be found in: Frank L. McVey, *The Gates Open Slowly: A History of Education in Kentucky* (Lexington, 1949); Thomas D. Clark, *A History of Kentucky* (2nd ed., Lexington, 1950); Alvin F. Lewis, *History of Higher Education in Kentucky* (Washington, 1899); Barksdale Hamlett, *History of Education in Kentucky* (Frankfort, 1914); Merle Curti, *The Social Ideas of American Educators* (New York, 1935); Charles F. Thwing, *A History of Higher Education in America* (New York, 1906); and Niels Henry Sonne, *Liberal Kentucky, 1780-1828* (New York, 1939).

a system of public schools, but the legislature did not respond to his plea. Instead, in 1821 the state established a "literary fund," made up of profits from the Bank of Kentucky, which was to be used to support a system of general education. At the same time a legislative committee was established to make a study of educational organizations and to outline a plan for common schools suited to the condition of the state. In the next year the committee submitted an outstanding report, which was not acted on by the legislature. The literary fund was not managed to the best interest of the schools, the Bank of Kentucky closed a few years later, and so this method of supporting education proved a miserable failure.

The distribution in 1836 of the United States Treasury surplus to the states with the provision that the money be used for education and internal improvements paved the way for the creation of a modern school system in Kentucky. The legislature set aside $1,000,000 of the federal funds to found and maintain a system of public education, although the intervention of the panic of 1837 stopped the payment of sums allotted to Kentucky, causing the school fund to be smaller than had been anticipated. Nevertheless, in 1838 the legislature provided that $850,000 should be devoted to schools, and in the same act it established the fundamental plan of the present school system. The constitutional convention of 1849 for the first time wrote provisions for "sustaining a system of Common Schools" into the constitution. Thereafter, though schools still faced tremendous problems, Kentucky was committed to the principle of state support of elementary education.

Meanwhile, early Kentucky legislatures had shown no more willingness to give continuous direct aid to higher educational institutions than to the elementary schools. Because of the failure of the land grants to create a permanent system of state academies and a state university, college education became in time almost a monopoly of religious denominations. Church control of higher education was not a new concept, of course, for it was traditional in Europe even before the New World was discovered, and it was the general practice in America during the colonial period. When the pioneers moved across the mountains to establish their homes in the Kentucky wilderness, they knew nothing of state-supported, state-controlled educational institutions. On the other hand, they were familiar with church-controlled schools on the seaboard, and they were willing as a matter of course for the churches to take the lead in educational matters in the West.

Among the religious denominations most active in pioneer Kentucky, only the Presbyterians were interested to any appreciable extent in education. They recognized even at that early date the need for a literate clergy, able to read and to reason, while Baptists and Methodists still depended on preachers who frequently held learning in contempt and who, relying on timely inspiration from above, could rouse a backwoods congregation to religious frenzy. The Presbyterians took the lead in establishing schools in Kentucky, and they demanded that the principles taught in these institutions be acceptable to them, no matter if financial support was provided by the state.

After taking the lead in educational matters, the Presbyterians soon found their dominance challenged, not to any great extent by rival sects, but by independent-minded men who had imbibed freely of the revolutionary spirit which prevailed in America and western Europe in the late eighteenth and early nineteenth centuries. Rebellion against established authority, belief in the principle of separation of church and state, devotion to liberty, exaltation of the individual, and acceptance of equalitarian doctrines led many Kentuckians to reject orthodox religious beliefs. The French influence was strong among Kentucky political and social leaders, who also learned much from Tom Paine, Thomas Jefferson, and other freethinkers in America and England. To the Presbyterians, the independents in the West were deists, Arians, or downright infidels, and in some instances the characterization fitted the facts.

In Kentucky, as in other states where the same influences were at work, the revolutionary spirit brought grave dissatisfaction with denominational control of schools. In some cases—Georgia and the two Carolinas, for example—a new type of state-supported institution was chartered; in others, efforts were made to remove the schools from the hands of the sectarians. The challenge to denominational control of education failed in Kentucky, largely because the Presbyterians were unbending in their determination and because the freethinkers comprised only a small segment of the population of the state. The challengers enjoyed a brief success, however, and erected a school which became for a few years the pride of the West, comparing favorably with older institutions on the seaboard.

Having made a noble beginning, Kentucky might today boast a state university many years older than the commonwealth itself, if events had taken a different turn. More than seventy-five years before the establishment of the college which evolved slowly and painfully into the present university, Kentucky pioneers placed in operation their first institution of higher learning, which shortly became in fact if not in name the state university. But for financial troubles and for involvement in squabbles which now seem almost fantastic, that earlier institution might still be the apex of the state system of public schools. But it would not be the present University of Kentucky, nor would it be located on the present campus. Nor, in all probability, would it bear the name of the present institution, for doubtless it would have retained its original title, Transylvania University. The connection between the two is tenuous and indirect, but in relating the story of the modern University of Kentucky, old Transylvania cannot be ignored.

The first step toward the establishment of a state-supported college in Kentucky occurred during the Revolutionary War when "Kentucke" was a part of Virginia. As early as 1776 Thomas Jefferson introduced in the Virginia General Assembly a bill providing for public schools and for the establishment of a state university. His program did not materialize at that time, but the movement for higher education soon bore its first fruits on the frontier. Action was taken in 1780 through the efforts of Colonel John Todd, one of two representatives sent in that year from Kentucky to the General Assembly, and of his uncle the Rev. John Todd, a Virginia Presbyterian minister who was deeply interested in the West because of his many friends and relatives who resided there.[2]

In May, 1780, the Virginia legislative body, in order "to promote and encourage every design which may tend to the improvement of the mind and the diffusion of useful knowledge, even among its remote citizens, whose situation a barbarous neighborhood and a savage intercourse might otherwise render unfriendly to science," donated 8,000 acres of escheated lands, formerly the property of loyal British subjects and lying within Kentucky County, "for the purpose of a publick school, or seminary of learning, to be erected within the said county as soon as the circumstances of the county and the state of its funds will admit."[3] Colonel Todd and

[2] Virginia's part in the founding and development of Transylvania Seminary is described in Virginius Dabney, *Liberalism in the South* (Chapel Hill, 1932); John S. Patton, *Jefferson, Cabell and the University of Virginia* (New York, 1906); and, William H. Foote, *Sketches of Virginia, Historical and Biographical* (2nd ser., 2nd ed., Philadelphia, 1856).

[3] This act is reprinted in William W. Hening (comp.), *The Statutes at Large: Being a Collection of All the Laws of Virginia, from the First Session of the Legislature in the Year 1619* (13 vols., Richmond, 1809-1823), X, 287-88, which contains all the laws pertaining to Transylvania passed up to 1792.

twelve other notable residents of the West were made trustees of this endowment.

Two months later an inquiry determined the eligibility for confiscation of the lands mentioned in the act. Among the jurymen who decided the case were the pioneer Daniel Boone and John Bowman, grandfather of the founder of the University of Kentucky.[4] No further action appears to have been taken for approximately three years, but immediate results were, perhaps, not anticipated. The frontier was embroiled in a war which claimed the lives of three of the trustees, and the act concerning escheated lands had declared that the donation "might at a *future* day be a valuable fund for the maintenance and education of youth."[5] Nameless, homeless, and altogether without substance, the new "publick school or seminary of learning" was as yet no more than a dream.

Nevertheless, the dream was not abandoned, and the return of peace to the frontier enabled Kentuckians once more to devote some attention to the need for educational facilities. A majority of the surviving members of the Board of Trustees convened under the act of 1780, only to discover themselves embarrassed by the ambiguities of the original law, which failed to state "whether a majority of the Trustees are sufficient to act," how vacancies on the board were to be filled, and whether or not the trustees had power to receive donations from individuals in support of the school. A petition to the Virginia General Assembly asked for clarification of these points.[6]

Early in May, 1783, the legislature responded with an act

[4] Indenture of Inquisition of Escheat of Lands of Pollison, Collins, and McKenzie, in Deed Book "F," Fayette County, 378; Indenture of Inquisition of Escheat of Lands of John Connolly and Alexander McKee, *ibid.*, 380.

[5] Italics inserted.

[6] This and later petitions are reprinted in James R. Robertson (comp.), *Petitions of the Early Inhabitants of Kentucky to the General Assembly of Virginia, 1769 to 1792* (Filson Club *Publications*, No. 27, Louisville, 1914).

that gave a name to the projected school, which actually came into existence nearly two years later. Twenty-five men, many of whom are outstanding in the history of Kentucky, were named to a self-perpetuating "body corporate and politic to be known by the name of the trustees of the Transylvania seminary" and were given all the "powers and privileges that are enjoyed by visitors and governors of any college or university within this state not herein limited or otherwise directed." In them was vested the original grant of escheated lands, as well as an additional appropriation of 12,000 acres "that now are or hereafter may become escheatable to the commonwealth," with the provision that the seminary should be allowed to hold 20,000 acres permanently free from public taxes.

Although called a seminary, the proposed institution, in line with a widespread practice of the time, was empowered to give the degrees of Bachelor and Master of Arts as well as honorary degrees. Twice each year the trustees were required to witness examinations at the school in order to determine the "fidelity of the teachers, and the diligence of their pupils," and always at the end of the second semi-annual tests degrees were to be conferred. The trustees were authorized to select a site for the school and to choose its personnel, who should continue in office during good behavior, and who, like the students, were exempt from militia duty. The trustees, the President, and all officers and instructors were required to take the oath: "I, A. B. do swear (or affirm) that I will, to the best of my skill and judgment, faithfully and truly discharge the duties of a trustee [or other officer as the case might be], required of me by an act, intituled 'An act to amend an act, intituled, an act to vest certain escheated lands in the county of Kentucky in trustees for a public school' without favor, affection or partiality. So help me God."[7]

[7] Hening, *Statutes*, XI, 282-87.

In conformity with the act of 1783 the first meeting of the new Board of Trustees convened at Crow's Station near Danville on November 10, 1783, with thirteen members, barely a quorum, present.[8] Soon after having chosen the Rev. David Rice as chairman, the board undertook to examine the status of its trust. Its primary concern was, of course, to place the seminary in operation as soon as possible, but an insurmountable obstacle prevented immediate action: the necessary funds were not available. Land comprised the school's sole endowment, and good land it was, yet at that period in Kentucky uncleared land was cheap and unproductive of returns. The urgent need was cash, which the board sought unsuccessfully to obtain by means of public subscriptions. The outlook was most discouraging, and on numerous occasions it proved impossible even to assemble a sufficient number of trustees for the transaction of business.

The board sought to fulfill its duties, nevertheless, and was eventually able to show some evidence of progress. Encouragement came early in 1784 with the news that one of the oldest friends of learning in the West, the Rev. John Todd of Louisa County, Virginia, had presented to Transylvania a "library and philosophical apparatus," valuable equipment for the beginning of a school, which unfortunately was not transported to Kentucky until 1789. Meanwhile, on November 4, 1784, a decision was reached to create a grammar school near Danville "at or near the Rev. Mr. Rice's present dwelling," and a committee was appointed to select a teacher. At long last, the "publick school or seminary

[8] The remainder of this chapter is based largely on the Records of the Proceedings of the Board of Trustees for the Transylvania Seminary for the dates indicated. Additional material is found in William H. Whitsitt, *Life and Times of Judge Caleb Wallace, Some Time a Justice of the Court of Appeals of the State of Kentucky* (Filson Club *Publications*, No. 4, Louisville, 1888); Robert Peter, "A Sketch of the History of Kentucky University and of Transylvania University . . ." (typewritten manuscript in Bureau of Source Materials in Higher Education, University of Kentucky Library); and the files of the Lexington *Kentucky Gazette.*

of learning" was to be put in operation. Three months later, on February 1, 1785, the first session of Transylvania Seminary, taught by the Rev. James Mitchell, began in the "dogtrot" home of the Rev. David Rice. Mitchell was first employed for three months, later induced to remain six months longer, and finally appointed for one additional year at a salary of £120, payable quarterly.

The trustees appear to have hoped that means for the payment of Mitchell's salary might be derived from the tuition of four pistoles a year paid by each student at the rate of one pistole (about four dollars) at the beginning of each quarter, but these funds proved insufficient. Since private donations also had not materialized, the trustees resolved to apply for further aid from the state. A petition presented to the Virginia General Assembly brought about the passage of an act appropriating one sixth of the surveyors' fees in the District of Kentucky to the use of Transylvania Seminary. The revenue from this source was disappointingly small, however, despite subsequent acts designed to strengthen the original statute, and in 1802 the Kentucky legislature abolished entirely this method of aiding its university.[9]

Keeping the school in continuous operation during the early period of its life was an impossibility. James Mitchell, who had married a daughter of the Rev. David Rice, returned to Virginia early in 1786, leaving the institution without a teacher, apparently for about three years. During this time the trustees, despairing perhaps of local aid in Danville or possibly considering Lexington a more convenient site, decided in 1788 to move the seminary to the latter town. Once more optimistic, they elected Elias Jones to serve as "professor" and voted him a salary of one hundred pounds a year. At the same time they provided that a "grammar master" should be employed as soon as twenty students ap-

[9] Kentucky's early laws are collected in William Littell (comp.), *The Statute Law of Kentucky* . . . (5 vols., Frankfort, 1809-1819).

peared and that an "usher" should be added to the staff if the enrollment should exceed forty.

Neither funds nor students materialized as rapidly as had been expected, and Jones probably never entered into his duties. At any rate, in April, 1789, the trustees rescinded their former order for his appointment, decided not to employ a professor at that time, and chose a committee to select a grammar master to conduct the school. A local newspaper advertisement brought a response from Isaac Wilson, master of the Lexington Grammar School. He was employed to begin teaching June 1, 1789, "at the Public School-house near Lexington." During Wilson's administration the institution, with a pardonable show of pride, held its first commencement in April, 1790; but in the next year the enrollment of students dropped from thirteen to five, and Wilson was dismissed. The Rev. James Moore then became grammar master, and during his tenure of office the seminary was established on a firmer basis.

Before 1793 the school could not boast even a permanent location. After having been moved to Lexington, it was conducted at first in the public schoolhouse, but this arrangement was only temporary. Late in 1790 the trustees received legislative permission "to raise by one or more lotteries, a sum not exceeding five hundred pounds, for the purpose of erecting an academy." The scheme was put into effect, but apparently it was financially unsuccessful, since in 1791 an effort was made to rent a schoolhouse and in 1792 James Moore taught classes in his own home. Under such circumstances there was a distinct possibility that the school might be moved to another town, an eventuality which Lexingtonians wished to prevent. Accordingly, a group of prominent men of the town in 1792 founded the Transylvania Land Company, which purchased three acres of land on the present site of Gratz Park, upon which stood an unfinished two-story building. The company then offered the whole property to Transylvania Seminary upon the condition that the school be permanently located in Lexington. In April, 1793, the Board of Trustees accepted this generous gift, the first of many donations of a similar nature which have been made to educational institutions by the people of Lexington, and Transylvania Seminary at last found a home.

Students now began enrolling in increasing numbers. It was found necessary to employ two assistants to the grammar master, and by December the authorities were able to insert a modest advertisement in the *Kentucky Gazette:*

> THE TRANSYLVANIA SEMINARY,
>
> Is now well supplied with teachers of Natural and Moral Philosophy, and the Mathematics, and of the learned languages.
>
> An English teacher is also introduced, into the College who teaches, Reading, Writing, Arithmetic, and the English Grammar. In this School great attention is paid to Reading; and that not confined to prose authors only, but to the Poets.
>
> This Seminary is the best seat of education on the Western waters; and it is to be hoped, the time is not far distant when even prejudice itself will not think it necessary to transport our Youths to the Atlantic States, to complete their education.
>
> Good boarding may be had in Lexington and its vicinity, on very moderate terms.

Smooth sailing apparently lay ahead, but new troubles soon arose, perhaps from an unexpected quarter.

Beginning in 1794 Transylvania experienced for the first time the sectarian bitterness which in one form or another was destined to bedevil it until long after the Civil War. The initial conflict arose when the Presbyterians not only withdrew their support from Transylvania Seminary, after the Board of Trustees had selected a head for the school outside the ranks of that denomination, but also established a rival institution. The choice of a man who was not a

Presbyterian might not in itself have caused a division, but the new appointee sinned in holding views far in advance of those professed by the leaders of the church on the frontier. The moral code of the West might be lax in some respects, but any departure from orthodox theology was not to be countenanced.

Transylvania Seminary was a state institution, and yet it was an institution in which the Presbyterians considered themselves peculiarly interested.[10] Their position was not without justification, for their efforts had brought about the establishment of the school and the first decade of its existence had passed under their watchful guidance. John Todd and his uncle the Rev. John Todd were Presbyterians, as were the Rev. David Rice, the Rev. James Mitchell, the Rev. James Moore, Judge Caleb Wallace, and many more of those who founded Transylvania and tenderly cared for it during its infancy. At first they dominated the Board of Trustees, but in the course of time they became a minority in spite of the fact that the board was self-perpetuating, electing whom it pleased to membership. Having lost control of policies, they did not hesitate to withdraw altogether when the majority of the trustees decided a matter of importance in a manner contrary to their wishes. Nor, it must be said, did they hesitate to return when the cause of the dispute had been eliminated.

The Rev. James Moore continued by annual appointment to serve as head of Transylvania Seminary until 1794, when the trustees did not re-elect him. Instead, by a vote of eight members to five on February 5 of that year they chose a newcomer to the West, the Rev. Harry Toulmin, a Unitarian

[10] The Presbyterian connection with Transylvania Seminary is discussed in Robert Davidson, *History of the Presbyterian Church in the State of Kentucky, with a Preliminary Sketch of the Churches in the Valley of Virginia . . .* (New York, 1847); and William W. Sweet, *Religion on the American Frontier,* Vol. II, *The Presbyterians, 1783-1840: A Collection of Source Materials* (New York, 1936).

minister and a man of broad views and outstanding ability who had been recommended for the post by Thomas Jefferson, or James Madison, or perhaps by both. At the same time the title "grammar master" was discarded in favor of "President," and Toulmin became the first to serve in that capacity.

The Presbyterian members of the board looked upon Toulmin, "a known disciple" of Joseph Priestley and "an apostate Baptist preacher," as a deist if not an infidel, and they refused to patronize a school which was under his direction. They endeavored to block his appointment by protesting that the election was illegal, but it was reaffirmed on April 7, 1794, and he took the oath of office on June 30 of that year. Shortly after their defeat in this matter the Presbyterian members of the Board of Trustees resigned. The Presbyterians withdrew their support from the seminary, and they carried out an earlier threat to set up a rival institution under their own control. At a session of the Transylvania Presbytery at Woodford Church, April 24, 1794, definite plans were agreed upon and the work of founding a school began. Although the institution was born as a result of a sectarian dispute and founded along strict denominational lines, its program and its operation were surprisingly liberal.

The Presbytery decided to establish first a grammar school, and later, "as soon as may be thought convenient," a public seminary was to be founded. It was decided to raise funds for buildings through public subscriptions, both locally and elsewhere, and to purchase a library and scientific apparatus. The seminary was to be always under the direction of a minister of the gospel, although "no endeavor shall be used by the president or other teachers to influence the mind of any student to change his religious tenets or embrace those of a different denomination any further than is consistent with the general belief of the gospel system & the practice of vital piety." The decisions of the Presbytery were written into a charter, granted by the legislature on December 12, 1794, which also authorized the Board of Trustees to fill vacancies within its own ranks and provided that the institution be called "Kentucky Academy."

Although its supporters worked zealously to establish the school, their progress was slow, and when the academy did come into existence its life was brief. The grammar school, which had been the first consideration, was put in operation immediately at Pisgah Church under the supervision of Andrew Steele, who was succeeded in 1796 by James Moore, formerly head of Transylvania Seminary. The trustees of the academy in a meeting held on March 10, 1796, resolved that "a permanent seat for the Kentucky Academy ought to be fixed on as soon as possible." Since funds were not available to purchase a site, a committee was appointed "to receive proposals from those, who may think proper to contribute land for that purpose, and to give assistance in erecting buildings thereon, for the use of the Seminary, or otherwise to increase the funds," but the school was finally located at Pisgah.

A scheme for obtaining private subscriptions had already been formulated, and gifts of land as well as money and agricultural produce were received. Donations came not only from Kentucky, but also from the seaboard states where two ministers, David Rice and James Blythe, had been sent to solicit funds. George Washington, John Adams, Robert Morris, and Aaron Burr were among the prominent men of the day who loosened their purse strings to aid the frontier school. The nucleus of a library was also obtained, partly from books collected by Dr. Blythe in the East and partly from a small library which had been placed in the hands of the Rev. David Rice for the use of theological students and which the Presbytery requested him to deliver to the trustees of the academy. The school also received in 1798 a valuable contribution from the Kentucky General Assembly, which endowed it with 6,000 acres of land, although the appropriation was made only a few months before Kentucky Academy ceased to exist.

As a matter of fact, while the campaign for subscriptions was in progress and long before state aid was granted, the trustees of the academy applied for reunion with Transylvania Seminary. The latter institution had suffered from the disaffection of the Presbyterians, although as time passed its condition improved somewhat. Harry Toulmin served as President for less than two years, during which the enrollment declined, after an initial increase, and the trustees failed to give him their wholehearted co-operation. On April 4, 1796, he presented his formal resignation, which was probably based on several factors: his small salary, hostility on the part of a large element of public opinion, and perhaps a legislative act which, had it been enforced, would have hamstrung the Board of Trustees by placing it under the control and supervision of the District Court in the district where the board should meet.

After the departure of Toulmin, the Board of Trustees recalled James Moore, now an Episcopal minister, to the presidency of Transylvania Seminary. Under his leadership, as had happened once before, conditions were improved. Greater efforts were made to augment the income of the institution by leasing the lands belonging to it, and arrangements were made for housing and boarding the students on the campus, an innovation in policy which had been recommended by Toulmin. The library was expanded, partly through purchases and partly by donations from friends of the school, until it contained in 1796 approximately four hundred volumes. Two years later the trustees arranged to employ a French teacher and boasted: "Education may now be had at the Transylvania Seminary on as extensive a plan, and as moderate terms as at any school in the Union. The Greek and Latin languages will be taught there, together with Mathematics, Geography; the Belles Lettres, and every other branch of Learning that makes part of the usual course of Academic Education."[11]

The resignation of Harry Toulmin, whose appointment had been so distasteful to the Presbyterians, removed the cause for their withdrawal from the support of Transylvania Seminary, and they soon indicated a desire for a reconciliation. On June 3, 1796, the trustees of Transylvania met to consider a feeler proposed by the "Kentucky Academy-society" regarding a possible union of the two schools. During the next few months both Boards of Trustees agreed to the consolidation, and with that end in view a memorial to the legislature was drafted. The project was delayed for two years, however, because, according to one explanation, "a few of the Trustees of Transylvania Seminary, were opposed to a union on any principle; believing it a scheme to bring the whole under the control and management of a particular religious sect."[12]

At the time these negotiations were in progress, the Presbyterians were receiving gifts for their own projected institution, and when the plan for union did not materialize they renewed energetically their campaign for funds and lands. Finally, at Pisgah in the fall of 1797 Kentucky Academy, under the direction of Andrew Steele, opened its doors for the reception of students. Early in the next year, as already noted, its endowment was increased by a grant of land by the legislature, which at the same time made similar donations to five other schools. Judge Caleb Wallace was largely instrumental in securing the passage of this act, which he hoped would be a step toward the formation of a real university, a project in which he was intensely interested.

The culmination of Wallace's plan was hastened by action on the part of the trustees of Transylvania Seminary, who

[11] Lexington *Kentucky Gazette,* January 17, 1798.
[12] *Ibid.,* January 18, 1828.

were at that time trying to relieve their financial difficulties and to strengthen their own school by a merger with another institution. They appointed a committee on October 1, 1798, to confer with representatives of Kentucky Academy and Lexington Academy on the subject of a possible union with either or both. On November 2 the committee reported a favorable response from the trustees of the Presbyterian school, and a consolidation of the two academies was agreed upon. The old opposition to the union had not disappeared, but it was pushed into the background by an urgent need for funds, of which it was believed the academy possessed a rather large surplus. This assumption was erroneous, however, as the old Transylvania trustees discovered to their disappointment after the union had been effected. Both boards agreed on the form of a petition to the General Assembly, asking for a charter for the new institution, to be called Transylvania University, which should begin its existence January 1, 1799.

Legislative action followed almost immediately, and "An Act for the Union of the Transylvania Seminary and Kentucky Academy" was approved on December 22, 1798. This law, which adhered rather closely to the desires of the petitioners, was in reality an amendment to the earlier Virginia and Kentucky enactments governing Transylvania Seminary, and these acts were declared still to be in force. As a matter of fact, no changes of importance were made. The most significant provision was that which named the twenty-one members of the new Board of Trustees, which included besides the Governor of Kentucky ten representatives from each of the boards of the two schools now united. Once more the Presbyterians were in control, since a majority of the trustees, including some clergymen, were of that denomination.

The first meeting of the trustees in 1799 was devoted to the task of organizing the university. James Moore, President of Transylvania Seminary and former head of Kentucky Academy, was the logical choice for acting President of the new institution. Moore also became professor of logic, moral philosophy, metaphysics, and belles-lettres; the Rev. James Blythe was appointed professor of mathematics, natural philosophy, and astronomy; and the Rev. Robert Stuart became professor of ancient languages. Some degree of substance was given to the title "university" by the establishment of two professorships which were new to the West: medicine, under Drs. Frederick Ridgely and Samuel Brown, and law and politics under George Nicholas. Appropriations of five hundred dollars and six hundred dollars respectively were made for the purpose of establishing law and medical libraries.

Although all interested factions co-operated in launching the new institution during a brief period of sectarian calm, its growth was by no means flourishing, nor was it in reality a university during the greater part of its first two decades. Neglect, factional quarrels, paucity of funds, and the effects of a foreign war were included in the combination of repressive factors against which it struggled. Its successes were few, and yet its very existence during the lean years served to impart to it some degree of endurance and to prepare it for the golden era which was to come.

The personnel of the faculty changed rapidly during the first part of this early period. The professorship of law and politics, "the first collegiate law professorships intended for other than undergraduates, which had any permanency," was left vacant in 1799 by the death of George Nicholas, who was "one of the ablest lawyers Kentucky ever produced."[13] The law class, reputed to include nineteen students, was then taught by a committee of lawyers selected from among

[13] Charles Warren, *History of the American Bar* (Boston, 1911), 253; Charles Kerr (ed.), *History of Kentucky* (5 vols., Chicago and New York, 1922), II, 1052.

the trustees, until James Brown was elected to the professorship later in the same year. Brown was removed from office in 1805, after which the post was filled by Henry Clay, who was then twenty-seven years old. Upon Clay's resignation in 1807 the trustees elected James Monroe, who was followed in succession by John Pope and Joseph C. Breckinridge. Perhaps all of these men lectured to some extent, but regular courses in law were not offered every year.

There was probably even less activity in the medical courses, where for years whatever teaching there happened to be appears to have been done in an individual capacity, and until 1817 appointments of professors were merely nominal. Drs. Samuel Brown and Frederick Ridgely are noted as the first in the West to deliver lectures on medicine, and the former is further remembered for his inoculation of hundreds of Lexingtonians against smallpox as early as 1802, "even before Jenner could gain the confidence of the people of his own country." No systematic instruction was given by them, nor was the situation much improved by reorganization of the medical faculty in 1809 and 1815. After the latter date the irregular classes increased in size, however, and another reorganization in 1817 placed the Medical Department on a more satisfactory footing. In 1817-1818 twenty students attended the course of lectures offered by: Dr. Benjamin Dudley, professor of anatomy and surgery; Dr. James Overton, professor of theory and practice; Dr. Daniel Drake, professor of materia medica and medical botany; Dr. William H. Richardson, professor of obstetrics; and Dr. James Blythe, professor of chemistry. At the end of the year, which had been enlivened by a duel between two members of the faculty, the first M.D. degree ever granted in the West was awarded John L. McCullough of Lexington.[14]

[14] Robert Peter, *The History of the Medical Department of Transylvania University*, prepared for publication by his daughter, Miss Johanna Peter (Filson Club *Publications*, No. 20, Louisville, 1905).

The Academic Department also had its troubles, although unlike the Departments of Law and Medicine it was able to remain in continuous operation. Its course of study was of an elementary character far below college level, to a great extent "accommodated to the public demand," and arranged so that it might be completed within a single year. The instructors were therefore forced "to concentrate much within a little compass; and their short-lived efforts . . . [were] for the most part, expended on minds not well prepared by previous management." Not until 1816 did the trustees order that "no student shall be suffered to dictate his own course, nor any parent or guardian, in his behalf; but that all shall be compelled to conform to a general routine prescribed, and that none shall attempt the more advanced branches of study till masters of those which precede." The limited course offerings and the poor quality of work done aided in keeping the enrollment at a low level, as did the effects of factional quarrels, the War of 1812, and competition with more vigorous institutions of learning.[15]

The school had only twenty-two graduates from 1799 to 1818, the first being Robert R. Barr, who received the Bachelor of Arts degree on April 7, 1802. About fifty students were in attendance in 1800, and the average annual enrollment for the next sixteen years did not rise above that mark.

The poor financial condition which had fettered the university at its birth improved slowly. The school was rich in land which, leased to tenants who paid a part of their small yearly rental in produce and who tended to waste valuable timber, yielded a revenue wholly inadequate for the support of a university. Yet these rentals, aggregating approximately three hundred dollars a year, constituted the sole permanent income of the school. Having little hope that conditions might improve under that arrangement, the

[15] Kentucky *House Journal,* 1815-1816, pp. 199-215.

trustees decided about 1805 to sell the lands and to invest the proceeds in stock of the Bank of Kentucky and the Kentucky Insurance Company. By 1816 the revenue from these investments reached approximately $3,000 a year, with an additional annual income of about $2,000 in prospect.

The sectarian intolerance which had led to the disruption of Transylvania Seminary was by no means ended by the formation of Transylvania University, but for a time it remained under cover, smoldering, with only an occasional outbreak to indicate the unceasing struggle. Two groups contested for control of the Board of Trustees and, through it, control of the school. On the one hand were the Presbyterians, who exercised an influence out of proportion to their numbers in the state and who were unyielding in their orthodoxy; on the other were men less interested in theology than in politics, in the enjoyment of life, and in building a school befitting their ideals of civilization and the culture which they were developing in the West. Or, viewed from a different angle, the two parties were composed respectively of "the friends of evangelical religion, and the open, or disguised, abettors of deism and infidelity."[16]

The first manifestation of the conflict between these two parties occurred in 1801, when a group of students presented to the trustees a petition containing certain charges against the Rev. James Welsh, who had succeeded the Rev. Robert Stuart as professor of languages. The trial that followed became a contest between the Presbyterians, supporting Welsh, and their opponents on the board. By a close margin the trustees finally voted to dismiss Welsh, but only after a number of students had left the university when it appeared that the sectarians had been victorious. Shortly afterward the complexion of the board changed, and the Presbyterians regained a control over it which they kept more than a decade.

[16] Davidson, *Presbyterian Church,* 298.

In 1804 James Moore left the presidency of Transylvania and devoted himself to the duties of rector of Christ Church. Although a group of students petitioned that he be retained and one of them later intimated that the office had been "wrested" from him, Moore probably resigned willingly. At any rate in 1802 he had indicated a willingness to step aside when an effort was made to obtain the services of the President of William and Mary College, and he remained loyal to the school after relinquishing his post. The board chose as his successor the Rev. James Blythe, who continued until 1816 to serve as acting President, and whose administration was most satisfactory to the Presbyterians.

The opposition, however, was able to prevent the board appointing Blythe permanently to the office, and at various times efforts were made to select for the post some man of wider reputation. In 1812 a committee was "appointed to obtain information whether a gentleman of talents and reputation can be procured to serve as a President of the University," but apparently it took no action. Another committee in the next year was instructed to employ the Rev. Dr. E. Nott, who, however, declined the offer. Meanwhile, Blythe continued to serve as acting President, much to the dissatisfaction of a large element of the public in central Kentucky. Beginning about the end of the War of 1812 a newspaper campaign was waged against him, which, though unorganized, led eventually to his resignation.

The pressure of public opinion led the trustees to become more active in their search for a President, who had to be acceptable to the Presbyterian element which still composed a majority of the board. On June 5, 1815, the Rev. Dr. John B. Romeyn was elected, and upon his refusal the Rev. Dr. Horace Holley of Boston was chosen. Neither had been consulted in advance, and apparently the appointments were made without a thorough investigation of the qualifications of the men chosen. Holley was accepted by the conservatives because of his position as a minister and without knowledge of his liberalism. When rumors of unorthodox theology on his part reached the disturbed Presbyterian majority on the Board of Trustees, they hastened to rescind the appointment. A committee had already been directed to inform him of his election, but, "before the committee had performed their duty, a board was convened, and the authority of that committee suspended; not because the capacity or talents of Doctor Holly [*sic*] were doubted, his moral conduct reproachable, or his christian deportment called in question, but merely because it was reported that he had adopted some sentiments formerly entertained by the celebrated orator Priestly [*sic*], which did not exactly quadrate with Calvanistic [*sic*] orthodoxy."[17]

The sectarianism of the board and its inability to obtain the services of an acceptable man to replace the unpopular Blythe caused the school to suffer and occasioned much public criticism. Late in 1815 a legislative committee undertook "to enquire into the situation of the Transylvania University" and, as a result of its findings, recommended "that a law ought to pass appointing new trustees . . . , to hold their offices for two years, and that biennial elections to supply the board shall be made by a joint vote of both branches of the general assembly."[18] The proposals were incorporated in a bill that passed the House but which the Senate failed to consider.

Blythe resigned in 1816, and the Rev. Robert Bishop, another member of the faculty, was placed in charge of the school until a permanent appointment could be made. The liberal minority of the trustees tried to bring about the election of Dr. Thomas Cooper, who later became President of South Carolina College, but their efforts were overruled. Instead, two ministers in quick succession were chosen, and each rejected the offer. Meanwhile, Lexington newspapers

[17] Kentucky *House Journal,* 1815-1816, pp. 201-202. [18] *Ibid.,* 199, 203.

warned of the necessity of restoring public confidence in the university if it was to survive. Horace Holley was again proposed as President in October, 1817, but his appointment was rejected by a small majority. On November 15 of the same year, his name was once more placed in nomination, and Joseph C. Breckinridge and Charles Humphries warned of the possibility of legislative action if the trustees, by setting up sectarian requirements, should not choose a man satisfactory to the public. When the vote was taken, Holley was elected by a bare majority, which included one Presbyterian minister and John Pope, "a politician of eminence, who had been chosen and relied on as a friend of the Presbyterians, but who betrayed their confidence."[19] The minority then withdrew or sat silent, and the election was declared to be unanimous.

The Presbyterians had not recovered from this blow when another struck with harsher impact. In February, 1818, the legislature took complete charge of the university, ejected the old Board of Trustees, "which had hitherto been under Presbyterian influence and control," and replaced it with a new board of thirteen members, of whom eight had been members of the former group. The trustees now included a number of outstanding public figures of the state, not one of whom, however, was a clergyman or "a professor of religion of any sect." A few weeks later Holley accepted the appointment which had been tendered him, and the new organization of the university was complete. The revolution against sectarianism had succeeded, the liberals were in control, and the Presbyterians began the organization of another college, Centre, which should be theirs alone. "From that time, with an ungodly Board of Trustees, and a Unitarian President, that [Transylvania] institution sent forth infidel graduates with great uniformity."[20]

19 Davidson, *Presbyterian Church,* 299.

20 *Ibid.,* 284-85.

Chapter Two

Transylvania's Golden Age

TRANSYLVANIA UNDER ITS NEW PRESIDENT ENTERED upon its period of greatest glory, rising in a few years from insignificance to a position among the leading educational institutions of the nation. Holley, who resigned the pastorate of Hollis Street Church in Boston to come to Kentucky, entered upon his duties with boundless enthusiasm. Before accepting the presidency, he investigated its possibilities by a personal visit to the scene, where he had been favorably impressed by the social life of Lexington, by the promises of support from state and local officials as well as from private citizens, and by the educational possibilities of the region. The salary of $3,000 a year was attractive, a new building on the university campus appeared adequate for classes, and he was promised "perfect liberty to take such part of the instruction as I like, and to model the institution at my discretion." Holley took charge of the school in November, and was formally inaugurated on December 19, 1818.[1]

Only two years were required to transform what had been "in fact a piddling indifferent, little grammar school, not equal to many of the private schools kept by individuals in its vicinity," into "one of the first literary institutions in America."[2] The first step in the reorganization occurred by order of the Board of Trustees after Holley's acceptance of the presidency (but before he formally assumed the duties of the office) and comprised a "solid, useful and comprehen-

[1] Letters from Holley to his wife, written during his visit to Lexington and describing his impressions, are published in Charles Caldwell, *A Discourse on the Genius and Character of the Rev. Horace Holley, Ll. D., Late President of Transylvania University* (Boston, 1828), 151-63.

[2] Cincinnati *Literary Cadet,* January 13, 1820.

sive scheme of education" patterned after the best models in the nation. No longer were students to be accepted into the school regardless of previous preparation; henceforth the applicant for admission to the freshman class was required to have a good knowledge of Greek and Latin grammar and literature, to "understand common arithmetic," to "have studied ancient and modern geography," and to "possess a good moral character." A grammar school was established for the benefit of those who were not prepared for college work, and at the same time provision was made for applicants who had "no knowledge of the dead languages" to enter the college as "irregular students."

No longer was one year's attendance in the college sufficient for a degree. The new organization provided a four-year course of study "with the view to the substitution of a solid, useful, and comprehensive scheme of education, to that superficial plan which is too often followed."[3] Under Holley's guidance the curriculum was broadened and enriched to meet his own views of a liberal education and to compare with the offerings of institutions with which he was familiar in the East. Latin and Greek were, of course, required, and the courses of study included also mathematics, history, speaking, navigation, composition, surveying, chemistry, pharmacy, ethics, logic, philosophy, politics, political economy (economics), astronomy, botany, and modern languages. Classes were conducted by both the lecture and recitation methods; and though the President thought Constantine S. Rafinesque's field trips in natural history were too radical, he realized the value of scientific apparatus for experimental use in the classroom.

John Roche was placed in charge of the Preparatory Department, and President Holley, whose teaching duties included Philosophy of the Human Mind, Moral Philosophy and the Elements of Civil Policy, Rhetoric, Logic, and Philo-

[3] *Niles' Weekly Register* (Philadelphia, 1811-1849), XV (1818), 132-33.

sophical Grammar, devoted his attention especially to the junior and senior classes. Other instructors included John F. Jenkins, John Everette (brother of Edward), Daniel N. Bradford, the Rev. Robert H. Bishop, Charles S. Morehead, Benjamin O. Peers, and Constantine S. Rafinesque, "the most learned man in America."[4] Students were encouraged to seek poise and self-expression by participation in weekly speaking exercises to which the public was invited. The public was also urged to attend examinations, where the candidate for a degree found himself harassed by questions from learned men in the audience as well as from his professors. Writing shortly after this period, Charles Caldwell recalled that

> the weekly declamation of the classes, in the chapel of the University, was regularly attended by the most enlightened portion of the citizens of Lexington, as a source of instruction and refined amusement; and the rhetorical and *belles lettres* exhibitions of the candidates for degrees, on occasions of public commencement, constituted the admiration and delight of crowded audiences, composed of the most cultivated and fashionable inhabitants of the West. For several years, a commencement in Transylvania was the gala [event] of the country. So flourishing . . . did the academical department of the University become.[5]

The Academic or Liberal Arts Department was only a part of the university envisioned by Holley, which he built with the aid of the trustees, state officials, and citizens of Lexington and central Kentucky. In the summer of 1819 he began a campaign to strengthen the languishing Medical Department, and he achieved a remarkable success. A faculty which included Drs. Samuel Brown, Charles Caldwell, Benjamin W. Dudley, William H. Richardson, James Blythe,

[4] Richard H. Collins, *History of Kentucky* (2 vols., Covington, 1874), II, 185. See also F. Garvin Davenport, *Ante-Bellum Kentucky: A Social History, 1800-1860* (Oxford. Ohio, 1943).

[5] Caldwell, *Discourse on Horace Holley,* 191-200.

and, later, Daniel Drake, was assembled; the library was strengthened by purchases abroad; and in 1827 a medical hall was erected. Students flocked to the institution from all parts of the South and West, the enrollment increased from twenty to two hundred within five years, and Transylvania came to rank among the outstanding medical schools of the United States.

Efforts to build a flourishing Law Department were less successful, perhaps because law might be learned in private offices in any locality and because a diploma was not required of those who practiced in the Kentucky courts. Instruction in law had been allowed to lapse before the overturn of the Presbyterian regime at Transylvania, and not until 1821 was the department reorganized under the administration of William T. Barry. Twenty students composed the first class, and with addition of Jesse Bledsoe to the faculty, the enrollment grew to 44 in the next year and to 48 in the session of 1823-1824. In 1824 Barry resigned and the enrollment dropped to thirty. For a while President Holley lectured in the Law Department, and efforts to employ one or more men of distinction as professors were unsuccessful. Bledsoe was discharged in 1825, and the Law Department became moribund.[6]

The success achieved by the new administration at Transylvania attracted attention in other areas. Thomas Jefferson in 1820 noted that "Kentucky, our daughter, planted since Virginia was a distinguished state, has an University, with 14 professors & upwards of 200 students." Writing to a friend he complained that, if the Virginia legislature did not "heartily push" the university of his own state, "we must send our children for education to Kentucky or Cambridge [Harvard]." Neither was a happy choice, for Harvard would

[6] See Transylvania University, *A Catalogue of the Officers and Students of Transylvania University,* for the years mentioned, for faculty membership and student enrollment.

make its enrollees "fanatics & tories," and those who went to Kentucky would remain there rather than return to their native state. His conclusion was that "if . . . we are to go a begging any where for our education, I would rather it should be to Kentucky than any other state, because she has more of the flavor of the old cask than any other."[7]

As its fame spread, Transylvania drew patronage not only from the South and West but also on occasion from Delaware, Pennsylvania, and even Massachusetts. The great majority of students, both from Kentucky and elsewhere, were enrolled in the professional schools. Medicine attracted most of the students, and the Medical Department continued to flourish long after the remainder of the university began its decline. The total enrollment of all departments was doubled and redoubled during the presidency of Holley. In 1818 the school had only 60 students, the number rose to 140 in 1819, and the enrollment reached a peak of 418 in 1826. During Holley's administration of nine years, 644 degrees were conferred, compared with the 22 degrees granted by the school from 1799 to 1818. It may be pertinent to note by way of comparison the enrollments of other institutions at about the same time. In 1821 Harvard had 286 students; Yale, 319; Union, 264; Dartmouth, 222; and Princeton, 150. Transylvania in that year registered an attendance of 282.[8]

The program of expansion could not have been carried on if the income of the institution had not been increased. Even during its palmy days the school was never prosperous, and after the panic of 1819 there was danger that a lack of funds might cause it to "retrograde to a mere grammar school." Yet the income was greater than ever before as the state, always niggardly toward Transylvania, and the citizens of Lexington, often generous, exhibited unwonted liberality. In

[7] Paul L. Ford (ed.), *The Works of Thomas Jefferson* (12 vols., New York, 1904-1905), XII, 154-55.

[8] *Niles' Weekly Register,* XX (1821), 63.

1819 the legislature granted to the university for two years the bonus of the Farmers' and Mechanics' Bank of Lexington, from which a revenue of approximately $3,000 was realized. The Medical Department was aided on two occasions: by a grant in 1820 of $5,000 to be expended for books and equipment, and by an act in 1822 authorizing a lottery designed to raise $25,000 for a new building. The university received approximately $10,000 specie from half the profits of the Branch Bank of the Commonwealth of Kentucky, appropriated to it in 1821, and in 1822 a 2 per cent duty was levied on auction sales in Fayette County for the benefit of the law library. From Lexington came donations of $6,000 in 1820 and $5,000 two years later. The most munificent gift the old Transylvania ever received was the bequest of Colonel James Morrison, former chairman of the Board of Trustees, who died in 1823. His legacy, including $20,000 for the endowment of a professorship and approximately $50,000 for the erection of a new building, is still remembered because of the hall which bears his name. The financial condition of the university was always precarious, since most of its uncertain revenues was used to pay debts and current expenses. No regular income could be expected from the state, and funds were never available to build up an adequate endowment.[9]

In spite of the eminence attained by Transylvania during his administration, President Holley found himself the subject of attack almost from the moment he accepted the presidency, and as time passed his enemies grew more and more bitter toward him. The strongest opposition emanated from the Presbyterians, who had lost control of the university in 1818 and to whom Holley came to represent the embodiment

[9] See Kentucky *Acts,* for the years mentioned; Lewis, *Higher Education in Kentucky,* 61; and Horace Holley, *A Discourse Occasioned by the Death of Col: James Morrison, Delivered in the Episcopal Church, Lexington, Kentucky, May 19th, 1823* (Lexington, 1823), 31.

of infidelity. Other denominations had rallied to his support during his first visit to Kentucky, but "the Presbyterians were not among the number of those who were easily deceived."[10] At least one member of that denomination feared that already "the Transylvania University is lost to the Christian community,"[11] and the Synod of Kentucky began its long-continued opposition to Holley by insinuating charges against him under the guise of explaining its reasons for establishing a denominational college.

It was known generally that Holley was a Unitarian and a liberal in religious matters, catholic in his viewpoint, holding himself above sectarianism, and finding good in all denominations. A frank statement of his position early in his administration met general approval except from the Presbyterians, who, however, found little basis at that moment for a concerted attack upon him. Their opportunity came in 1823 when the President, in an eulogy to James Morrison, explained his views more fully. From that time forward he was to his opponents a Socinian, an Arian, and an infidel who must be removed from the university. The Lexington newspapers finally refused to print the rabid charges against him, but his attackers expressed themselves through numerous pamphlets and through the columns of newspapers in neighboring towns. His supporters were not as prolific in their writings as were his opponents; and Holley, having been advised to remain aloof from the sectarian squabble, maintained a dignified silence.

Not only were Holley's religious views questioned and condemned, but other accusations were hurled at him and at the Board of Trustees. Charges of extravagance and of "politics" were heard, investigating committees were sent by the legislature to probe the condition of the school, and the university

10 Davidson, *Presbyterian Church,* 303.

11 "A friend to learning and piety," in Lexington *Western Monitor,* December 26, 1818.

became involved involuntarily in the Relief–Anti-Relief and the New Court–Old Court fights. In 1825 it suffered another attack from an unaccustomed quarter. Governors Gabriel Slaughter and John Adair had always urged support of Transylvania, but Governor Joseph Desha struck it a staggering blow. In his message to the legislature on November 7, 1825, he uttered charges, as amazing as they were untrue, of "unbounded liberality" on the part of the state toward the university and of extravagant expenditures by officials in charge of the institution. Holley was singled out for special attention by a statement that his compensation was "twofold higher than is paid to the highest officers of our State government, and wholly disproportioned, as well to the services rendered, as to the resources of the institution." Perhaps his most injurious blow was the declaration that "as the University is now managed, it seems that the State has lavished her money for the benefit of the rich, to the exclusion of the poor; and that the only result is to add to the aristocracy of wealth, the advantage of superior knowledge."[12]

Shortly after this evidence of the Governor's unfriendliness toward him, Holley resigned, but he was persuaded by his supporters to retract his resignation and to remain at his post. His action, however, naturally caused a widespread feeling of uncertainty as to the future of the school, and the enrollment suffered a sharp decline. Another attack by Governor Desha in 1826 and a reduction in the President's salary in the same year led Holley finally to sever his connection with Transylvania in 1827. At last the nonsectarians were decisively defeated in their efforts to build a great university, and the golden era of Transylvania was at an end.

The enrollment declined to 286 by January, 1827, and to 184 by December of the same year; and Governor Desha was able to say smugly of the institution that "for a short period, it appeared to flourish, and seemed to be gaining an extensive

[12] Kentucky *Senate Journal,* 1825, p. 14.

celebrity. Latterly, it has fallen as rapidly as it rose." In his opinion, even if it could "be placed in the most prosperous state, little would be done towards promoting the great causes of general education," and yet he professed to consider it "too important to be abandoned." His hints of incautious expenditures on the part of the trustees led to a legislative investigation which cleared the board of all such accusations and at the same time showed the need for financial aid from the state.[13] That aid was not forthcoming, however, and the university was forced to continue its struggle for existence under the handicap of inadequate revenues. Relief was sought at various times by placing the school partly under denominational control, but each church was primarily interested in the welfare of its own small college and Transylvania was of secondary importance. The institution could hardly have continued to operate had not the citizens and town of Lexington repeatedly come to its rescue.

All departments of the university suffered a decline in enrollment after the resignation of President Holley, but the greatest shock came to the Academic Department. Within a short time the Medical School regained its former importance, and the Law School, reopened in 1829, also prospered for a time. Each was operated almost independently, its faculty included men outstanding in their respective fields, and tuition fees plus donations from individuals enabled it to pursue its course regardless of the general condition of the university. The Academic Department, on the other hand, had owed much of its prestige to the personality of Holley, and when that prop was gone, it slumped immediately and operated on the verge of collapse for many years.

For more than a year after the resignation of President Holley, the school existed without a President, while Drs. Caldwell and Dudley alternately acted in that capacity on

[13] *Ibid.*, 1827-1828, pp. 9, 264-68, 371.

public occasions and the Academic Department was managed by its faculty. The trustees were able to offer little inducement to anyone who might have been interested in accepting the position, for aside from tuition fees, the meager revenue of the school was derived from fines, forfeitures, and the sales tax on auctions, all of which paid into the treasury from $100 to $200 per year. In 1828 the situation was somewhat relieved when citizens of Lexington subscribed a sum of $3,500 annually for four years. With this assurance of a steady income for at least a brief period the trustees were able to induce Alva Woods, a Baptist minister, to relinquish the presidency of Brown University and take over the administration of Transylvania.

Once more the institution began to rise from somnolence, slow though the change may have been. The total enrollment experienced a steady, though slight, increase, reaching 362 in the last year of Woods' connection with the school. The outstanding achievement of the new administration was the revival of the Law School, which had ceased operation in 1825. President Woods' program of improvement was, however, cut short in 1829 when on the night of May 9 the main university building was destroyed by fire. Much of the scientific apparatus was damaged and the law library was burned. The property loss was estimated at about $40,000, most of which was not recovered, since one policy of $10,000 on which the premiums had been paid by the town of Lexington constituted the total insurance.

After this misfortune an effort was made to change the relationship between Transylvania and the state by making the university the head of the whole system of public education in the state, with the duty of training teachers for the common schools. Even the proponents of the scheme held little hope for its adoption at that time, and it was relegated to the background, only to crop up again a few years later. Discouraged by the losses resulting from the fire and by the uncertain revenues of the institution, Woods resigned his post in 1830, and Transylvania was once again without a President.

The position was not filled for three years in spite of considerable public dissatisfaction with the situation, and a widespread "impression . . . that the operations of the University cannot go on without a President at the helm."[14] During the interregnum a stroke of good fortune came to the school when in 1831 Henry Clay, executor of the Morrison will, was authorized to turn the residue of the estate over to the trustees. With the funds thus obtained it became possible to replace the old main building which had burned in 1829. Almost immediately construction began on the new, commodious "Morrison College," completed in 1833 and still in use, which is admired today as an outstanding example of Greek revival architecture.

After a series of acting Presidents, the administration of the university was entrusted to one of its own alumni, Benjamin O. Peers, an Episcopal minister and the Principal of the Lexington Eclectic Institute, who assumed the duties of his new position in 1833. President Peers suffered no illusions concerning the task which lay before him, and from the beginning he regarded his administration as an experiment designed to conciliate public opinion and "to demonstrate that an institution after repeated failures under much more advantageous circumstances, can force itself into prosperity almost without resources, and in despite of numerous and appalling difficulties."[15] Events proved the difficulties to be even greater than Peers had anticipated, and the experiment failed. The increase in enrollment was too slight to be encouraging, and Peers had the misfortune to become involved in a controversy with the Board of Trustees which led to a

[14] Frankfort *Commentator,* May 10, 1831.

[15] Benjamin O. Peers, *Inaugural Address Delivered at the Opening of Morrison College, Lexington, Kentucky, November 4th, 1833* (Lexington, 1833), 25-26.

Senate investigation and to the severance of his connection with the university in 1835.

Again and again the trustees presented pleas to the legislature for aid, pointing out in one instance "that the present income of the academical department is hardly sufficient for the employment of two illy paid professors in the College Proper, and a principal and assistant in the preparatory department, with the other necessary contingent expenses."[16] The legislature turned a deaf ear, and the necessary aid was not forthcoming. Another President, Thomas W. Coit, also an Episcopal clergyman, was chosen to succeed Peers, but after nearly three years he too gave up the hopeless struggle.

Shortly before the end of Coit's administration the Medical School was threatened with disruption. That college had continued to flourish even during the worst of the depression which gripped the Academic Department, and it maintained its enviable reputation. The departure of President Holley had caused its enrollment to drop, but two years later it had climbed again to more than two hundred students. Its buildings, including an "excellent Anatomical Amphitheatre" and a medical hall constructed in 1827, escaped the fire which consumed the main university building in 1829. In 1828 the department began publication of the quarterly *Transylvania Journal of Medicine and the Associate Sciences* under the editorship of John Estin Cooke, one of the members of a distinguished faculty which included Drs. Benjamin W. Dudley, Charles Caldwell, William H. Richardson, Charles W. Short, and Lunsford P. Yandell. With an attendance larger than that of any other medical school in the United States except the college at Philadelphia, the Transylvania Medical Department appeared able to weather any storm.[17]

[16] Kentucky *Senate Journal,* 1834-1835, p. 300.

[17] Charles Caldwell, *A Report Made to the Legislature of Kentucky, On the Medical Department of Transylvania University, February 15th, 1836* (Lexington, 1836). See also Kentucky *Senate Journal,* 1836-1837, pp. 358-62; *ibid.,* 1839-1840, *Appendix,* 149-50.

A quarrel which sprang up in 1837 threatened to destroy the school but ended by aiding it, at least temporarily. The city of Louisville sought either the removal of the Transylvania Medical Department to Louisville or the establishment of a rival school in that city, the latter possibility having been discussed for some time previously. Dr. Caldwell, who became involved in a bitter controversy with his colleague Dr. Dudley in 1837, was most active in an attempt to move the Transylvania department and had the support of Cooke, Short, and Yandell. The effort aroused the indignation of Lexingtonians and caused the trustees to dismiss Caldwell and to reorganize the school. The disturbance also awakened the people of Lexington to a realization of the needs of the institution, and they rallied to its aid. The town in 1838 donated $70,000, a part of which was used to construct a new medical building, completed in 1840. An additional sum of $40,000 was subscribed by the "Transylvania Institute," a company of citizens of Lexington organized "to contribute, by subscription and otherwise to the success and prosperity of Transylvania University" and incorporated by legislative act on February 20, 1839.

The reorganization of the Medical Department was completed in 1838. Among the professors who composed the new faculty were Drs. Dudley, Richardson, J. M. Bush, James C. Cross, Nathan R. Smith, Thomas D. Mitchell, and Robert Peter, who had begun his long career as a teacher in the university in 1833. The department was now more prosperous than it had been in years. The library was enlarged by purchases abroad, and the enrollment grew yearly until about 1844. After that date, confronted by ever-growing competition from rival institutions in larger cities, the Transylvania Medical Department declined. The Civil War struck it a fatal blow, for not only was the school suspended during the war years, but in 1863 its building and equipment were destroyed by fire.

The Law Department, which had been revived during the administration of President Peers, did not at any time approach the Medical School either in numbers or in reputation, although it did compare favorably for a number of years with other law schools in the United States. Like the Medical Department, it was conducted virtually independently of the rest of the university. The salary of the professors depended exclusively upon the revenue from tuition fees, and the only aid derived from the state was intended for the benefit of the law library. After the department was reopened in 1829, its first session, attended by nineteen students, was presided over by John Boyle. Boyle's successor, Daniel Mayes, in 1831 lectured to twenty-five embryo lawyers. As the enrollment increased, George Robertson was employed to assist Mayes; and when the latter resigned, A. K. Wooley and Thomas A. Marshall became members of the law faculty, to be followed later by Madison C. Johnson, Francis K. Hunt, and George B. Kinkead. After 1842 the enrollment, which had reached a peak of seventy-one students, decreased until on the eve of the Civil War the department required the services of only one professor.

Meanwhile, far-reaching changes had taken place in the Academic Department of the university. In 1838, after the resignation of President Coit and the schism in the Medical School, the outlook for the future was even darker than usual. In an effort to find a remedy for conditions the legislature provided for a new Board of Trustees, five in number, which was appointed with instructions to "open a correspondence . . . with the Presidents of the principal Universities in the United States, and such other persons as they may think proper, with a view to obtain information as to the best mode of managing and governing Transylvania University."[18] On the basis of their findings the trustees recommended that the university be endowed by the state, that

[18] Kentucky *Acts,* 1837-1838, p. 250.

provisions for the education of poor boys and for teacher training be set up, and that agriculture, mining, and civil engineering be added to the usual courses of study.

When the legislature showed no inclination to follow these recommendations, the town and people of Lexington came to the aid of the languishing institution in 1839 and in return were given the controlling voice in the management of its affairs. In addition, "the Mayor and Board of Councilmen, of the City of Lexington, and the members of the Transylvania Institute, may send one scholar to Morrison College, for each and every five hundred dollars which they have, or may hereafter, subscribe, and shall fully pay."[19] Funds raised by the Transylvania Institute made possible the erection of a dormitory, and the outlook for the future became somewhat brighter; although the trustees, realizing the inadequacy of its resources, vainly urged once again that the university be made a part of the common school system.

It was hoped that under the new organization and with the reawakened support of the people of Lexington, the revenues of Transylvania might be increased by tuition fees from a large student body and that the Academic Department might be revived. The Rev. Robert Davidson was promoted from a professorship to the presidency in 1840, but after a brief and unsuccessful struggle he was forced to resign against his will in 1842. In the latter year the trustees, discouraged by the dilapidated condition of Morrison Hall and by the ever-increasing debt and despairing of aid from the state, recommended that the Classical Department be placed in the hands of the General Conference of the Methodist Episcopal Church of the United States. Negotiations with the Kentucky Conference of that denomination had already begun, and it was believed that the General Conference would be glad to accept the offer. The transfer to the Methodists was made without legislative sanction, and

[19] *Ibid.*, 1838-1839, p. 301.

in the autumn of 1842 Transylvania opened under its new patrons. The Rev. H. B. Bascom, a professor in Augusta College, who had been prominent in the negotiations preceding the transfer, became acting President.

Under the management of the Methodists Transylvania appeared to be embarked upon another golden era, and for a while its enrollment exceeded that of any previous year, even including those of the Holley administration.[20] The times, however, were not propitious for the construction of a great university upon such a basis, despite a sanguine hope that "The day of darkness, under which the University has been so long shrouded, seems at last to have passed away, and the great light of hope risen upon its fortunes, by which a prospective advancement is seen to bear its honorable name, high above the lofty titles of even Harvard and Yale."[21] The General Conference of the Methodist Church of the United States did not adopt the school in 1844 because of the imminence of a division of the church into northern and southern branches, but the first General Conference of the Methodist Episcopal Church, South, held in 1846, accepted the responsibility. After an initial period of success, the fortunes of the institution, haunted by internal dissension and lack of support, again began to decline. Discouraged, President Bascom resigned in 1849. In 1850 the General Conference of the Methodist Episcopal Church, South, abandoned the school to the Kentucky and Louisville conferences, which in the same year returned it to the trustees, a part of whom were appointed by the city of Lexington as in 1839.

Under that arrangement Transylvania drifted until 1855,

20 The Methodist connection with Transylvania is discussed in Earl P. Barker, *The Contribution of Methodism to Education in Kentucky* (Nashville, 1937); and, William E. Arnold, *History of Methodism in Kentucky* (2 vols., Louisville, 1935-1936), as well as in the legislative documents and the Lexington newspapers of the period.

21 "A Visitor," in Frankfort *Commonwealth,* September 2, 1845.

when the legislature reorganized it as a normal school integrated with the common school system and placed it under the direct control of the state. A system was worked out whereby each county was allowed to send as many students "free of all charges of instruction" as it had representatives in the General Assembly, provided these students bound themselves to teach in the common school of their respective counties for as many years as they had attended the university. To help meet the expenses of such an arrangement, an annual appropriation of $12,000 from the common school fund was provided. For the first time in the history of the university, the state showed a willingness to support the institution regularly by appropriations and to make it in reality the state university.

In the first year after the establishment of the Normal School, over two hundred students were enrolled, and the future of Transylvania seemed brighter than it had for a generation. The Rev. Lewis W. Green, former President of Hampden-Sidney College, was placed at the head of the institution, but he resigned in 1857 to become President of Centre College. Meanwhile, a vociferous group protested the use of common school funds for the benefit of the university, asserting that such a diversion of funds was unconstitutional. The strong and growing opposition succeeded in bringing about the repeal of the act of reorganization, and the experiment of state support and control over Transylvania ended after only two years' trial.

After desertion by the state the school quickly "lapsed back to a local mediocrity."[22] During the Civil War its libraries were scattered, much of its equipment destroyed, and one of its more important buildings burned; and the once proud university became merely a high school, under the supervision of James K. Patterson. In 1863 the legislature rejected an offer made by the trustees to establish the

[22] Peter, "Sketch," 43.

new Agricultural and Mechanical College in connection with Transylvania, and in 1865 the latter institution united with Kentucky University, thereby losing its separate identity and giving up its historic name.

Kentucky University, the institution with which Transylvania was combined in 1865, came into existence in 1858, but its beginnings may be traced to a school which was founded at a much earlier date. In the late 1820's, shortly after the resignation of Horace Holley from the presidency of Transylvania University had ended an era which had demonstrated to pious denominationalists the dangerous infidelity inherent in secular education, the Baptists of Kentucky, as did other sects, undertook to establish a college of their own. After a half dozen years of the customary vicissitudes attending a struggle for existence without adequate funds, their school, Georgetown College, became torn by internal dissension—a contest between the orthodox Baptists on the one hand and on the other, three members of the faculty who had imbibed the teachings of Alexander Campbell. Learning of impending dismissal, the three heretics resigned in 1836. Upon their own initiative and responsibility, yet confident of aid from the Disciples of Christ who were especially numerous in Georgetown, they established there a rival institution of higher learning.[23]

Named in honor of Francis Bacon, the school, which began operation without even a Board of Trustees, was chartered in 1837 with the wholly unnecessary limitation "that the real and personal estate acquired by this corporation, shall at no time exceed the yearly rent or value of ten thousand dollars."[24] Elder Walter Scott, the first President, re-

[23] A. R. Milligan, "Historical Review of Kentucky University Read at Fortieth Anniversary of Union with Transylvania" (typewritten manuscript in Bureau of Source Materials in Higher Education), contains material pertinent to Bacon College.

[24] Kentucky *Acts,* 1836-1837, p. 275.

signed shortly after his election and was succeeded by Elder D. S. Burnet, who also served as professor of intellectual and moral science. The President, four other professors, an assistant professor, and the Principal of the Preparatory Department composed the first faculty. With 203 students enrolled during the session of 1836-1837, the launching of Bacon College was highly successful. The size of the first student body, so encouraging to the friends of the college, was due in part to the support of the Christian Church, and perhaps to a greater degree to the fact that the School for Civil Engineers which had been connected with Georgetown College transferred bodily to Bacon College with its professor, T. F. Johnson, who was one of the founders of the latter institution.

Despite an auspicious beginning, the school, dependent for revenue upon tuition fees alone, was far from prosperous; and the unpleasant fact soon became apparent that it could not long continue in operation without endowment and buildings. A campaign for contributions in 1839 failed, and the trustees then sought relief by offering to locate the college "permanently where the heaviest subscription should be obtained, provided the whole subscription should amount to $50,000 in scholarships at $500 each." Largely through the efforts of James Taylor, a lawyer, the requisite pledges were forthcoming from Mercer County, and later in 1839 Bacon College was moved to Harrodsburg. A reorganization of the faculty accompanied the change in location, and a new President, Samuel Hatch, was chosen. After one year's service he in turn was succeeded by James Shannon, who remained in office until the operations of the college were suspended.

At Harrodsburg the institution had for the first time a campus and buildings of its own, but it was little, if any, more prosperous than it had been at Georgetown. Its enrollment decreased, averaging about half that of the school's first session. The generous pledges of support proved easier to get than to collect, and it was said that "a professor first earned his salary, and then riding a hired horse, would spend a few weeks in collecting it from subscribers to the college in different counties."[25] In 1847 a campaign for funds resulted in subscriptions for $11,000 for the payment of debts, and the trustees declared that "Bacon College may now be regarded as permanent."[26] Without continued support the air of permanency passed. In 1850, when the compensation for the previous session was "less than the trustees could ask the professors to accept for another," the faculty was dissolved. To avoid suits which might be brought by holders of scholarships still outstanding, the trustees maintained the fiction of continuous operation by allowing Samuel Hatch to conduct a high school in the college buildings. After Hatch left in 1855 the institution no longer showed life.

Even before Bacon College ceased operations, efforts were under way for its revival and endowment. The first statewide meeting of the Churches of Christ in Kentucky pledged itself in 1850 to raise $20,000 for the purpose of establishing a chair of sacred history, in 1852 a campaign was begun by the churches and by the trustees of the college, and in 1853 Albert G. Talbott, a member of the Board of Trustees, "prosecuted a plan for an endowment of $100,000." When none of these efforts succeeded, the friends of the institution lost hope, "and even its board . . . in despair almost abandoned it." At least one member of the board, however, refused to admit defeat, and as a result of his labors and sacrifices a new university was erected upon the ruins of the old, poverty-stricken college.[27]

[25] Milligan, "Historical Review," 9.

[26] Frankfort *Daily Commonwealth,* January 14, 1848.

[27] Bacon College, *Minutes of a Meeting of the Donors and Friends of Bacon College Held at Harrodsburg, Ky., May 6, 1857* (Harrodsburg, 1857), tells of John B. Bowman and the founding of Kentucky University.

John B. Bowman, a Mercer County farmer thirty-one years old, an alumnus and a trustee of Bacon College, watched with concern the failure of the campaign for funds, and "feeling deeply the importance and necessity of the work as an auxiliary in the cause of Education and Christianity in Kentucky, and relying alone in confidence upon Him who is the giver of all . . . , determined, with a full sense of all the difficulties, to make a final and vigorous effort for its accomplishment." After discussing the matter with A. G. Talbott, Bowman called a meeting of the Board of Trustees and submitted to it a plan of endowment which provided for the collection of at least $100,000, one third of which should be raised in Mercer County, the home of the college. The project was approved, and Bowman deserted his own private affairs to devote his full attention and energies to carrying it out.

He enlisted the aid of Major James Taylor, who within a short time raised in Mercer County $30,500, "to which amount he was himself the largest contributor." Bowman added nearly $8,000 from the same area, then enlarged the scope of his activities by canvassing other counties in central Kentucky. The response was most heartening, and within the space of 150 days approximately $150,000 had been subscribed.

In May, 1857, a group of "Donors and Friends of Bacon College" assembled in Harrodsburg to decide upon the disposition of the funds. In his report to that body Bowman indicated that his plans went far beyond the mere resurrection of a small denominational institution, and he warned that those "brethren and friends" who had pledged their support

> feel that they are contributing to an institution which promises to meet in all its arrangements the present crisis in our Church and Society. In a word, little, if anything was contributed to Bacon College as it is, or as it has

> been; but the prospect of establishing an Institution more liberal in all its appointments,—permanent in its nature—and auxiliary to the cause of sound morality and pure Religion in our state—this and this only has opened the hearts of the brethren, and to such a work only have they contributed. It is, therefore, assumed that the Board will faithfully carry out the wishes of the donors in these respects, by laying, broad and deep, the foundation of a school for young men.

Stirred by his enthusiasm, the meeting approved his report and appointed a committee "to propose and present to the Trustees of Bacon College the Amendments deemed necessary to its charter."

The committee and the trustees agreed on all points except a name for the new institution. The preparatory school, which was put in operation in 1857, was called Taylor Academy in honor of the Harrodsburg lawyer who had helped raise subscriptions for the college. Along the same line of thought, "Bowman University" was proposed as the name of the school as a whole, but John B. Bowman modestly objected. No agreement had been reached when the charter was sent to Frankfort for legislative action, and the name of the school was omitted from the draft of that document. When no further delay was possible, Representative Philip B. Thompson "filled the blank Kentucky University and then wrote to the other members of the committee that if the name were unacceptable to the trustees it could be changed afterward."[28]

The new charter, approved by the legislature and signed on January 15, 1858, provided in addition to the change of name that the management of the school should be in the hands of a board of at least thirty curators, chosen from the counties which had contributed as much as $15,000 to the endowment. The Christian Church in Kentucky was safeguarded in its ownership and control of the institution by a

[28] Milligan, "Historical Review," 18.

requirement that a minimum of two thirds of the Board of Curators belong to that denomination.

Meanwhile, even before the charter had been approved, many of the donors to the school were becoming impatient, and the establishment of Taylor Academy in 1857 reflected a desire of the trustees "to allay a popular demand for what it was thought would be a premature opening of the collegiate department." The trustees were already carefully selecting a faculty for the college, a task completed by the new Board of Curators, and on September 19, 1859, "the doors of Kentucky University were thrown open . . . under weeping skies and almost on the verge of a disastrous civil war." Two days later, Robert Milligan, A.M., was formally installed as its first President.[29]

Kentucky University, born on the eve of troublous times, suffered from the Civil War; yet it was later claimed that none of the endowment nor a week of exercises was lost during the struggle.[30] The enrollment, of course, was affected, dropping from 194 students in the first session to 62 in the fourth. The college buildings also suffered, for they were seized by the Confederates to use as a hospital after the battle of Perryville and later destroyed by fire in February, 1864. Since Bowman failed in an effort to purchase Harrodsburg Springs for the use of the college, after the fire, classes were "conducted after the manner of a Sunday School" in the Harrodsburg Christian Church.

On September 20, 1864, a meeting of the curators and donors was held to determine the future of the now homeless school, and a committee consisting of Bowman, Professor Henry H. White, and President Milligan was appointed to select a new location. This trio, after failing to secure a favorable response to a scheme to obtain suitable buildings and grounds in Mercer County and after considering bids

29 *Ibid.*, 18-21.

30 Frankfort *Commonwealth,* November 3, 1871.

from Louisville and Covington, finally decided in favor of Lexington as the site of the university. From Mercer County now came unexpected opposition to removal, quieted only by Bowman's personal pledge to refund to every citizen of that county "who might claim it, the full nominal value of all unpaid coupons which were subscribed and paid by them to the endowment of the University; also all the Bacon College scholarships subscribed and paid in full by any citizen thereof."[31]

Lexington was chosen by the committee because of a most attractive offer from the trustees of Transylvania University, which had fallen upon lean years. Authority to transfer control of Transylvania to a denomination in return for pecuniary aid had been granted by the legislature in 1862, and even two years earlier the trustees had proposed union with Kentucky University. In 1865, after the decision for union had been reached, Bowman met a representative of Transylvania to work out the plan in detail. At the same time he conferred with the Committee of Agriculture of the Kentucky House of Representatives, which was debating the disposition of lands granted by Congress for the establishment of an agricultural college.

Two legislative acts resulted from these conferences: one providing for the establishment of the Agricultural and Mechanical College of Kentucky as a college of Kentucky University, and the other authorizing the union of the latter institution with Transylvania. By the act of consolidation, approved February 28, 1865, all the funds and property of Transylvania were transferred to Kentucky University, which also assumed the obligations of the older school. Should the location of the new institution ever be changed from Fayette County, however, the consolidation should cease, and Transylvania should resume its corporate existence.

[31] John B. Bowman, "Report," in Kentucky University, Announcement, 1865-1866 (manuscript).

Details of the new organization were hastily worked out during the summer months, and on October 2, 1865, in the halls of old Transylvania the greater Kentucky University began its first session.

Chapter Three

The Founding of the Agricultural and Mechanical College

On July 2, 1862, President Abraham Lincoln signed an act which has had far-reaching consequences in American education, and under whose terms appeared the institution which later developed into the University of Kentucky. Passage of the act, which bears the name of Justin S. Morrill of Vermont, marked the culmination of a long period of agitation in the United States for the establishment of agricultural schools. In Europe during the eighteenth century a number of agricultural societies had come into existence, and courses in agriculture were taught in certain schools. In colonial America agricultural societies were active, agricultural fairs attracted attention, and agriculture was included (on paper, at least) in the course of study adopted by the governors of one educational institution, King's College, now Columbia University.[1]

The traditional emphasis on the classics continued in colleges in the United States far into the nineteenth century, but at the same time an increasing number of institutions offered instruction in the sciences, particularly in chemistry, botany, zoology, and geology. More directly related to agricultural education were schools established in the 1820's and

[1] The founding of land-grant colleges is discussed in Alfred C. True, *A History of Agricultural Education in the United States, 1785-1925* (United States Department of Agriculture, *Miscellaneous Publications*, No. 36, Washington, 1929); Ellwood P. Cubberley, *Public Education in the United States: A Study and Interpretation of American Educational History* (rev. ed., Boston, 1934); Earle D. Ross, *Democracy's College: The Land-Grant Movement in the Formative Stage* (Ames, Iowa, 1942); and I. L. Kandel, *Federal Aid for Vocational Education: A Report to the Carnegie Foundation for the Advancement of Teaching* (New York, 1917).

afterward, some of which perhaps owed their origin to American initiative, while others definitely were influenced by the Fellenberg manual-labor movement in Europe. Philipp Emanuel von Fellenberg, a Swiss disciple of Johann Heinrich Pestalozzi, established in 1806 in his homeland an institution which included a large farm, workshops of various kinds, a literary unit for the education of the wealthy, a unit for training in the occupations of the middle class, and an agricultural unit for the training of farm laborers and rural teachers. Fellenberg's ideas were widely copied. In the United States they led to the establishment of manual-labor schools in at least ten states by 1830, and later they influenced to some extent the development of agricultural and mechanical colleges.

A different type of school, in which instruction in theory as well as practical work in agriculture was offered, began to appear in the United States after 1820. The Gardiner Lyceum in Maine was established in 1821 as a private school with state assistance to train "scientific farmers and skillful mechanics," and other institutions of similar nature followed. More significant was the first American technical college, founded by Stephen Van Rensselaer at Troy, New York, in 1824. The school, later called Rensselaer Polytechnic Institute, under the direction of Amos Eaton broke with tradition and offered training in a wide variety of scientific and vocational fields, which included agriculture during the early years of its existence. It has been said that "This institution undoubtedly had considerable general influence on the movement for scientific education relating to agriculture and mechanic arts which culminated in the land-grant act of 1862. It was well known to those leaders . . . who were promoting the establishment of colleges and other public agencies for the promotion of agriculture. Some of its students had direct relations with this movement."[2]

[2] True, *Agricultural Education*, 42.

THE PRESIDENTS

John Augustus Williams — Joseph Desha Pickett
James Kennedy Patterson — Henry Stites Barker

The "Revolution of 1828" which elevated Andrew Jackson to the presidency marked the rise to political power of the common man, who in addition to making his influence felt in government undertook to obtain for himself and his children a higher standard of living and new opportunities for social and cultural advancement. The panic of 1837 and the resulting depression intensified class consciousness among farmers and laborers and brought among these groups greater dissatisfaction with their position in the economic and social structure of the nation. Efforts to deal with the ills which beset the country, and which were not well understood, led to the numerous reform movements characteristic of the "fabulous forties." Educational reforms of all sorts were advocated, and especially noteworthy was the movement for agricultural education, a movement in which the more philosophical advocates sought to enlist the support of farmers in general, pointing to greater knowledge and specialized training as means of improving their condition.

Reluctance to submit to additional taxation for the support of new schools delayed the plans of the reformers and permitted private institutions to take the lead in establishing courses in agriculture and in the sciences related to agriculture. Yale, Harvard, and Amherst were among the colleges which assumed leadership in this regard, and beginnings were made elsewhere. Farmers' College, located near Cincinnati in 1846, was one of a large number of agricultural and technical schools established by individual or community effort in nearly all parts of the country during the years before the Civil War. No other school of this type was as outstanding as the People's College of New York, begun in 1853, and most of them were of little importance.

The inability of most of these institutions to acquire needed income and to achieve the success desired for them demonstrated to reformers the need for governmental assistance to agricultural education. Thomas Jefferson, who in

1800 included agriculture among the sciences which should be taught in the projected University of Virginia, was a forerunner of a large number of men who in the first quarter of the nineteenth century labored vainly for state support of instruction in agriculture. They worked before the times were ripe for the success of their efforts, and their work was done largely on an individual basis. Significantly, achievement of their objectives began to come only after the organization of vigorous agricultural societies in the individual states and after the establishment of agricultural periodicals which proved highly effective in propagandizing rural folk and politicians.

Renewed agitation for state aid to agricultural education started in the 1830's, intensified after the panic of 1837, and finally began to bear fruit in the decade before the Civil War. Proposals for state-supported schools which would give instruction in agriculture were made by 1837 by legislators or agricultural societies in several states, including Maryland, New York, Michigan, and Pennsylvania, but without immediate result. In Kentucky, nearly a quarter of a century before the passage of the Morrill Act, the State Agricultural Society presented to the legislature on January 7, 1839, a memorial "praying for the passage of a law establishing and endowing a school of Agriculture for the state of Kentucky."[3] The Senate Committee on Agriculture, to which the memorial was referred, recommended postponement of action because the session was drawing to a close. Even if there had been time to consider the matter, the committee pointed out, "the state of the ordinary revenue is not such as would justify so large an appropriation of money as would be necessary to carry out the measure contemplated by the memorialists." The Senate group insisted that an

[3] The courses of the various plans may be followed in Kentucky *Senate Journal,* 1838-1839, pp. 103, 219-23; *ibid.,* 1839-1840, pp. 49-52, 164, 312; Kentucky *House Journal,* 1839-1840, pp. 528-31.

appropriation from the school fund for the purpose designated would not be proper, "because that fund is pledged to the support of a System of Common Schools, and cannot, without a breach of faith, be directed to any other purpose, however desirable it may be." Upon the recommendation of this committee the legislature delegated John Lewis to gather information concerning agricultural schools both in the United States and abroad. Lewis' report showed an awareness of developments in agricultural education to that time. After describing the organization of certain schools, Lewis warned that "in schools of agriculture, the most useful of all arts, we cannot lose sight of those principles of general instruction which tend to form *enlightened citizens* of a republican government," and he cited the necessity "for an academical department, embracing a wide literary scope."

A singular plan for providing agricultural education, painlessly as far as taxes were concerned, was presented early in 1840, when James Guthrie introduced in the Kentucky Senate a bill providing for the creation not only of a college but also of lower grade schools where agriculture might be taught. According to this measure the state was to be entirely exempt from financial responsibility for the proposed institutions, which were to be established and supported by state and county agricultural societies. Each of the societies to be organized in the various counties would be authorized to purchase and hold not over 500 acres of land upon which to establish an agricultural school and an experimental farm, as well as a library and a "county lyceum." When twenty or more county societies should organize, each was empowered to choose delegates to a state society. To these representatives was given the power "to cause an agricultural college to be established, and to fix the section of the State where the same shall be located; and to prescribe the number of professors, and rules and regulations for its government." The state and county societies were empowered to raise funds by the sale of stock with a par value of $100. The bill was favorably received by the Senate, where it passed by a vote of 24 to 13, but the lower house refused to concur, and the scheme was abandoned. In 1857 the State Agricultural Society (the third in a series of short-lived organizations bearing the same name) urged the legislature to provide for agricultural education and experimentation. No action followed, perhaps partly because of public indifference and partly because of the panic which struck the country in the same year.

Several states, including New York, Pennsylvania, Maryland, Massachusetts, Michigan, and Iowa, were more successful than Kentucky in establishing agricultural schools, though there was no uniformity among their institutions. Most of the states did not provide for agricultural training and as time passed an increasing number of leaders of the industrial movement came to favor and to agitate for federal aid. Precedents had already been set in federal grants of land for various purposes, including education, and in the establishment of the Military Academy. The most inviting prospect for federal assistance was the Smithson fund, over the disposition of which there was much uncertainty. In 1840 Solon Robinson, one of the great agricultural reformers of this country, helped organize the Agricultural Society of the United States, whose main purpose seems to have been to secure the Smithson bequest for the establishment of a national agricultural college. In the same year in which the national society was organized, the Kentucky State Agricultural Society also recommended that the Smithson legacy be applied to the establishment of agricultural schools.

Two years earlier, in 1838, Charles L. Fleischman, a graduate of the Royal Agricultural School of Bavaria who had become a naturalized citizen of the United States, presented to Congress a memorial in which he described agricultural education in Europe and urged the establishment in this country of schools devoted to science, mechanics, and agriculture. Another interesting memorial was presented to Congress early in 1841 by Captain Alden Partridge, onetime President of Norwich University in Vermont, a man who may have had some influence on Justin S. Morrill's ideas regarding federal aid to education. At any rate Partridge's memorial is thought to contain the first proposal that Congress use the proceeds of the sale of public lands for the endowment of institutions which should offer "a broad curriculum, including the natural and economic sciences with their applications to agriculture, engineering, manufactures, and commerce, as well as military science and practice." It is worthy of note that the funds derived from such land sales were to be distributed among the states in proportion to their representation in Congress.[4]

Of the memorials and petitions presented to Congress during the 1840's and 1850's urging assistance to agricultural schools, the most influential came from Illinois, where Jonathan Baldwin Turner was working for the establishment of a state university and evolving a comprehensive plan for federal aid to the states for the purpose of agricultural education. The second Illinois Farmers' Convention in 1852 resolved that Congress should be requested to aid educational institutions by the sale of public lands, and in February, 1853, the state government adopted resolutions asking the support of Congress for the plan. The Illinois delegation in Congress was instructed to try to secure the passage of a federal law "donating to each State in the Union an amount of public lands not less in value than five hundred thousand dollars, for the liberal endowment of a system of industrial universities, one in each State in the Union to cooperate with each other, and with the Smithsonian Institution at Washington, for the more liberal and practical education of our industrial classes and their teachers."

[4] True, *Agricultural Education,* 83, 88.

Though there was evidence of widespread interest in the proposal, Congress took no action on it.

By request of an Illinois congressman, Turner in 1854 embodied his ideas in a bill, which was not introduced, however, because in the same year President Franklin Pierce made known his opposition to land grants to state institutions. Proponents of Turner's plan asked the United States Agricultural Society for aid in applying pressure on Congress, but the opposition of the southern members of the society was so marked that the organization postponed action until the next meeting, when it registered its approval by a slight majority. Meanwhile, the accession of James Buchanan to the presidency in 1857 led the advocates of land grants for educational institutions again to approach Congress. Turner remained active in behalf of his plan, speaking, writing letters, and distributing a pamphlet which he had composed. Senator Lyman Trumbull of Illinois in October, 1857, wrote Turner that the idea expressed in his pamphlet was "a grand one," but that Congress would not be likely to favor a request for land grants from the new states which had already received large grants for various purposes. Consequently, he suggested, the chances of success would be better "if some of the old States would take hold of the matter."

In December, 1857, Justin S. Morrill of Vermont introduced a bill whose provisions were similar in many respects to the ideas advocated by Turner and his supporters. Strangely, it is not clear to what extent, if any, Morrill was influenced by Turner, or Captain Partridge, or others who had worked for approximately the same objectives. Morrill, who had long been interested in practical education, had been a delegate at the meetings of the United States Agricultural Society when the Illinois plan for federal land grants had been discussed, though there is no evidence that he participated in the discussions. Turner's daughter later declared that her father, after the receipt of Senator Trumbull's letter of October 19, had sent a number of papers and documents to Morrill and had asked him, a New Englander, to introduce a bill. On the other hand, Morrill never publicly acknowledged an indebtedness to Turner, and more than once in referring to the famous act which bears his name he said: "Where I obtained the first hint of such a measure, I am wholly unable to say." Actually, the measure was "the culmination of the long movement for agricultural and technical schools, . . . and it is altogether likely that Morrill derived the ideas incorporated in the bill from various sources connected with that movement."[5]

The bill weathered the storm of southern and Democratic opposition and passed both houses of Congress, only to meet disaster at the hands of President Buchanan. Buchanan, a Democrat who was dominated to a large extent by the southern leaders of his party, gave six reasons for his veto of the measure, including the alleged financial inexpediency of the project at that time and his conviction that in granting federal aid to education in the states Congress had gone beyond its powers under the Constitution. The veto was sustained, and not until a change of administration had occurred did Morrill venture to introduce his bill again, late in 1861. By that time state-rights Southerners were no longer present in numbers sufficient to impede its progress, minor objections were overridden, and in June, 1862, it passed both houses of Congress.

The Morrill Act granted to each state 30,000 acres of public land for each senator and representative in Congress to which that state was entitled by the census of 1860. States such as Kentucky, in which no public lands existed, were to receive "land scrip" which might be sold and the proceeds applied to the purposes of the act. No state was allowed to use its scrip to locate land outside its borders,

[5] *Ibid.,* 91-94, 97-99.

and not more than one million acres could be located in any one state. All revenues from the sale of land or land scrip were to be invested in safe stocks yielding interest at a rate not less than 5 per cent a year.

The principal was to remain forever undiminished, and the interest was to be applied to the "endowment, support, and maintenance of at least one college" in which the primary aim should be "to teach such branches of learning as are related to agriculture and the mechanic arts in such manner as the legislatures of the States may respectively prescribe in order to promote the liberal and practical education of the industrial classes in the several pursuits and professions in life." "Other scientific and classical studies" were not to be excluded; and in accordance with the spirit of the time, military training for students was required. States which wished to avail themselves of the opportunities offered by the act were required to express acceptance within two years after its approval by the President and to provide at least one college within five years.

In view of earlier proposals in Kentucky for agricultural education the state might have fulfilled more readily the conditions imposed by the Morrill Act if the generous offer had been extended during normal times. At the time the possibility of federal aid became a reality, however, Kentucky was less concerned with educational problems than with internal divisions and with her effort to maintain an anomalous neutrality in the face of invading armies. Nevertheless, Governor James F. Robinson in his message to the legislature on January 8, 1863, called attention to the Morrill Act, recommended a "faithful consideration" of the subject, and indicated that he expected a prompt response to the proffer of aid. Legislative action followed as promptly as he could have wished, and within a fortnight he signed the "Act accepting the donation of lands to Kentucky for the endowment of Agricultural Colleges," which authorized such "steps as may be necessary to obtain the land scrip to which the State of Kentucky is entitled, under the provisions of the act of Congress."

Looking forward to the actual establishment and operation of an agricultural school, the General Assembly entrusted to the Board of Directors of the State Agricultural Society the task of investigating and reporting the advantages and inducements offered by various communities for the location of the institution. It was expected that a number of towns and counties might compete with one another in their offerings, and one writer pointed out with needless alarm that "new dangers . . . impend and threaten on every hand; and none seems more formidable . . . than the simultaneous offer of so many college buildings, in so many towns and villages, when common sense at once decides that these buildings ought to be in the midst of the college farm."[6] The expected competition did not materialize, and after advertising for bids for approximately six months, the president of the Board of Directors of the State Agricultural Society reported that only one proposal, from Transylvania University, had been received. Acceptance of the offer was postponed "in order that every portion of the State might have full time to present its claims and advantages for the location of the Agricultural College." Continuation of the advertising campaign yielded no further results, however, and, after an investigation, the agricultural board in December, 1863, recommended without reservation that the General Assembly accept the proposal offered by the trustees of Transylvania, which provided for the surrender of all the university property to the state, "to be managed in such manner as the State shall prescribe, provided, though, it shall be made the site or location of the Agricultural College."[7]

[6] Frankfort *Tri-Weekly Commonwealth,* February 28, 1863.
[7] Kentucky *House Journal,* 1863-1864, pp. 48-49.

Two months later, on February 19, 1864, the Kentucky Senate by unanimous vote passed a bill incorporating an agricultural college and connecting it with Transylvania. Shortly afterward the General Assembly adjourned, and the bill did not reach the House of Representatives until January of the next year. The time limit set by Congress was rapidly approaching; and if Kentucky expected to retain her land scrip, it was necessary that she establish an agricultural school soon. Yet the proposed union of the new college with Transylvania was not favored by the lower house, where an effort had already been made "to find a more eligible place." Opposition to accepting the Transylvania offer was based in the main upon the shaky financial condition of that school and the probability, so distasteful to the legislators, that monetary assistance from the state would be required to enable the agricultural college to begin operation. No alternative appeared, however, and during January, 1865, the lower house reluctantly took up the Senate bill and then amended it by substituting one more nearly in conformity with its own views. Consideration of the latter was suddenly halted on February 3, when R. J. Browne moved to commit it pending amendments while the legislature should conduct an investigation of the obligations of Kentucky University growing out of its location at Harrodsburg.

This precipitate action in regard to the bill was in reality an abandonment of the scheme of annexing the proposed state institution, the agricultural college, to the existing state university, Transylvania. Furthermore, it marked the appearance of a new possibility which seemed more attractive to the legislature, since apparently it would not require an appropriation from state funds. The idea had been suggested to Bowman, at that time engaged in his self-appointed task of resuscitating Kentucky University, who, with the successful culmination of his efforts, became the founder of the Agricultural and Mechanical College of Kentucky.

Kentucky University had determined to seek a new location after its disastrous fire in Harrodsburg in 1864. Negotiations with Transylvania and the city of Lexington had led to a decision to move the Disciples of Christ school to Lexington and there to unite it with the remains of the old state institution of higher learning. Before the project could be consummated, however, it was necessary to secure the approval of the General Assembly. Early in 1865 John Bowman, serving as general agent of Kentucky University, summoned to Frankfort a special committee which had been appointed by the Board of Curators for the purpose of seeking the necessary legislative action. The other members of the committee did not appear, leaving Bowman to do the work alone.

While in Frankfort he held a conference with the chairman of Transylvania's Board of Trustees and with the Committee on Agriculture of the House of Representatives, and from that meeting emerged full-grown the plan of organization which was shortly put into effect. Results followed swiftly. On February 7, 1865, only four days after the decision of the House to commit the bill calling for the annexation of the agricultural college to Transylvania, another substitute bill appeared and was rushed through the General Assembly in spite of opposition from citizens of Harrodsburg, who objected to the removal of Kentucky University, and from certain "parties resisting the connection of the Agricultural and Mechanical College" to that institution.

The measure, approved February 22, 1865, provided that, since the Board of Curators of Kentucky University proposed to move that institution to Lexington and to consolidate it with Transylvania, and since the enlarged university proposed "to raise an additional one hundred thousand dollars to purchase a farm and erect all the necessary buildings and improvements to carry on the operations of an Agricultural and Mechanical College, and connect therewith a model or experimental farm with industrial pursuits," the "Agricultural and Mechanical College of Kentucky, located in the county of Fayette, in or near the city of Lexington," be established as a college of Kentucky University. When the organization should be completed (and the act was not to go into effect until then) the curators should receive the income from funds obtained from the sale of the land scrip granted by Congress and should apply such funds to the operation of the Agricultural and Mechancial College. In return, the state retained the right to send to the school free of tuition charges three students from each representative district, who should be entitled to attend classes in all other colleges of the university except those in law and medicine.

In the act the legislature attempted to quiet the fears of those who, remembering the history of Transylvania, opposed the union of the state college with the denominational university. It provided that the Agricultural and Mechanical College was to be unmistakably a state institution, operated under the watchful supervision of a Board of Visitors appointed by the Governor, and that the income from its endowment might be stopped at any time if the General Assembly considered that Kentucky University was not fulfilling its contract. Furthermore, the organization of the college was to be strictly nonsectarian. In order to insure impartiality, the act of 1865 required "that a majority of the professors of said college shall not at any one time belong to the same ecclesiastical denomination," and that

> In the appointment of professors, instructors, and other officers and assistants of said college, and in prescribing the studies and exercises thereof, and in every part of the management and government thereof, no partiality or preference shall be shown to one sect or religious denomination over another; nor shall anything sectarian be taught therein; and persons engaged in the conducting, governing, managing, or controlling said college and its studies and exercises, in all its parts, are hereby consti-

> tuted officers and agents of the whole Commonwealth, in faithfully and impartially carrying out the provisions of this act for the common good, irrespective of sects or parties, political or religious.[8]

Six days after the passage of this act the Governor approved another statute which provided for the consolidation of Transylvania and Kentucky universities; at the same time the commissioners of the Sinking Fund were authorized to sell, "at such time and upon such terms as they may deem best for the interest of Kentucky," a part or all of the land scrip donated to the state by Congress. The commissioners were further directed to invest the proceeds of such sales in "interest-bearing bonds of this State, or of the United States, at their discretion; the principal of which bonds shall be forever held sacred for the purpose directed in the act of Congress aforesaid; and the interest thereof, as collected, shall be paid over as directed by law."[9]

The legislature had now prepared the way, and the next step in the task of erecting the Agricultural and Mechanical College devolved upon the Board of Curators of Kentucky University, or rather, upon John B. Bowman, the general agent of the board. Bowman, who was pressing steadily toward his goal of creating a great university, took in stride his new responsibility.[10] He set out immediately to raise the huge sum required by the state for the purchase of land and buildings. Within three months he obtained from the citizens of Lexington subscriptions for more than the necessary amount, and he was able to report his success to the General Assembly before the end of its session. Unnoticed in the enthusiasm of the time was the possibility for future

[8] Kentucky *Acts,* 1865, I, 45-48.

[9] *Ibid.,* 68-69.

[10] This account of the founding of the Agricultural and Mechanical College is based on Kentucky University, Announcement, 1865-1866; Kentucky University, *The Annual Report of the Treasurer of Kentucky University with the Financial History and Condition of the Institution . . .* (Lexington, 1871); and Kentucky University, *Catalog . . .* , 1865-1866.

disagreement in regard to the purpose for which the fund was raised. According to the act of 1865 it was to be expended in the purchase of a farm and the erection of buildings and improvements to carry on the operations of the Agricultural and Mechanical College; but Bowman declared, apparently without contradiction, that the money was to be used "for the purchase of grounds and erection of buildings for [all] the various departments of the University." His interpretation appears to have been entirely legal, and in 1865 it gave no cause for alarm; but thirteen years later the supporters of the state college had reason to regret their carelessness in allowing the title to the lands and buildings bought with their donations to be vested in Kentucky University instead of in the Agricultural and Mechanical College.

In June, 1865, Bowman submitted a report of his activities to the Board of Curators, which indicated its approval. At the same time the curators ratified the scheme of consolidation with Transylvania, whose trustees had already signified their concurrence. Bowman also presented to the curators a plan of organization which was accepted, and the board then ordered the first session of Kentucky University in Lexington to begin in the fall of 1865. Accordingly, the buildings of Transylvania were repaired, the scattered equipment of that venerable institution was collected and pooled with that owned by Kentucky University, and "on the 1st Monday in October" the enlarged university began operations "under the most flattering auspices." During this first year classes were conducted in the College of Science, Literature, and Arts, the College of the Bible, the College of Law, and the Academy, with a total enrollment of approximately three hundred students from "some ten or twelve states of the West and South."

Meanwhile, preparations were being made for the opening of the Agricultural and Mechanical College, which, according to the terms of the land-grant act, had to take place be-

Ashland

Home of Henry Clay, residence of J. B. Bowman, Regent of Kentucky University

fore July 1, 1867. Early in 1866, "after a muture [*sic*] consideration of the advantages of the many desirable locations which were offered, and in harmony with the wishes of a very large majority of the citizens of Fayette who had contributed to the object," Bowman purchased as a site for the school "Ashland," the homestead of Henry Clay, for which he paid $90,000. In addition, for $40,000 he purchased "Woodlands," the estate of J. B. Tilford, which adjoined Ashland and the town and included buildings suitable for immediate use. Together these two estates comprised a tract, 433 acres in area, "of as rich and beautiful land as can be found in America, with a few buildings well adapted to boarding-houses and farm purposes, with fine shrubbery, and fruits, flowers, vines, gardens, lawns, and woodlands, the results of fifty years labor and expense, and which improvements alone could not now be put upon the grounds for the sum paid for the whole estate." It is doubtful that any other of the newly established agricultural colleges, many of which were located in isolated areas among primitive surroundings, could boast a more favorable site.

Bowman now reported to the Governor that Kentucky University had fulfilled the conditions required of it for the establishment of the Agricultural and Mechanical College, that steps were being taken to employ a faculty, and that the opening of the school only awaited action by the state in placing at its disposal the interest arising from the proceeds of the sale of the land scrip. Once more a dangerous delay threatened, for the scrip had not been sold. Unfortunately for Kentucky, large amounts of public lands were being thrown upon the market under the terms of the Morrill Act and the military bounty system, with a resultant reduction in price. At the same time the operation of the Homestead Act reduced the demand for land scrip. Consequently, when Madison C. Johnson, agent of the commissioners of the Sinking Fund, attempted to sell Kentucky's share of the scrip, he found that he "could not obtain 50 cents per acre as a bid." Kentucky officialdom was disturbed. Upon the recommendation of Johnson and Governor Thomas E. Bramlette, the legislature adopted a resolution instructing the members of Congress from this state to work for an amendment to the Morrill Act which would allow Kentucky to "locate said land scrip in such parts of the public domain as are not otherwise appropriated."[11] Pending the outcome of this move, and in order to insure the opening of the Agricultural and Mechanical College within the specified time limit, the legislature by an act approved February 10, 1866, appropriated $20,000 to be paid to the treasurer of the Board of Curators of Kentucky University. This appropriation was in the nature of a loan, since the state reserved the right to reimburse itself from the interest derived from the sale of land scrip. This right, however, was never exercised.

The sale of the land scrip constituted a sore point both before and long after the event. Since the scheme for amending the Morrill Act had little chance for success, two equally unpleasant alternatives faced the state if it intended fulfilling its obligations under the act: either to sell the scrip for less than half its original value, a step which would bring upon the responsible officers charges of wasting the congressional grant; or to support the college by legislative appropriations until an advantageous disposal of the scrip could be effected. In view of the times and the historic reluctance of Kentucky legislatures to support state institutions of higher education, the latter possibility was too much to expect. The appropriation of $20,000 was designed merely as a stopgap to permit a breathing space in which a solution might be found. At the invitation of Bowman, who was eager to have some assurance for the future, the Governor of the state, the Board of Visitors of the Agricultural and Mechanical College, the

[11] Kentucky *House Journal,* 1865-1866, pp. 419-20.

commissioners of the Sinking Fund, and the Board of Directors of the State Agricultural Society met with the Executive Committee of the Board of Curators of Kentucky University at Ashland on June 4, 1866, "for the purposes of general conference in regard to the interests of the College." Describing the meeting, Bowman wrote:

> After a very free consultation and cordial expression of approval and co-operation with us in what was being done for the upbuilding of the College, there was a unanimous concurrence in the recommendation made by the Governor, and the Hon. L. J. Bradford, the distinguished President of the Board of Visitors and of the State Agricultural Society, that the land scrip should be put upon the market immediately for sale, and that the College should be organized as early as possible. In accordance therewith, I understand the Commissioners have resolved to sell, and perhaps the most of it will be sold at once.[12]

In view of this meeting there appears to be little justification in the censure sometimes directed at the commissioners of the Sinking Fund and at their agent, Madison C. Johnson, who actually sold the scrip. Johnson had already reported that land scrip was bringing less than fifty cents an acre and that he had postponed selling it, meanwhile making "arrangements for obtaining immediate information as to any favorable change in the market." These facts were known to the group which assembled at Ashland on June 4, and yet it recommended an immediate sale. The meeting, of course, had no power to authorize or to direct action on the part of the commissioners of the Sinking Fund, but the latter body can hardly be blamed for carrying out the recommendations of a group which included high state officials as well as men directly connected with the school, all of whom might be expected to have the best interests of the college at heart.

12 John B. Bowman, "Annual Report of the Regent," in Kentucky University, *Catalogue,* 1865-1866, p. 56.

Nor should it be forgotten that Bowman and the Executive Committee of the Board of Curators of Kentucky University were present at the meeting which expressed "a unanimous concurrence" in the recommendation that the scrip be sold at once.

Before the month was over the first sale was made, and by the end of January, 1867, the entire allotment had been disposed of, yielding a total of $164,960. This sum, raised to a round figure, $165,000, and invested in state bonds, became the permanent endowment of the Agricultural and Mechanical College. From this endowment the school could expect an annual income of only $9,900, in addition to the revenue from the farm and shops and from fees paid by students.

To all who had expected the state to realize a great sum from the sale of her land scrip, both the selling price and the income from the endowment were shamefully small. Bowman especially was disappointed, for at the time he began his campaign for a union of the agricultural college with Kentucky University land scrip was worth one dollar an acre. He therefore had expected the state to realize at least $330,000 from the sale of its scrip, and he had conjured up a vision of the future in which the agricultural college, with an annual income of around $20,000 from its endowment, would be a source of strength to his own institution. When the state procrastinated in disposing of its grant, land values depreciated, and Bowman's dreams became less sanguine.

The actual endowment and annual income were only half the sums anticipated, but Kentucky University's obligations under its contract with the state were not diminished, for it was still constrained to furnish lands, buildings, and a faculty for the agricultural school, as well as to provide free tuition for approximately three hundred students for the state. Nevertheless, there appears to have been no disposition at that date to abandon the original project. The Board of Curators of Kentucky University already had accepted the loan of $20,000 from the state, had assumed the obligations contracted by Bowman in the purchase of Ashland and Woodlands, had approved a plan of organization for the new college, and in fact had placed it in operation before the entire allotment of scrip was sold. Perhaps the board hoped for future legislative aid to supplement the endowment, a surmise which seems creditable in the light of subsequent pleas for assistance; or perhaps it believed the endowment sufficient, for an annual income of almost $10,000 for an educational institution appeared large to Kentuckians of that day. Whatever the reasons may have been, the work was continued, and Bowman declared that "for one, I was determined to carry out in good faith, and to the letter, our part of the contract."[13] And Bowman's will was the will of the curators.

Kentucky was not the only state whose agricultural college did not receive the fullest advantage of the grant given to it under the terms of the Morrill Act. The haste with which most of the older states in the East and South sought to dispose of their holdings was reflected in low prices and sales to speculators who were able to purchase large quantities of scrip. Rhode Island sold hers for the lowest price of all, between 41 and 42 cents an acre; North Carolina, like Kentucky, received 50 cents; New Hampshire and Ohio, 53 cents; and Indiana, 54 cents. A small number of speculators bought most of the scrip, and by 1866 or 1867 Gleason F. Lewis of Cleveland, Ohio, who eventually acquired approximately five million acres, enjoyed a virtual monopoly in the field. The states which were able to hold their scrip until a later date realized larger returns than those which sold before 1870, as did those southern states which for a time

[13] John B. Bowman, "Report of the Agricultural and Mechanical College of Kentucky, made to the Governor of the State of Kentucky" in Kentucky *Documents*, 1868, II, No. 11, p. 8.

had not been given a share in the grant. These later sales brought the average return from the land scrip up to $1.65 an acre. New York's Ezra Cornell used a part of his state's scrip to take up Wisconsin land which ultimately increased tremendously in value and so provided a large endowment for the agricultural college which he fostered.[14] Unfortunately, Kentucky had no one with the fortune and the foresight of Cornell.

[14] United States Office of Education, *Survey of Land-Grant Colleges and Universities,* directed by Arthur J. Klein (*Bulletin* No. 9, Washington, 1930); Paul W. Gates, *The Wisconsin Pine Lands of Cornell University: A Study in Land Policy and Absentee Ownership* (Ithaca, N. Y., 1943).

Chapter Four

The College Belies Its Promise

ONE SESSION OF KENTUCKY UNIVERSITY, THAT OF 1865-1866, was held in Lexington before the Agricultural and Mechanical College was opened, but plans for the organization of the latter school were being perfected during that year and the next summer. The Board of Curators in February, 1866, accepted the legislature's loan of $20,000 with its conditions and in July selected for the new school a faculty which included John Augustus Williams, presiding officer; Professors Robert Peter, James K. Patterson, and Alexander Winchell; and W. E. Arnold, tutor. The college was to be located upon the estates purchased by Bowman for that purpose, and it was decided to use the existing buildings "for University purposes, although many of them were in a poor state of preservation." Accordingly, hurried preparations were completed, and the Agricultural and Mechanical College opened its doors on October 1, 1866.[1]

In order to understand the organization of the college during the first dozen years of its existence, one should first consider the structure of the university of which it was an important division, a structure which had been conceived and built by John B. Bowman. Bowman was a man with a vision, which, though its outlines were indistinct in the beginning, grew in clarity during his years of devotion to the school, until finally for a brief time it became concrete reality, far from perfect in detail but in general as he had

[1] Kentucky University, Minutes of the Board of Curators, and, Kentucky University, *Catalogue,* provide most of the material for the early years of the Agricultural and Mechanical College. Additional data may be found in Lexington newspaper files.

conceived it. His ideas reflected the thinking of the leaders of the movement for industrial and agricultural education who had spoken and written for more than two decades before he founded the new Kentucky University. He shared with other agrarians the belief that the traditional colleges and universities ignored the needs of all save the upper stratum of society. He joined in the demand for the democratization of education and participated in the movement, strongly supported by the Kentucky State Agricultural Society and other farmers' organizations throughout the country, for the creation of schools for the benefit of the "industrial classes," including those who depended upon the soil for a livelihood. In addition, his thinking was conditioned by a strong, conventional Christian outlook.

Bowman had seen too many schools of higher learning, including his own alma mater, rise, struggle against tremendous odds, and finally disappear. He had seen their high hopes, their inability to arouse popular interest, their dismal poverty, and their futility. He had noted that all were constructed in general along similar lines, and he had come to believe that they were all woefully inadequate, that they were not suited to the times nor to the civilization in which they struggled vainly for survival. He was firmly convinced of the need for educational institutions, but equally as firm was his conviction that a new type of school was necessary. He was willing to abandon his private interests and spend years in the task of erecting the kind of institution which would answer what he conceived to be the needs of Kentucky and the Mississippi Valley at that time.

As early as 1859 he had spoken of the character of American civilization and of a somewhat grandiose "mission of the American people," and had declared that

> As a people . . . we need an education, and educational institutions, peculiar. We need them, not modeled after those whose charters were planted by kings, popes,

and potentates, which answered for their country and times; but we need them founded upon a more modern, American, and Christian basis. We might here modestly hint, that our Puritan Fathers, who came across the ocean in their Pilgrim barks, bearing their patents royal, and laying the foundation of a Yale, a Harvard, and a William and Mary, some two hundred years ago, cramped by the spirit of their times, were but copyists of the now antiquated English models; and most all our smaller colleges have been but dim photographs of the same. It was perhaps reserved for the great Jefferson, after laying aside the robes of his country's highest honors, and breathing intensely the American spirit, to dedicate the evening of his life to the noble work of projecting and building up the first American University, after a liberal and more improved model. And it stands to-day a splendid monument to his undying fame. But alas! he, be it spoken with reverence for his immortal name, failed to breathe that loftier purer spirit of Christianity into his work, which alone can form true life of all correct collegiate government and discipline. Especially do we need them here in the great heart of the nation, in this Mississippi Valley, whose "Father of Waters" drains nearly half the states and territories of the Confederacy, rich in all the elements of growth and greatness, capable of being the granary of the world, and the nursery of empires, the realities of whose wealth and resources are even now more than had been fabled of any orient clime, whose people are teeming and swarming in from all parts of the civilized world, and running to and fro with all the activity of giant youth; here this valley spreads out before us, comparatively undeveloped and uncultivated, and is a field especially inviting to the intelligent farmer and scientific mechanic, the educated teacher and the minister.[2]

At another time he stated that his efforts had never been directed toward building a school for one particular locality, nor had he limited his plan to include a "single *College*,

[2] John B. Bowman, "Introductory Address of John B. Bowman Delivered Before the Board of Curators, Harrodsburg, Ky., on Wednesday, 21st September, 1859."

with a hundred or two boys, with four or five teachers grinding away for their bread upon the old tread-mill of the bygone ages. We had more than enough such sickly half-starved things, called Colleges all over the land, which the people had begun to look upon rather as a curse than a blessing." To the contrary, he envisioned "a University for *young men,* with a grade of scholarship equal to that of any other in our country, furnishing the very highest advantages of education, both general and professional, and which, especially in its ministerial, normal, scientific, and agricultural and mechanical departments, would meet the wants of the great Mississippi Valley." Moreover, his was to be a school for the masses, and as his ideas matured he expressed them in the following words:

> I have but one desire in all this matter; I want to see accomplished through this Institution, the *greatest good* to the *greatest number* of our poor fallen race, thus giving the *greatest glory to God.* I want to build up a people's institution, a *great free* University, eventually open and accessible to the poorest boy in the land, who may come and receive an education *practical* and suitable for any business or profession in life. I want to cheapen this whole matter of education, so that, under the broad expansive influences of our Republican institutions, and our advancing civilization, it may run free, as our great rivers, and bless the coming millions. Hitherto, our Colleges and Universities have been accessible only to the few, such are the expenses attending them. We therefore want a University with all the Colleges attached, giving education of the highest order to all classes. We want ample grounds and buildings and libraries, and apparatus, and museums, and endowments, and prize-funds, and professors of great heads and hearts, men of faith and energy. Indeed we want everything which will make this institution eventually equal to any on this continent. Why should we not have them? I think we can.[3]

[3] Bowman, "Report," in Kentucky University, Announcement, 1865-1866.

Small wonder that a man of such ideals and such boundless enthusiasm was able to lead others and to impart to them some measure of his own spirit. Small wonder that his campaigns for funds opened the pocketbooks of men, both within and outside his own church, who had grown tired of similar pleas in the past. His services in the cause of education called forth "a universal sentiment of gratitude," and his name was placed in the same rank with those of the "founders of the best educational establishments in Europe."[4] For a time almost his every effort was successful, but at last he came in conflict with a force greater than his own enthusiasm. Bitter sectarian opposition had destroyed Transylvania's hopes, and the appearance of a similar spirit ended Bowman's effectiveness as an educator, disrupted his university, and saddened his last days. But before that opposition came into the open, he had laid the foundations of what might have become a great school.

The organization of Kentucky University no less than its guiding philosophy was conceived by Bowman, although the details of that organization were worked out by a committee of the Board of Curators appointed for that purpose. As finally put into effect the scheme included a number of features which departed from customary practice. No provision was made for a President of the university. Instead, each college of the university was governed by its own presiding officer and faculty, and the general supervision of the institution as a whole was "committed to a Regent who is elected from among the Curators and is Ex officio Chairman of the Executive Committee and whose duty it is in connection with the Executive Committee to see that the general laws and statutes of the University are faithfully carried out." The Regent, who was not connected with any faculty, thus served as the chief administrative officer of the university and

[4] Lexington *Kentucky Gazette,* July 14, 1866.

at the same time as the representative of the donors and of the Board of Curators, an arrangement which, it was claimed, gave "unity to the whole plan."

Within the university each college, of which six were provided for in the original plan, was divided into schools or departments. A professor, aided by adjunct professors, instructors, and tutors where needed, was placed in charge of each school, and one of the schools of each college was conducted by the presiding officer, who thus served also as a teacher. All presiding officers, all members of the faculties of the various colleges above the rank of instructor, and the Principal of the Academy composed the Senate of the university over which the Regent presided as chairman ex officio. The entire system of schools and colleges was somewhat cumbersome and inefficient, since many courses were duplicated in, and a number of professors divided their time between, two or more colleges.

Degrees were considered secondary in importance to scholarship and thoroughness in any given course of study. A student enjoyed a wide choice in the selection of courses, for after he had matriculated in one college he found open to him without additional expense classes in all others with the exception of law and medicine. If he chose, he might "graduate" in any school of the university after one year's residence, provided he had completed all the required studies of that department and had "observed habitually all the rules and regulations of the University." If he desired a degree, however, it was necessary that he receive certificates of graduation from a prescribed number of schools in any one of the colleges. In other words, "a young man may study what he pleases, remain as long as he may choose, receive his certificate in any one of the schools, but he cannot receive its academic degrees without having completed in a satisfactory manner" certain required courses. He might also receive a master's degree after having gained the baccalaureate, if he remained in residence an additional year at the university, if he could pass "a satisfactory examination before the proper Faculty in at least three elective branches," and if he paid ten dollars to the library fund. No honorary degrees were conferred.

Such was the general plan of Kentucky University both before and after the Agricultural and Mechanical College was organized, and such was the system of which the state school was made a part. To those who were charged with the task, however, the establishment of that college presented many new and difficult problems. Different views were held in reference to its character and design, and the all-important question lay in choosing the subjects to be taught. Much had been said and written on the subject of agricultural colleges, but no one, not even Senator Morrill himself, had a definite plan for their organization.[5] John B. Bowman characteristically adopted the problem as his own and energetically sought a solution, visiting some of the schools already in operation, examining all available material on the subject, and carefully studying the appropriate laws, both federal and state.

He already believed steadfastly that something more was needed "than the everlasting Latin and Greek and Mathematics, whose myths and forms have hung ghost-like so long in the halls of those hoary institutions [of the old type], and whose slavish worship has crushed the spirit and constitution of many a toil-worn student." He believed the needs of the day were "*science* in its widest ranges," English, literature, modern languages, and the fine arts. According to his views, Americans were "not willing longer to admit that the Law and Medicine, and Divinity, are the only learned professions; but they are determined to exalt and dignify labor, and to ennoble the profession of the great

[5] Henry S. Pritchett, "Introduction," in Kandel, *Federal Aid for Vocational Education,* v.

masses of men upon whose shoulders mainly rests the fabric of our social and Republican institutions—I mean the *Farmers* and *Mechanics*."

From a close examination Bowman concluded that in the Morrill Act Congress had declared the leading objective of the Agricultural and Mechanical College to be "to promote the liberal and *practical* education of the industrial classes in the several pursuits and professions of life." The Kentucky legislature had further provided for the establishment of an experimental farm on which, as well as "in the Mechanical Arts, there shall be provided to the students opportunity for industrial pursuits, at stated times, whereby Agriculture and the Mechanical Arts may be practically learned." Furthermore, the students who so desired were to have the opportunity of earning their support by work on the farm or in the shops.

Practical experience was therefore to be one of the objectives of the school, and yet something more was contemplated than the mere establishment of farms and shops where such experience could be obtained. On the other hand, the erection of a great polytechnical institution was not contemplated, nor was it possible with the means available. The course of study was to be liberal and to cover a wide range of subjects calculated to impart a "*practical* business education." The institution was to be a college for the masses, particularly for those who had neither the time nor the means to pursue a "thorough collegiate and classical course." Labor was to be given dignity, and strict discipline was to be enforced. By a system of combined study and labor, Bowman proposed "to give all young men more practical views of life and true manhood, as well as of experimental knowledge in the useful and honorable pursuits of Agriculture and the Mechanical Arts." With these aims in view an effort was made to establish an educational machinery which should maintain a program of study, labor, and drill.[6]

The original organization of the Agricultural and Mechanical College provided for eleven schools, although all of them did not begin operations immediately. John Augustus Williams, who served as the presiding officer of the college for one and a half years, also conducted during that time the School of Philosophy. The School of English Language and Literature during its first year was headed by Robert Graham, who at the same time presided over the College of Science, Literature, and Arts. Other schools and their professors were: Mathematics, Henry H. White; Chemistry and Experimental Philosophy, Robert Peter; Natural History, Alexander Winchell; History, James K. Patterson; Commercial and Business School, John H. Crutcher and A. B. Smith, who were at the same time instructors in Hollingsworth's Commercial College; and Military Tactics, William E. Arnold. The Schools of Modern Languages, Civil Engineering and Mining, and Fine Arts were without instructors in 1866.

Requirements for admission of the prospective student to the "regular collegiate course in the Agricultural College" were similar to those found in other land-grant colleges of the day: that he be at least sixteen years old, that he "present satisfactory evidence of good moral character and industrious habits," and that he pass an entrance examination upon "English Grammar; Geography; Outlines of History; Ray's Arithmetic, Part III; Ray's Algebra, Part I." Any applicant who found himself unable to pass the examination was allowed to enter the Academy, where he might qualify himself for admission to the college.

Announcements, catalogs, and other mediums of publicity used by the school frequently made much of the legislative

[6] Bowman, "Annual Report," in Kentucky University, *Catalogue,* 1865-1866, p. 57; *ibid.,* 1866-1867, pp. 76-79.

act of 1865 which permitted each representative district of the state to send to the college three students, free of tuition charges, for each member of the General Assembly from that district—these so-called "state students" to be chosen by a majority of the justices of the peace in each district. Although this provision was retained until long after the separation of the college from Kentucky University, at no time did the enrollment of the state students approach the maximum number. In the early years the savings effected by an individual under the provision were slight. According to the catalog of 1866-1867 the yearly tuition fee amounted to thirty dollars, which could be discharged by tuition coupons available at half price, and five years later the fee was reduced to only five dollars. The state students were in some respects a privileged order, since in addition to escaping tuition fees, they found reserved for their use all rooms on the estate set apart as living quarters, leaving other students to seek lodging in private homes. Military drill, however, was required of all alike, with the exception of those to whom the faculty "for sufficient reasons" might grant exemption.

Likewise, manual labor upon the farm or "at such of the Mechanical Arts as are carried on in connection with the same" was compulsory upon all who could not claim exemption because of physical disability. In this matter the college was adopting a policy popular among those who favored industrial education and already in operation in other land-grant institutions. Theoretically, this labor would provide the student with opportunities to apply the knowledge acquired in the classroom, to obtain healthful exercise, and to earn a small income from his efforts. Actually, the "practical work" feature of the new agricultural colleges was not successful, for at many of them, as at the Michigan State Agricultural College, the manual labor consisted of felling trees, digging up swamps, and building barns, fences and bridges, in addition to performing the ordinary farm chores.

Compulsory labor was not popular with students in general, although few were as daring as a class at the Massachusetts Agricultural College which went on strike because of a conviction that the work assigned to it was not educational. Eventually, after persistent trial, in most land-grant colleges the system was abandoned.

At the Agricultural and Mechanical College student laborers were divided into two classes: those who wished to support themselves in whole or in part while attending school and the remainder of the student body. The former were required to work four hours each day for six days a week for a stipend ranging from five to ten cents an hour. The second class labored only two hours a day for five days each week in the "Ornamental and Experimental Grounds and Gardens" for no compensation save "physical exercise and practical instruction." Upon the recommendation of the superintendents of the estates, the faculty was empowered to suspend in whole or in part all manual labor during the winter months.

On the whole, during the first four years of its life the Agricultural and Mechanical College fulfilled the hopes of those who had worked to establish it, even though it was not the kind of institution which agricultural leaders had envisioned. As in the case of the university of which it was a part, it experienced for a time an annual increase in enrollment which, though not spectacular, was healthy and steady, and appeared to presage a bright future for the school. Kentucky University, at least momentarily, claimed to be the outstanding school of the entire Mississippi Valley, and the Agricultural and Mechanical College attracted a larger number of students than any other division of the university. To observers who saw the growing enrollment and other physical signs of progress, the connection of the state college to the sectarian university seemed to have justified itself.

Even the first session, begun hastily after inadequate preparations and among numerous uncertainties, was pronounced a success. Actually, that view of the situation was open to question, for the task of organization proved difficult. The opening date meant little to many prospective students, who appeared on the scene at their own convenience throughout the year. The first semester began in October, by December nearly eighty young men had enrolled, during the next month the attendance reached 120, and at the end of the academic year the records showed a total of 190 matriculates. As in other southern and western states, many of those who appeared, especially among the appointees, were found to be unprepared for college work and were shifted to the Academy. Others were dismissed for breaches of discipline, but the majority quickly fell into the routine of study, labor, and drill. Their irregular entrance all through the year necessitated the organization of more classes than had been contemplated and forced the college to add temporarily to its teaching staff.

After the first year the school was better able to care for its students, and the process of enrollment followed a more conventional pattern. Until the autumn of 1870 each session brought to the university more students than had attended during the previous year, and the Agricultural and Mechanical College led all the divisions of the larger institution. The enrollment reached 220 students in 1867-1868, 285 entered during the third year of the school's existence, and in 1869-1870 a peak of 295 was reached. The number dropped to 211 during the next year, rose to 216 in the following session, and from that point declined annually until 1876, when 110 students enrolled as compared to 94 the previous year. Again, the same trend in general was evident in the university as a whole. Abolition of the Academy and the rise of other colleges in the Mississippi Valley, as well as other events, were cited to explain the diminishing attendance, but a more valid explanation lay in the dissension between Bowman and his opponents in the Christian Church.

In spite of the comparatively large enrollment of the Agricultural and Mechanical College during this period, its graduates were few in number. The first degree ever conferred by the institution, the Bachelor of Science, was received in June, 1869, by William B. Munson of Astoria, Illinois, and the second, in the next year, by T. Volney Munson of the same address. By the summer of 1878 only twelve degrees had been granted.

Had a student been forced to leave the college in 1867 without completing his course of study, he could have returned a decade later and found himself upon familiar ground. Professor White still conducted the School of Mathematics, using for the most part the same reliable textbooks; Professor Peter's department had evolved in name from the School of Chemistry and Experimental Philosophy, through a period during which it was called simply the School of Chemistry, to the School of Chemistry and Physics in 1876; and Patterson's School of History had become the School of Civil History, with minor changes in the courses offered. During the decade, the School of Philosophy became the School of Mental and Moral Philosophy, which was conducted by Patterson after the session of 1868-1869; John Shackelford succeeded J. D. Pickett as head of the School of English Language and Literature in 1871; and Francois M. Helveti in 1869 became a fixture in the School of Modern Languages.

The School of Natural History, the School of Civil Engineering and Mining, and the School of Military Tactics were each conducted by a succession of professors during the period. The catalog did not publish the name of the professor of the School of Fine Arts, if there ever was such a person. A School of Natural Philosophy appeared in 1869 and disappeared five years later, a Department of Telegraphy made a brief appearance on the scene in 1873-1874, and a meteorological observatory was established in 1872.

Though the school was named the Agricultural and Mechanical College, courses in agriculture and mechanics were not to be found in the curriculum. These fields were new to American education, qualified instructors were wanting, and throughout the country there was disagreement over the content of and the method of teaching such courses. In the Kentucky college the professors of chemistry and experimental philosophy and of natural history were supposed to point out, where possible, applications of science to the fields of agriculture and mechanics, and two of the features that distinguished this school from other liberal arts institutions were its farm and its shops. Required to devote a certain portion of their time to manual labor, students received practical training, with very little of the theoretical, in agriculture or mechanics. Perhaps any other successful farm or shop in Kentucky could impart equally good instruction.

Regent Bowman modestly gave credit for the success of the first session of the college to the members of the faculty and in particular to John Augustus Williams, its first presiding officer. Williams, a graduate of Kentucky University, brought to his new position in 1866 a wealth of experience in organizing, teaching in, and administering educational institutions, and an experienced hand was needed to guide the affairs of the infant state college. His connection with it was so brief, however, that his work left little impress upon its development. In January, 1868, in the middle of the second session of the college, he resigned his post as President in order to return to Daughters' College, "his school for young ladies at Harrodsburg," which he had left in other hands upon coming to Kentucky University and which was now in need of his attention. His connection with the school at Lexington was not completely severed at his departure, since on June 26, 1868, he was elected a curator of Kentucky University.

After Williams resigned, Professor Joseph Desha Pickett of the School of English Language and Literature was appointed acting presiding officer of the college. Although he entered upon the duties of his new position on February 3, 1868, he was not formally elected until June 25 of that year, and at the latter date, because a majority of the Board of Curators was not present, he was elected temporary President—that is, he was chosen merely "to fill the vacancy in said office until the next meeting of the Curators." His term of office was no longer than that of his predecessor, and its brevity was equaled only by the burdens it imposed upon him. In the second term of the session of 1867-1868 he not only discharged the duties of presiding officer but at the same time continued to conduct his regular courses in the School of English Literature and, in addition, taught classes in Moral Philosophy and Sacred History, tasks which took from four to five hours each day.

To add to his troubles, Pickett soon found himself at odds with the faculty over which he presided. Believing in one particular case involving the application of the law of arrest in the school that his colleagues did not second his efforts in enforcing rules and regulations, he submitted to the Executive Committee on April 7, 1869, a letter containing his resignation. When the matter was presented to the curators at their regular session in June, they withheld approval of the resignation until a committee could investigate Pickett's charges. By June 10 misunderstandings had been cleared up, and Pickett withdrew his original declaration, still maintaining, however, that "the Faculty was not sufficiently decided in its action to meet the case." On the next day the Board of Curators accepted his resignation as professor of English language and literature in the Agricultural and Mechanical College but at the same time requested him to act as presiding officer of the college during the commencement exercises being held at the time. The board then appointed him to a post in the Bible College and adopted resolutions expressing appreciation for his faithful and zealous application to duty.

When John Augustus Williams resigned the presidency of the Agricultural and Mechanical College, the Board of Curators of Kentucky University embarked upon a long continued search for his successor. Pickett, even after being elected to the position, served only on a temporary basis, although no other candidate appeared on the scene during his incumbency. Upon his resignation the matter was brought to a climax, and during the next few months the search for a presiding officer continued amid mounting confusion.

On June 10, 1869, the curators settled the problem to their own satisfaction by electing Isaac Errett of Alliance College, Ohio, to the post. Elder Errett was at first interested in the offer, but an investigation convinced him of the advisability of rejecting it. In truth, the inducements to accept a position in a struggling college at a low salary were such that the officials were hard pressed to find a candidate for the post. Since the Board of Curators had adjourned before Errett's refusal became known, the choice of a President devolved upon the Executive Committee, which also had to select a head for the College of Arts.

During the summer the positions were filled by temporary appointment, and the catalog of the institution stated that John Augustus Williams would become the new President of the College of Arts and that Henry H. White would occupy the same position in the Agricultural and Mechanical College. Later, however, when the catalog actually was issued it carried an inserted notice to the effect that Williams had been compelled by circumstances to decline the presidency of the College of Arts and that White had been chosen to replace him in that position. Early in August James K. Patterson was appointed to the presidency of the

Agricultural and Mechanical College,[7] and he was formally elected to the office on June 9, 1870, at the next meeting of the Board of Curators.

Within the space of approximately three years five men had been chosen as presiding officers of the Agricultural and Mechanical College, and three of that number actually had served. In 1869 Patterson was not the first choice of the curators, nor even the second, but for forty-one years thereafter no governing board had to choose another President for the Agricultural and Mechanical College.

Compared to their worries in regard to a presiding officer, the curators found the administration of the physical plant of the college a light task. The estates were large enough for almost any expansion the future might require: they included fertile lands for both experimental and commercial farming; they were rich in historical tradition; and potentially they were nearly ideal for the site of such an institution. Some of the buildings, however, were in a state of poor repair. They had never been intended, nor were they particularly suitable, for dormitories, classrooms, and shops. Nevertheless, both the finances and the time for a program of construction were lacking, since it was imperative that the school open before July 1, 1867, in order that the land grant not be forfeited. The existing buildings had to answer for the moment, and others would be erected as soon as possible. To prepare for future construction and to provide funds with which to retire the notes signed by Bowman when he purchased the estates, a Real Estate and Building Fund was established, and Bowman undertook to increase it by means of popular subscriptions.

His plans for aid did not, however, evoke the generous response to which he had been accustomed in the past. For a

[7] Mabel H. Pollitt, *A Biography of James Kennedy Patterson, President of the University of Kentucky from 1869 to 1910* (Louisville, 1925), 97.

time promises were secured, notably from a supposedly wealthy manufacturer and from citizens of Bourbon County, but the manufacturer actually paid only a part of his subscription, and as the university became torn with sectarian dissension its appeals for money fell on deaf ears. In consequence, few additions were made to the physical plant, which in the beginning must have been almost as remembered by a student of a slightly later date:

> Ashland contained 324 acres; and Woodlands, 109 acres. The broken line of two straight parts, which separated these estates, is the line running from the middle of east Main Street to the middle of east High Street, and now forming the rear boundaries of the resident lots on Ashland Avenue and which face approximately west. Woodlands extended in a straight line along the Richmond Road for a distance of 861 yards. The opposite boundary extended in a straight line along the Tate's Creek Road for a distance of 871 yards.
>
> Woodlands was first known to the writer in February, 1878. It was then a beautiful tract of land, covered in most part by native forest trees, many of which are yet standing in the present Woodland Park, and others on what are now resident lots. With the bluegrass sod, there was little or no undergrowth except planted shrubbery. This was abundant on the side adjacent to the city, especially around the principal buildings. There was an open field in the obtuse corner formed by the Richmond Road and the boundary with Ashland, containing some ten or fifteen acres which had been cultivated.
>
> The Tilford residence, which then served as quarters for the A. & M. College, faced toward the city and parallel with the Tate's Creek Road. It was situated on the natural crest or hilltop about eighty yards back from where the city auditorium now stands. It was a rectangular, two story brick building containing about fourteen rooms, with the front wall of the building convex outward. Four of the first floor rooms, one projecting from each corner of the main structure, were quite small. There was one large elongated room on the second floor, over the front entrance hall, which would seat perhaps

one hundred persons or more. This room was used by the college for chapel services and also for lectures and recitations. On both floors, a hall extended centrally from the front to the rear. There was a covered porch in the rear extending between the two projecting corner rooms, and with its ceiling two stories above its floor. A large attic served as armory and general storeroom. There was also a rough dirt basement. Connected with the building at the rear, there was a one story brick structure of two rooms, used as kitchen and dining room for students.

About on the site of the present auditorium, there was an old, dilapidated frame house, the lower rooms of which were occupied by the janitor's family, and the two upper rooms by students. Near this building, toward the main building, there was a small, one room, brick house used by students. Southeast, and near the main building, there was a two story brick building of two rooms, also occupied by students. Near the main building on the east, stood a two room cottage, framed with the planks upright, also serving as quarters for students.

A small open field by the road just south of the main building, was used by the Commandant as a drill ground.

All the lands between Woodlands and the Ashland home was cleared and subject to cultivation.

In location, in beauty of landscape, in fertility of soil, in historic associations, in convertability to serve the purposes and needs of a great school embracing arts, science, agriculture and mechanics, this body of land was not inferior to any other tract of equal size in the State.[8]

The Board of Curators tendered to Bowman, who refused to accept a salary for his services, the use of the mansion at Ashland, where he established his residence. Other buildings on the estates were similarly offered to Presidents Milligan and Graham and to professors with families. Bowman's plans for locating all parts of the university on the estates, for erecting residences, dormitories, lecture halls, and other buildings, and for a program of beautification of the campus

[8] Merry Lewis Pence, "The University of Kentucky," part 1, pp. 15-17 (4 parts, typewritten manuscript).

were destined never to progress further than a mere beginning. His design to make practical farming on the lands a source of income to the institution was more successful, and most of the annual harvests of wheat, corn, and other grains, sorghum, hemp, and vegetables were large and profitable. In addition to the field crops, Bowman in 1869-1870 erected a large barn and stables, "procured a lot of cows," and added dairying to the expanding activities of the college.[9]

Ashland was chosen as the site of the Mechanical Department, which was partially organized in 1868 with the erection of temporary shops for carpenters, wagonmakers, and blacksmiths and with the reception of a steam engine donated to the university by Colonel William H. Grainger of Louisville.[10] Later in the same year G. W. N. Yost of Pennsylvania appeared at Ashland with a mowing machine which he had just invented and which he wished to test. Pleased with the performance of his machine, mellowed by the hospitality accorded him, and interested in the aims of the college as they were stated to him by Regent Bowman, he subscribed $25,000 to aid the work of the institution. A part of the subscription was paid in cash which the Regent used to construct a brick building, "sixty to one hundred and forty-five feet, two stories high, with tower three stories," known as the Ashland Mechanical Works, which was equipped for the manufacture of agricultural implements, especially Yost's Climax Reaper and Mower. In this factory approximately one hundred young men were given an opportunity to learn a trade and at the same time to earn money to help pay for their education. In addition, students were employed in the college paint shop, in the shoe shop, in constructing new buildings and repairing old ones, and in manufacturing

9 Kentucky University, Minutes of the Board of Curators, June 8, 1870, p. 176.

10 Bowman, "Report of the Agricultural and Mechanical College of Kentucky, made to the Governor of the State of Kentucky," in Kentucky *Documents,* 1868, II, No. 11, pp. 19-20.

Ashland Mechanical Works

Mechanical building of the Agricultural and Mechanical College at Ashland

brooms "under the guidance and instruction of a Shaker . . . hired for this purpose."[11]

Indeed, Ashland and Woodlands, combined as the estate of the Agricultural and Mechanical College, were the scene of many diverse activities. Particularly during the late 1860's was there an air of bustle and enthusiasm about the school as students in ever-increasing numbers made their appearance to take advantage of its opportunities. During the next decade, however, the pace slackened and the enthusiasm declined. By the end of the period fewer voices were heard in the classrooms, fewer hands were available for shop work, and the farm was no longer a source of profit. Earlier plans and dreams were abandoned, and an air of comparative quiet, almost of apathy, settled over the college and its estates.

[11] Kentucky University, *Catalogue*, 1869-1870, pp. 89-91.

The surprising extent into which the Agricultural and Mechanical College entered the manufacturing field may be illustrated by a list of the output of the Ashland Mechanical Works for one year:

22 two-horse wagons
64 two-horse plows
43 one-horse plows
60 cultivators
2 coal carts
50 patent trucks
135 mowers painted and put up
22 mowers painted and repaired
8 buggies painted and repaired
2 rockaways painted and repaired
1 Omnibus painted and repaired
35 senior combined Climax machines
4 light spring wagons
2 two-horse spring wagons
1 milk wagon
5 AA harrows
6 sets doubletrees
1 dray
16 tables for Commercial College
1 bank counter
30 benches for Agricultural and Mechanical College
1 machine for making brooms
5 hay rakes
5 patent improved clothes-horses

Chapter Five

Sectarian Controversy

AS MIGHT HAVE BEEN EXPECTED, THE UNION OF THE Agricultural and Mechanical College with Kentucky University was not endorsed by certain elements in the population of Kentucky. During the short time which elapsed between the proposal of the scheme of union and the passage of the legislative act of 1865, opposition had appeared; but under Bowman's influence and impelled by the necessity for haste, the General Assembly moved so rapidly toward a decision that the opposition lacked time to organize. It was consequently overridden, but it did not disappear in the face of defeat. Rather, it remained as a discordant note in the harmony of general good will and bright hopes for the success of the institution.

Thoughtful men of various groups may have experienced misgivings concerning the wisdom of repeating an experiment which had proved disastrous in the past, but it remained for less distinterested persons and organizations to give voice to vigorous protest against the connection of the state college to the sectarian university. To other religious denominations, particularly the Baptists, the Methodists, and the Presbyterians, it appeared that the Christian Church, through somewhat mysterious and doubtless corrupt means, had prevailed upon the legislature to single it out for special favors which amounted to state subsidization of that particular sect. Jealous and apprehensive of the growing power of the Christians, these other denominations turned their attention toward the problem of rectifying the mistake which had been made. If they had been able to present a united front, they might have achieved tangible success, but their distrust of one another prevented co-operation, with the result that their first efforts accomplished little beyond the creation of an undercurrent of dissatisfaction with the operation of the college.

The first notable protest came from the Baptists in 1867, after the end of the first session of the college, and took the form of an address drawn up by a committee of the General Association of that denomination and presented to the people of Kentucky through the newspaper press. This forthright document charged the Christians with being the only sect in the state "that has sought to subsidize a State institution to sectarian interests," and accused them of using foul means to secure that institution in such a hurried fashion that the voice of the people could not be heard upon the matter. Furthermore, it protested against "the action of the Legislature as tending to the union of Church and State"; against "making a State Institution a sectarian one, . . . thereby making, what was designed to be a benefit to all a benefit to one sect"; and "against the Legislature embracing and caressing one sect more than another, and lavishing upon it the patronage and prestige of the State, as not only an act of the grossest injustice in itself, but as tending to breed widespread distrust and discontent." Advocating "an Agricultural and Mechanical College that is a State institution and not a sectarian one; one that shall be under State control and not sectarian; and one that shall be a benefit to the whole State and not to a mere sect only," the Baptists appealed to the people of Kentucky to undo the wrong perpetrated by the legislature. They suggested that the members of the legislature of 1867 be instructed to repeal the act "whereby the A. and M. College was turned over into the hands of the Campbellites, and practically made a sectarian institution."[1]

The Presbyterians would probably have taken similar ac-

[1] Lexington *Kentucky Statesman,* July 19, 1867.

tion if a wise old preacher-politician, Robert J. Breckinridge, had not intervened to convince them of the folly of such a course. Both the advice of Dr. Breckinridge and the cautious policy of his church are surprising, the former because of that individual's admitted reputation of not "being particularly inclined to peaceful measures, or to prudent measures," and the latter because of the usual aggressiveness of that denomination. Nevertheless, when in a meeting of the Synod of Kentucky in 1867 a motion was made to instruct a committee to draw up a report on the Agricultural and Mechanical College question, Breckinridge arose to state that in his opinion they had "better not move in this business." He pointed out the dangers of making more enemies at a time when the church was faced with grave schism within its own ranks and the hazards of becoming involved in a political feud. In stressing the latter point he expressed a view which was supported by other opponents of the college merger: that "the Legislature last year, and the year before, made a political bargain with the Campbellites, by which they gave them over the Transylvania University, with all its funds, and then the grant of land, making them residuary legatees, and lending them money besides; and the supposed consideration was to be taken out at the ballot box, in a running account."

In addition he reminded the Synod that the fight had already been begun by the Methodists and Baptists, and he cautioned his listeners against risking "what little life we have left in such a crowd as that." The proper procedure, therefore, was not to organize the Presbyterian Church "in a crusade as to who is to get and hold that Agricultural College fund," but for the members to act individually as men and as voters to exercise their influence in the matter.[2] Impressed by Breckinridge's advice, the Synod tabled the motion and thus refrained from official protest concerning the

[2] *Ibid.*, October 15, 1867.

status of the college. There could have been no doubt, however, about where the Presbyterians stood on the question, for Breckinridge's statement was published, and his words expressed for himself and his church an unyielding opposition to Christian control of the Agricultural and Mechanical College.

Such attacks naturally brought the defense into action, and the newspapers of the state became the battleground for the opposing factions. One of the earliest writers for the defense referred sarcastically to "certain very zealous sectarian gentlemen [who] have thought it to be their duty to make a systematic and very energetic crusade against this institution, evidently under false impressions in regard to its endowment and its management"; and he undertook to enlighten them concerning the history of the college. He characterized the Christians as public benefactors because of their assumption of responsibility for the institution at a time when its loss to the state seemed imminent. He pointed to guarantees against sectarianism which were written into the act of 1865, he stated that the law was being strictly observed, and he appealed for tolerance and for support of the school.[3] Similar statements were made by others, particularly by Regent Bowman, who in the press and in his annual reports repeatedly declared that the Agricultural and Mechanical College was the property of the state and was not being subverted to sectarian use.

The outbreak of this controversy and the strength of the group opposed to the union of the Agricultural and Mechanical College with Kentucky University brought action from the legislature late in 1867. In consideration of the widespread belief "that the law establishing the Agricultural and Mechanical College of Kentucky is disregarded or evaded, and is controlled by a religious sect for sectarian ends and purposes, which belief is giving great dissatisfaction, and the

[3] *Ibid.*, October 1, 4, 1867.

people are demanding investigation," the General Assembly by joint resolution provided for the appointment of a committee to investigate the matter.[4] This committee proceeded to Lexington where it invited testimony from all who desired to appear before it, summoned witnesses, and concluded that the existing arrangements provided no cause for complaint.

If the opposition was discouraged by the outcome of the investigation, it was soon to find a new point of attack. In June, 1869, the Board of Curators of Kentucky University had decided upon Isaac Errett as President of the Agricultural and Mechanical College. Elder Errett declined the post and the curators were forced to continue their search for a presiding officer. A Lexington paper, the *Kentucky Statesman,* remonstrated with the board for its apparent determination to confine its choice to a member of the Christian Church. The *Statesman* suggested that the Board of Curators, in view of its responsibility to the state, should elect a properly qualified educator without regard to his religious affiliation. The *Apostolic Times,* an uncompromisingly sectarian periodical edited by leading Disciples in Lexington, published an aggressive reply in which it accused the *Statesman* of meddling and rashly stated that the policy of the curators was to have "only a man of their own religious faith as the permanent president of the College."[5]

Such an avowal brought others into the dispute. Charges of violation of the charter were expressed, and the legislature was exhorted to look into the matter. A warm fight was in the making, but before it had progressed to any great length the Board of Curators abruptly settled the issue by choosing James K. Patterson, a Presbyterian, as head of the college and thus cut the ground from under the opposition.

To this point the Christian Church had maintained a

[4] Kentucky *Acts,* 1867-1868, I, 76.
[5] Lexington *Apostolic Times,* September 2, 1869.

EARLIEST KNOWN PHOTOGRAPH OF THE FACULTY OF THE AGRICULTURAL AND ME-
CHANICAL COLLEGE, ABOUT 1870

Standing, left to right: Commandant of cadets (unidentified); Francois M. Helveti, languages; Albert R. Crandall, natural history; James G. White, mathematics

Seated: Dr. Robert Peter, chemistry and experimental philosophy; President James K.
Patterson; unidentified; John Shackelford, English

united front against all attacks and had been able to go successfully about the business of organizing and conducting its university. Its opponents had not been silenced, but they had been frustrated at every turn and could only mark time until an opportunity more favorable to their cause should appear. Unfortunately for the Christians, for the university, and for John B. Bowman, the church itself split into bitterly antagonistic factions and thereby aided in its own defeat. For nearly a decade the Agricultural and Mechanical College, as an innocent bystander, suffered from a struggle which did not concern it directly but which caused its enrollment to drop and its prestige to decrease. The quarrel among the sectarians finally led to a severance of the Agricultural and Mechanical College from Kentucky University, a victory which had proved impossible for the opposition alone to accomplish.

It is an irony of fate that the tremendous success of the Lexington Christian Church in expanding its membership should have contributed to the troubles which arose.[6] By August, 1869, the congregation had grown too large for its house of worship, but a proposal to erect another building evoked only a spirited discussion, a negative decision, and the appointment of a committee to investigate the possibility of enlarging the existing structure. When the committee reported the impracticability of the latter scheme, another place of worship became a necessity for a part of the congregation. After months of discussion, the Christians in April, 1870, purchased the property of the First Presbyterian Church on the corner of Broadway and Second Streets and established the Broadway Christian Church, not as an independent congregation but as a branch of the Main Street Church, with the stipulation that "the whole brotherhood of the city . . . be kept united in one congregation, with a

6 The Records of the Church of Christ in Lexington, Kentucky, 1869 to 1871, relate the course of the schism.

common treasury, so long as it may be found practicable to do so." It was also decided to provide additional buildings in the future if the need should arise, but always the worshipers were to remain members of one large body. No provision was made for the establishment of independent churches, and any effort in that direction was certain to be opposed.

Unfortunately for the interests of peace within the ranks of the church, secession appeared early in 1871 and started a controversy notable for its length and vindictiveness. In April of that year a small group, which included Regent Bowman and Professor J. D. Pickett of Kentucky University, protested against maintaining the rule of one Board of Elders over the entire Christian Brotherhood in Lexington, left the larger congregation, and founded the Second Christian Church. Pointing to the unwieldy size of the larger body as a reason for their action, the secessionists attempted to withdraw peaceably and to maintain friendly relations with the Main Street Church. The latter body, however, refused to co-operate. It censured the bold spirits who had dared to take such a step without prior consent, and when compromise proved impossible, expelled them from the Christian Church as disorderly schismatics. A crusade against the excommunicated brethren was then waged by the editors of the *Apostolic Times,* Elders John W. McGarvey, Moses E. Lard, and L. B. Wilkes, who composed the nucleus of what one of their opponents called the "terrible, iron-hearted, iron-handed dynasty" in control of the Main Street Church.[7] Their attitude was absolutely uncompromising, and as time passed their attacks became more and more bitter.

Representatives of both factions in the quarrel were connected with Kentucky University, and their struggle soon involved that unhappy institution, greatly to its detriment.

[7] L. L. Pinkerton, open letter, April 3, 1871, in Lexington *Kentucky Statesman,* April 4, 1871.

In October, 1871, the College of the Bible was the scene of an act illustrative of sectarian intolerance. For some time it had been customary for the professors to alternate in leading the morning prayer during chapel exercises, but after one of their number, J. D. Pickett, had been expelled from the Main Street Church he was no longer considered fit to exercise this privilege. Consequently, President Milligan and Professor McGarvey informed Pickett that they were opposed to his conducting the service any more, and when his turn to pray again appeared, a student was called on in his stead. Pickett protested vigorously and presented the Board of Curators with a pretty problem which uncovered a split within their own ranks.

The board met in special session and appointed an investigating committee to consider Pickett's protest. After conducting a brief hearing, the committee recommended six resolutions, which were adopted, apparently meant to be a compromise settlement of the dispute. It was recognized that President Milligan had the right to invite anyone whom he chose to conduct devotional services or to withdraw such an invitation if he wished, and that Pickett, as long as he held a professorship, was "entitled to all the rights which any other member of the Faculty enjoys, the prerogative of the President as such only excepted."[8] The Lexington *Daily Press,* November 27, 1871, sarcastically stated that the decision of the board seemed to indicate that "everybody was to blame and everybody wasn't."

Interesting though the Pickett case may have been, it was only a minor incident of a much larger struggle in which control of the university was the bone of contention. Bowman's liberal aims in regard to the school and his desire to make it a benefit to the whole state, even if it were under the control of one religious sect, did not please the more nar-

[8] Kentucky University, Minutes of the Board of Curators, November 22-23, 1871, pp. 206-18.

row leaders of the Lexington Christian Church, and after his disaffection from the latter body his removal from the regency became the object of a relentless campaign. On November 1, early in the controversy, the Louisville *Ledger* published an article, copied by other papers friendly to Bowman, which deplored the attempt to displace the Regent and declared that should he be forced to resign, the state, the donors, and Transylvania would withdraw their interests and leave the Christians to "work out their own ideal in their own way." As interpreted by Bowman's opponents, this article meant that if the Regent was not allowed to continue his control, he would destroy the university, and thereafter they repeatedly charged him with an ambition to rule or ruin.

Many of those who had deplored the connection of the Agricultural and Mechanical College to Kentucky University blamed Bowman for the union and had stated their opposition to him and his plans. As the quarrel between Bowman and his church developed, however, most of his onetime opponents rallied to his support. Pointing to the great work which he had done in building an institution for the benefit of the people, they demanded that he be allowed to continue his constructive program. One writer stated that "it may be that the Regent is 'as a heathen and a publican,' but so long as he affords a place where even the poorest may learn to be a preacher or a lawyer or a mechanic, and that at the smallest cost, or at no cost if he chooses to work, then the people of Kentucky prefer that he shall manage the institution which he himself created." Another considered it preposterous that McGarvey, Lard, and Wilkes should hope to oust Bowman in view of the popular knowledge of what he had done for the school. This particular writer then declared that "it looks too much like the work of pigmies against a giant—of envious schemers against a genuine philanthropist of large heart and broad views."[9]

[9] Lexington *Daily Press,* November 11, 23, 1871.

More important to Bowman than the support of outsiders, who after all were powerless to aid him, was the loyalty of a majority of the Board of Curators whose decisions regarding the university were final. In the early stages of the conflict Bowman had the satisfaction of knowing that though a minority opposed him bitterly, the board was behind him. In November, 1871, goaded by the attacks on him, he charged McGarvey, Wilkes, and Curator W. T. Withers with circulating "slanderous and unjust reports affecting his character as a Gentleman & as a Regent and as Treasurer of Ky. University," and appealed to the board for an investigation. A committee appointed in accordance with his request saw the dangers inherent in the situation and, instead of conducting an investigation, prevailed on Bowman to drop his charges "pending negotiations looking to a reconciliation of parties." At the same time the curators seized the opportunity to show their loyalty to the Regent by three resolutions:

> 1. That the entire history of the University is proof of undividing devotion on the part of Regent Bowman to the interests of the Institution marked by a self sacrifice (being without salary or reward) as also a success rarely if ever equalled.
>
> 2. Our records from the beginning ever open to the inspection of all interests are demonstrations beyond doubt not merely of eminent financial skill but of unflinching integrity in the management of all its finances.
>
> 3. That therefore we express our fullest confidence in Regent Bowman not merely as regards his fidelity in the past but also his competency to carry . . . [the university] forward to still higher success—and unequalifiedly [*sic*] commend the Regent to the confidence as we bespeak for him the cooperation of the friends of education everywhere.[10]

In spite of the support which he might receive from a majority of the curators and from the people of the state,

[10] Kentucky University, Minutes of the Board of Curators, November 24, 1871, p. 221.

the fact remained that Bowman was *persona non grata* to the leaders of the Christian Church, whose determination to remove him did not falter. A spokesman for this group, commenting in a scathing article on the action of the board, uttered a prophecy which proved more correct than perhaps even he dared hope. His statement was direct and definite:

> Upon the score of financial skill and energy, we shall not question the Regent's "competency." But competency alone will not serve him for the future. Unless he retrace his steps back into the Christian Church in such manner as to restore him to the full confidence of the Christian brotherhood in Kentucky and elsewhere he has ended his work for Kentucky University. He will never promote its prosperity more. Sundered from his brethren in Christ, Regent Bowman is dead. The sooner he recognizes this unpleasant fact and acts accordingly, the wiser will he show himself. The Christian Church in Kentucky will never give him their thousands again so long as he stands where he now stands. The Board may pass and re-pass resolutions of indorsement and confidence, but they will nevermore wake a response in the hearts of the Christian brotherhood so long as Regent Bowman is not of them. If it must be so, I ask him to learn even from an enemy.[11]

The truth of this declaration was not evident in 1871, but nevertheless Bowman was rapidly losing his effectiveness. He fought valiantly, refusing to admit defeat, but the odds against him were overwhelming. Two factors combined to undo all that he had accomplished to 1871 in building his university: the depression of 1873, which brought severe financial difficulties; and the stern, well-organized opposition which worked incessantly for the removal of the Regent.

Accompanying and merging with the conflict over Bowman's control of the university was a larger struggle in which the same factions were arrayed against one another. This

[11] Lexington *Apostolic Times,* November 30, 1871.

dispute centered about the question of ownership of the university, and on that point the Christians possessed a decided advantage. They cited the charter and the history of the institution to prove that the university, with the exception of the Agricultural and Mechanical College, belonged to them, and to them alone. At the same time they accused Bowman of attempting to wrest from them their rightful property. Their opponents, on the other hand, appealed to the same facts as proof that the Christians could not claim exclusive ownership. According to this point of view, ownership of the university resided partly in the state and partly in the hands of the donors, who were members of many sects. The Board of Curators endeavored to calm the tempest by a declaration of policy to the effect that they would continue to administer the university "in strict accordance with its Charter under the auspices of the Christian Church."[12] The *Apostolic Times* rejected such a solution, declaring six days later that whatever the relation of the university to the Christians might be, it certainly was not under their "auspices." They either owned it, or they did not own it—the question was as simple as that—and they challenged their opponents to do their worst.

Charges and countercharges flew thick and fast as the dispute sank further into the realm of personalities. Bowman was accused of mismanagement of the finances of the university and of trickery in holding the title of Woodlands for a brief period in his own name, as well as of trying to seize the control of the institution from its rightful owners. When he tried to defend himself, he precipitated even more violent attacks and found himself involved in bitter personal feuds. His supporters lacked nothing in aggressiveness, and the battle raged merrily. Echoes of the struggle reached the halls of the legislature, but an investigating committee in

12 Kentucky University, Minutes of the Board of Curators, November 24, 1871, pp. 221-22.

1872 declared that the contract between the university and the state had not been violated. In the opinion of the committee it would be undesirable to take from the school the income from the agricultural fund, for "to do so would seem like an attempt to injure a great college which is not only non-sectarian, but broad, Catholic, and comprehensive in its spirit and scope."[13]

The possibility that the existing arrangement might be ended by removal of the Agricultural and Mechanical College caused great concern among the people of Lexington who had been generous in their contributions in order to bring the institution to their city. Their apprehension was increased by a growing willingness among the Christians to part with the college if its retention stood in the way of their exercising complete dominance over the university. Lexingtonians in general ardently desired to keep the whole university in their town, preferably under the existing management. Their most able spokesman was the indefatigable Dr. Robert Peter, whose efforts brought upon himself the maledictions of the *Apostolic Times* and the censure of the Board of Curators, which found him guilty of "gross violation of good order in the publication of many articles in our city papers in which various charges were made against some of the Curators & Professors."[14] Nevertheless Dr. Peter continued to publish arguments in support of Bowman and in opposition to sectarian control of the university.

Buffeted by pressure from the opposing factions, the Board of Curators found itself in an unenviable position, and most of its meetings were as "harmonious as a thunder storm."[15] Its efforts to pursue as nearly as possible a middle course failed dismally in regard both to reconciling the antagonists in the quarrel and to excluding from its meetings any con-

[13] Frankfort *Kentucky Yeoman,* March 19, 1872.

[14] Kentucky University, Minutes of the Board of Curators, June 13, 1872, p. 240.

[15] Lexington *Daily Press,* June 19, 1872.

sideration of church troubles and personal feuds. Exchanges among the curators themselves became so bitter and frequent that as a last resort the board on July 13, 1873, adopted resolutions pleading for peace and for the resignation of any member who could not work in harmony with his fellows. Bowman immediately offered to vacate his posts as Regent and treasurer as a means of restoring peace, but he withdrew his resignation at the unanimous insistence of the Board of Curators.

Shortly afterward, the Executive Committee, interpreting these resolutions to mean that any official of the university (not only the curators, who were alone mentioned in the original) who disturbed the "harmony and peace of the institution should resign or be separated from further official relationship with the University," and finding that "Tutor E. B. Smith and Professor J. W. McGarvey did, in disregard of the expressed wish of the Board, publish articles improper and intemperate in their character and calculated to reopen questions of strife and discord," asked the two offenders to resign. Smith complied with the request, but McGarvey refused and was thereupon suspended from his duties in the Bible College. Since Bowman was chairman of the Executive Committee, McGarvey blamed him for its action, and the case developed into a struggle for supremacy between the two men, each backed by his partisans.

The Board of Curators met in September to consider this latest development in the imbroglio and found awaiting it petitions from various Christian churches over the state, all demanding that McGarvey be reinstated and that the regency of the university be abolished. The question to be decided was whether to revoke or to ratify the action of the Executive Committee in suspending McGarvey, and the board invited statements from the principals in the case. The hearings were highly sensational, for they provided an opportunity for airing all the accusations and counteraccusations of the preceding years, and at times the maintenance of any semblance of order proved a difficult task. Finally, after a stormy three-day session, by a strictly partisan vote the Executive Committee was upheld and McGarvey was formally ousted from his professorship.

The decision was a triumph for Bowman, but the victory was almost as costly as a defeat. It is true that his most bitter enemy had been removed from the university, but that enemy had not been silenced. McGarvey now pursued with renewed vigor and with the full co-operation of the Christian Church of the state his unrelenting war on Regent Bowman. After their defeat in the Board of Curators, the Christians emerged with a twofold program: to gain a revision of the charter of the university which would place that school absolutely in their own hands, and to separate the Agricultural and Mechanical College from the university, since retention of the college might endanger the attainment of their primary objective. Accordingly, late in 1873 a form for petitions to the legislature was drawn up in Lexington and sent to congregations over the state for adoption. When the General Assembly convened in January, 1874, it received a large number of these petitions, and it also received remonstrances from the old Board of Trustees of Transylvania University and from citizens of Lexington and Fayette County opposing any changes in the charter. The matter was settled by the Senate when it rejected a bill which would have removed the Agricultural and Mechanical College, and the charter of the university remained undisturbed.

Yet the Christians continued their campaign. At the same time the depression deepened, and Bowman found his difficulties growing ever greater. The failure of the "Short Line" railroad and of the Commercial Bank of Kentucky swept away part of the funds of the university, and though urged by the curators to raise new subscriptions, Bowman found the task beyond even his unquestioned ability. On the contrary, earlier contributors began withdrawing their promises of support, bringing the university dangerously near bankruptcy. Each year the number of students decreased, and at one time the Executive Committee felt itself constrained to deny the truth of a report that the university would not open for its regular session. More dangerous to the Regent's control of the school was a gradual change in the complexion of the Board of Curators. Some of his former supporters weakened under constant attack and went over to the enemy, and others, discouraged, resigned their posts, allowing the opposition to increase in number.

Bowman himself became more arbitrary under the constant strain of his position, and he tended to ignore the Executive Committee when it disagreed with him in the management of university affairs. A crisis occurred in 1877 when the Executive Committee suspended him from the regency until the Board of Curators could meet to act on his case. Before the whole board he defended himself by a report characterized as "a bold, violent and an aggressive document," which served notice that he did not intend surrendering without a struggle. It was apparent that he still commanded a majority in the Board of Curators, and after several days of debate which was called "almost interminable and at times energetic, if not angry," the board resolved not to ratify the action of the Executive Committee in suspending the Regent. At the same time, however, D. S. Goodloe replaced Bowman as treasurer of the university.[16]

The reinstatement of Bowman as Regent did not end the struggle. Bowman was reluctant to turn over to Goodloe the treasurer's accounts, and the board at its next session found it necessary to issue specific orders to him. Again angry charges were hurled at him, the debate waxed warm, and a new effort was made to remove him. And now, at long

[16] Lexington *Kentucky Gazette,* June 13, 16, 1877; Kentucky University, Minutes of the Board of Curators, June 12-14, 1877, pp. 361-74.

last, his enemies were successful. By a vote of 19 to 12 the office of Regent was abolished, and Henry H. White was chosen as the first President of the university.

No longer would Bowman administer the affairs of the university for whose existence he, more than any other man, was responsible. He was still a member of the Board of Curators, but he ceased attending its meetings after the board ordered him to give up all documents in his possession and to vacate the mansion at Ashland, and after it refused to listen to his protests. On July 25, 1879, his seat on the board was declared vacant, thus ending his last tie with the school to which he had devoted his best years.

The leaders of the Christian Church, having at long last won their fight against Bowman, were exultant. At about the time when the regency was abolished, the Agricultural and Mechanical College was taken from the university, leaving nothing to bar the church from controlling the latter institution. It was now to be unquestionably a denominational school, and the vision of a great nonsectarian institution had long since faded and vanished. The curators in the future would run the school according to the wishes of the Christian Church, and that they understood their position is indicated by an appeal which they issued in 1878:

> We announce to the Christian brotherhood, the citizens of Lexington and vicinity, and the general public, that the protracted struggle to obtain possession and control of Kentucky University for its rightful owners, has at length been crowned with signal success. The Regency has been abolished, and Prof. H. H. White has been elected President of the University. An Executive Committee has also been elected, all of whom are members of the Christian Church, of Kentucky, and are in full sympathy with the church. The desire of the brotherhood has at length been achieved, and we now appeal to them to rally around the University.[17]

[17] Lexington *Daily Press,* July 7, 1878.

Chapter Six

The College Stands Alone

HAVING ONCE SETTLED THE PROBLEM OF ESTABLISHing the Agricultural and Mechanical College by connecting it to Kentucky University, the legislature was reluctant to disturb that arrangement even after it became apparent that the state school was being seriously injured by the controversy over the control of the university. As the drastic fight between Bowman and the Christians approached a climax, however, the condition of the college could no longer be ignored. Its enrollment had dropped to a startlingly low ebb, and rumors were being circulated to the effect that its funds were not being applied to their proper uses. Heretofore, no investigation had uncovered any violation of the charter, but in 1877 the Board of Visitors reported that the Board of Curators, in the interest of economy, had suspended certain classes in the College of Arts and that these courses were being taught in the Agricultural and Mechanical College, consuming "so large a portion of the State fund . . . as to leave a sum inadequate to provide proper instruction in branches peculiar to an Agricultural and Mechanical College." Consequently, in the view of the Board of Visitors, the existing connection of the two institutions could no longer be considered advantageous to the state.[1]

Governor James B. McCreary had already suggested, without result, that the legislature consider the possibility of removing the college, and now backed by the report of the Board of Visitors, he became more insistent. In a message to the General Assembly in January, 1878, he traced briefly the history of the institution, recalled how hopes for its

[1] Kentucky *Documents,* 1877, III, No. 22, pp. 5-6.

success had been disappointed, and stressed the need for legislative action. One of three possible courses might be chosen, said he: to make it an independent state institution, to connect it with some other college or university, or to let it remain as it was. The Governor himself believed that it could be conducted with greater benefit to the people as a state institution, and he suggested that by the addition of a small annual appropriation to the income from the endowment, a state normal college might well be connected with it. But the decision rested in the hands of the General Assembly, whose members as agents of the people were urged by McCreary to examine most carefully all matters connected with the school.

Shortly afterward, the legislature established a joint committee to look into the affairs of the college, and hearings began in Lexington. Witnesses were summoned, volunteers were permitted to testify, and altogether the investigation was more thorough than any which had taken place previously. Some of the statements were particularly interesting. An agent of the state Grange appeared before the committee to plead for separation of the college from Kentucky University. Regent Bowman declared that the state had an interest in the estates of Ashland and Woodlands as long as the Agricultural and Mechanical College remained there, but he admitted that he did not know what claim the state would have on the property if the college was divorced from Kentucky University. Dr. Peter thought that the whole trouble might be settled by a modification of the charter which would allow "the interests represented in the general endowment fund . . . [to] have representation in the Board of Curators," and reminded his listeners that the state had never surrendered her right in the old Transylvania endowment. Professor Shackelford believed that the best interests of the public could be served by erecting an independent agricultural college. J. W. McGarvey agreed to the desirability of separation, not so much for the benefit of the college but "because the Christian Church did not want any State aid or any appearance of it."[2]

At the conclusion of its investigation the legislative committee reported that the connection between the college and the university should be severed, and the legislature speedily enacted into law the several recommendations included in the report. The act, approved March 13, 1878, first repealed "so much of the act approved February 22, 1865, . . . as establishes the Agricultural and Mechanical College of Kentucky as one of the colleges of the Kentucky University, and so much of said act as places said Agricultural and Mechanical College under the control of the curators of the Kentucky University, and as allows said curators to receive the interest on the fund arising from the sale of land scrip granted to the Commonwealth of Kentucky by act of Congress." The repeal was to become effective July 1, 1878. The law next created the Agricultural and Mechanical College Commission, whose membership was specifically named and which was directed to make arrangements with the officials of Kentucky University for the temporary operation of the college on its existing site until its final location could be chosen. If agreement with the university should prove impossible to achieve, the operation of the college was to be suspended until other arrangements could be made.

In addition, the commission was directed to take steps toward mapping out the future of the college. It was empowered to "advertise for and receive proposals and offers from counties, towns, or cities, or non-sectarian institutions of learning, in lands, buildings, money, apparatus, &c., or either of them, for the permanent location of said Agricultural and Mechanical College; and after receiving said proposals and offers, they shall report the same to the next regular session of the General Assembly, and shall recom-

[2] Lexington *Weekly Press,* January 30, 1878.

mend that place which shall present the best and greatest inducements, all things considered." At the same time the legislature instructed the commission to ascertain the number of departments which should be included in a first-class state university, taking into consideration the geography and resources of the state as well as the needs of the people, and to recommend a detailed plan for the organization and equipment of such a school. Whatever the future might bring, one thing was certain: "the said Agricultural and Mechanical College shall forever remain a State institution, free from all ecclesiastical entanglements or control." Such was the declaration of the Kentucky legislature, which had at last learned a lesson self-evident for more than fifty years.[3]

The Agricultural and Mechanical College Commission had comparatively little trouble in concluding an agreement with the Board of Curators of Kentucky University.[4] Negotiations began April 11, 1878, when the former group assembled at the Phoenix Hotel in Lexington and discussed the problem in general terms with the Executive Committee of the university. No decision could be reached at that time, and the meeting adjourned after the commission had appointed a committee of five from its membership to conduct a further investigation and to confer at greater length with the Executive Committee. A later session could take no action because of the absence of a quorum, but it fixed a date for another meeting to be held in Louisville, to which the commissioners urged the curators to send representatives who should be authorized to enter into a definite contract for the continuance of the Agricultural and Mechanical College for the next two years.

On the appointed day, July 5, 1878, the two groups convened at the Galt House in Louisville to work out a final agreement. The curators had chosen as their agents R. M.

[3] Kentucky *Acts,* 1877-1878, I, *Public Acts,* 46-51.
[4] Lexington newspapers carried full accounts of the negotiations.

Bishop, E. D. Sayre, George Stoll, W. T. Withers, John B. Bowman, F. K. Hunt, and Madison C. Johnson (the last two members because of their knowledge of legal matters), who stated that Kentucky University was willing to allow the Agricultural and Mechanical College the use of the buildings, apparatus, and other physical equipment on the Woodlands estate, as well as an amount of land to be determined. The proposal also included free instruction in each institution for students in the other, as had been the custom in the past. Since this plan differed little from that presented by the Agricultural and Mechanical College Commission, a compromise was easily reached. Bowman's proposal that the whole of both the Ashland and Woodlands estates be tendered to the state for the use of the college was rejected: by the Agricultural and Mechanical College Commission on the ground that the state had no use for so much property, and also by his own committee, which rebuked him for trying to go beyond the original instructions outlined by the Board of Curators.

The final agreement provided that for two years the Agricultural and Mechanical College should continue in possession of the buildings and equipment formerly used by it, and that for the same length of time it should have exclusive control of land to be selected by the Board of Visitors from both the Ashland and Woodlands tracts, "not exceeding one hundred acres, until the students of said college exceed one hundred in number, and then an additional acre for each additional student," as required. Expenses for repairs and insurance were to be defrayed by the university. Provision for the offer of free instruction by each institution to the students of the other was also included in the settlement, which meant in its entirety that the college, although now under the exclusive control of the state, would continue to operate with little change from its original status.

The responsibility for continuing the work of the college

devolved upon the old Board of Visitors, created in 1865 to look after the state's interest in the school, which now served as a Board of Trustees until the reorganization in 1880. On July 12, 1878, the Board of Visitors met in Lexington to select officers and teachers. It was agreed unanimously, "as a matter of course," that James K. Patterson should continue as President of the institution, and James G. White was elected to the post of treasurer. The board created an Executive Committee, composed of J. P. Metcalfe and W. C. P. Breckinridge of Lexington and C. A. Hardin of Harrodsburg. The faculty included men already connected with the college and with some reputation as educators. Governor McCreary urged the people of Kentucky to take advantage of the privileges now offered, President Patterson let it be known that he would grant free tuition to all who might apply, and the enrollment began to increase immediately. Indeed, the prospects of the school appeared better than had been the case for several years.

Now that the immediate future had been assured, there still remained the much more difficult task of fixing a permanent location for the college. In that problem the citizens of Lexington were particularly concerned, for their contributions had brought the institution to their city, and they felt that its removal would be a grave injustice to themselves. They also believed their city to be the logical site for the college: "Where else in our State can a more suitable tract of land be offered for its location? Where is agriculture carried on with greater success? In what other region can such a display of improved horses, cattle and other animals of the farm be daily exhibited?"[5] In the midst of the struggle over the ownership of the university they contended that morally, if not legally, Ashland and Woodlands belonged to the Agricultural and Mechanical College. That there was some doubt over ownership of the estates was indicated by

[5] Lexington *Daily Press,* April 7, 1878.

the inclusion in the agreement between the Board of Curators and the college commission of a provision that the rights and interests of both parties in the property should be left open to future adjustment.

Yet there could be no denying the fact that the title to these estates had been vested in Kentucky University, and when the college commission began advertising for bids for the permanent location of the agricultural school, Lexington was forced into action. Since no grounds existed for an appeal to the courts, in June, 1879, the donors and citizens of the town, convinced of the weight of their moral claim to the property, presented a petition to the curators of Kentucky University asking that a portion of Ashland and Woodlands be offered to the state. A committee appointed by the Board of Curators to study the request recommended that it be granted, but dissension immediately appeared. Curator Crenshaw voiced his opposition "to having the college here on any condition," R. M. Gano disapproved any "donation to build up a rival institution," and others spoke in similar, selfish vein. In spite of the efforts of a minority under the leadership of W. T. Withers and George Stoll, the Board of Curators, "owing to the financial condition of the University, and for other considerations," formally rejected the demands of the petitioners.[6]

Stirred by this act of gross injustice, as they firmly believed it to be, and by the very real danger of losing the college entirely, the now wrathful citizens of Lexington refused to accept the decision of the curators as final. Once more they asserted that their donations had been made for the specific purpose of buying land on which to locate the agricultural school, and that Kentucky University was therefore morally bound to concede to the community at least a part of the estate. The popular clamor showed no sign of

[6] Kentucky University, Minutes of the Board of Curators, June 10, 11, 1879, pp. 400, 403-405.

abating, and it resulted in a special session of the Board of Curators to reconsider the petition. In issuing the call for the meeting, George Stoll, A. M. Barnes, and D. S. Goodloe pointed out that since the good will of the community was essential to the welfare of Kentucky University, the claim which had been advanced should be met fairly, without evasion. If just, the demand should be granted. If not, its injustice should be clearly demonstrated.

When the board assembled on July 24, 1879, Curator Withers proposed that the Woodlands estate be tendered to the state as the permanent site of the Agricultural and Mechanical College, with the condition that should the school ever be moved, the lands and buildings would revert to Kentucky University. John Shackelford submitted an amendment which provided that both Ashland and Woodlands be offered for the use of the college, but only in case it were restored to its former connection with the university. The curators refused this opportunity to sidestep the real issue, which they believed should be settled at once and forever. Returning to Withers' motion, they then rejected it by a vote of 18 to 10 and thereby permanently divorced the future University of Kentucky from its original home.

The decision was a bitter disappointment to the people of Lexington. There was no time to waste in further recrimination, however, since within the week all bids for the permanent location of the college had to be in the hands of the state commission. Determined to retain the institution in their community, they had not pinned their hopes entirely on the possibility of securing Woodlands but also had resolved upon an alternative site. Late in June the city had agreed to set apart its old fair grounds or city park for that purpose, and Lexington's bid for the permanent location of the college included the offer of this property to the state.

Other towns also considered the advisability of bidding for the college. Frankfort had long wanted it and proposed uniting it with the military institute conducted by Colonel R. D. Allen at Farmdale, near the city. Cynthiana desired it, as did other communities, but none could match the inducements offered by Bowling Green and Lexington, which emerged as the only real contenders in the race. Bowling Green proposed that the school be connected with Ogden College of that city and was therefore able to tender to the state the special inducement of buildings ready for immediate use, as well as a farm and a donation of $30,000 in cash. Not to be outdone, Lexington offered in addition to its city park $50,000 in bonds, of which $30,000 was subscribed by the city government and the remainder by the Fayette County Court. The Agricultural and Mechanical College Commission considered the latter bid the more attractive and recommended to the legislature that Lexington be chosen as the permanent site of the institution.

Still the question was not definitely settled, for the General Assembly had to take action, and that august body moved with a degree of slowness most maddening to Lexingtonians who feared that the college might yet be taken from them. They were especially disturbed by reports that John C. Underwood, chairman of the commission which had recommended acceptance of the Lexington bid, was now working in behalf of his own home town Bowling Green. At the same time certain partisan supporters of the denominational school, Kentucky University, tried to prevent the location of the Agricultural and Mechanical College in Lexington. Curator W. T. Tibbs, who professed to blame the troubles of Kentucky University upon its connection with the state school, went so far as to declare that "the Board of Curators feel that the State is under 'moral obligations' to relieve us as far as possible by removing the A.

and M. College from the scene of discord already occupied permanently by the University in accordance with the requirements of the charter."[7]

The apprehensions of Lexingtonians were quieted late in January, 1880, by the passage of two acts which authorized the city of Lexington and the Fayette County Court to make the donations which each had promised and to levy taxes for payment of their bonds. On February 6 the Governor approved an act locating the college in Lexington under the conditions expressed in the bids, which had provided that if the land and the buildings to be erected with the proceeds from city and county bonds should ever cease to be used by the college they should revert to their donors.

Now that the question of its location had been settled, the independent Agricultural and Mechanical College (or State College, as common usage unofficially named it) was definitely established by an act of incorporation and a supplementary act, approved by Governor Luke Blackburn on March 4 and April 23, 1880. The government, administration, and control of the school were thereafter to be vested in a Board of Trustees whose members should be:

> (1). His Excellency, the Governor of Kentucky, who shall be *ex officio* chairman thereof;
> (2). Twelve men, discreet, intelligent, and prudent, who shall be nominated by the Governor of Kentucky, by and with the advice and consent of the Senate, and who shall hold their office for six years, four retiring and four being appointed at each regular session of the General Assembly;
> (3). And four who shall be elected by the alumni of the institution so soon as said alumni shall exceed one hundred, and shall also hold their office for six years, two being elected and two retiring every two years.

Any vacancies which might occur were to be filled by the remainder of the trustees, the replacements to serve out the

[7] Lexington *Daily Press,* August 24, 1879.

unexpired terms of the members for whom they were substituted. The law required regular meetings to be held in Lexington on the Tuesday immediately preceding the annual commencement, although special sessions might be called when necessary. From their own number the trustees should choose a secretary, a treasurer, and an Executive Committee of five members residing near the seat of the college. Except for a provision that no preference be given any religious denomination in choosing the President, professors, and instructors, the trustees were given complete and unrestricted power to organize and manage the institution under the terms of the laws affecting it.

Few departures were made from the provisions of the original charter. The principle of free tuition to selected students from each representative district was retained, but the number of appointees from each division was lowered from three to two, and by the supplementary act, to only one. In recognition of the need for trained teachers in the public schools and in response to a demand for the establishment of a normal school, the legislature provided free tuition to one student from each county "who has been engaged in teaching, or whose immediate object is to prepare for the profession of teaching," and also empowered the faculty "to grant certificates to teachers, students of the college, valid in any county in Kentucky, under the conditions and limitations prescribed by the common school law."[8]

On March 9 Governor Blackburn, as authorized by law, appointed twelve men, who were then approved by the Senate, to the first Board of Trustees of the Agricultural and Mechanical College: William B. Kinkead, R. S. Bullock, James F. Robinson, Jr., John G. Simrall, L. J. Bradford, P. H. Leslie, A. R. Boone, B. J. Peters, Don Carlos Buell, P. P. Johnston, B. F. Buckner, and W. H. Wadsworth.

During the last week in March, the Governor, the Board

[8] Kentucky *Acts*, 1879-1880, pp. 5-7, 10-12, 18-19, 38-42, 101-104.

of Trustees, and a special joint committee of the legislature met in Lexington to examine the existing condition of the college and to study its needs for the future. A visit to Woodlands convinced the observers that the buildings and facilities then in use were wholly insufficient and that an early removal to the new site, which they found to present "an elevated, picturesque, and healthful appearance," was much to be desired. After considering in general terms the courses of study to be offered and conferring with President Patterson and other members of the faculty, the visitors came to the inescapable conclusion that the income from the land grant alone was not adequate for the successful operation of an institution which would be a credit to the state. Additional revenue was vitally necessary, and the investigators agreed unanimously that it could be obtained only by means of a state tax levied specifically for the benefit of the college. Convinced of the urgency of the matter, both Governor Blackburn and the joint committee recommended that the General Assembly lose no time in providing additional funds. These funds, they suggested, could be raised by "a tax of one cent on the one hundred dollars' worth of taxable property in the State for the first year, three quarters of one cent . . . for the second year, and one half of one cent . . . annually thereafter."[9]

In view of the fact that such a proposal had never before been seriously considered by a Kentucky legislature, Representative W. C. Owen must have been impressed with his own boldness when he introduced in the lower house a bill embodying the recommendation of the joint committee. The progress of the bill was beset with many difficulties. A few legislators, perhaps fearful of committing themselves on an issue which promised to be highly controversial, sought safety in flight from the Capitol to the refuge of their homes.

[9] Kentucky *Senate Journal,* 1879-1880, pp. 982-84.

The opponents of the measure were poorly organized. The denominational colleges had not at that time been aroused to the threat to their own security which they soon envisioned, and consequently they were not ready for concerted action against the bill. Mercer County still resented its loss of Kentucky University, and the Mercer representatives refused to vote for state aid to a college in Lexington. In general, however, central Kentucky supported the appropriation, as did the Louisville delegation, the "Ohio River counties from Union to Greenup," and the "counties along the Tennessee line, from Christian to Wayne."[10] Victory in the lower house was attained by the margin of only one vote more than the majority of the whole house, a majority required by the constitution in the passage of a money bill, and the Senate was only slightly more favorably disposed toward the measure.

The act, which was signed by the Governor on April 29, 1880, did not follow completely the suggestions of the joint committee, but it retained the principle of a special tax, which should be collected "for the purpose of endowing the Agricultural and Mechanical College of Kentucky, and enabling it to purchase the apparatus, machinery and implements necessary for its successful operation, and for the purpose of making proper provisions for the maintenance and conduct of a normal department in connection therewith, for the proper instruction of common school teachers, and for the payment of the necessary salaries to its officers, professors, and instructors, &c., and for the purpose of purchasing a library for the use of the college and the defrayment of the other necessary expenses of said college." State revenue officials were required, beginning in 1880, to assess and collect an annual levy of a half cent on each one hundred dollars value of taxable property in the commonwealth, to keep the income thus obtained separate from other funds, and to pay it to the treasurer of the college as quickly as it was

10 Lexington *Daily Press,* May 1, 1880.

collected. Only property owned by Negroes was exempt from this special tax.[11]

Passage of this act heralded a new day for higher education in Kentucky, and its significance can hardly be overestimated. The legislature of 1879-1880 deserves honored remembrance for breaking with the traditions of the past, for taking a step which was bound to bring vigorous opposition, and for establishing a precedent for the support of the university of the future. Other Kentucky General Assemblies had been confronted with the same problem, but unwilling to commit themselves and the state to direct, continuous aid to institutions of higher learning, they had chosen to try other, less expensive expedients. Those expedients had failed, and their failure had been amply demonstrated by nearly a century of futile struggle to build a creditable university upon an insecure financial basis. By facing the issue squarely the legislators in 1880 committed the state for the first time to a sensible and fundamental policy of supporting its colleges.

The act, of course, did not end the financial worries of the Agricultural and Mechanical College for the future, nor even for the moment. In fact, there soon appeared a very real danger that it would be repealed or be nullified by the courts as a result of a well-organized campaign against it. The reactionaries were defeated, however, mainly because of the heroic efforts of President Patterson, and the tax was retained. Still, the income from all sources, from the state, the Morrill grant, and student fees, was discouragingly small, and the college was destined to struggle through many years of depression in which progress was exasperatingly slow. Yet after 1880 it was assured of a steady revenue, and its officials were able to move ahead with a new feeling of security and with the hope that Kentucky would eventually provide adequate support for its only institution of higher learning.

[11] Kentucky *Acts*, 1879-1880, pp. 137-38.

The Agricultural and Mechanical College in 1878 had begun its new life in a distressingly feeble condition.[12] Its previous dozen years had been almost barren of permanent gains, and the legislature, by divorcing it from its ill-fated connection with Kentucky University, restored it to the uncertainties of the year of its birth. It owned no land, no buildings, and no equipment. Its agricultural, mechanical, and military features virtually had been abandoned, and its enrollment had dropped to a seriously low ebb. It had no home, and it faced the prospect of a precarious existence for an uncertain length of time while its fate was being decided.

On the other hand, the outlook was not altogether disheartening. A constant, though small, income could be expected from the original endowment under the Morrill Act, there was the assurance that the legislature would attempt by some means to provide for the future, and the college could boast a corps of experienced teachers. The faculty, appointed by the Board of Visitors at its meeting on July 12, 1878, included President Patterson as professor of civil history and political economy; John Shackelford, Jr., English language and literature; Robert Peter, chemistry and experimental physics; J. D. Pickett, mental and moral philosophy and modern languages; James G. White, mathematics; A. R. Crandall, formerly with the State Geological Survey, natural history; and Lieutenant R. G. Howell, military tactics and civil engineering. James Crawford became superintendent of the labor department; E. T. Elgan, N. B. Hays, N. J. Weller, and M. L. Pence received appointments as tutors. Few changes in the curriculum were possible because of the lack of funds and the temporary nature of the agreement with Kentucky University. Nevertheless, the Board of Visitors did to a slight extent enlarge the scope of

[12] The separate existence of the Agricultural and Mechanical College after 1878 is reflected in the issuing of bulletins and the keeping of records apart from those of Kentucky University. Used for this study are the *Annual Reports, Annual Registers,* and Minutes of the Board of Trustees.

instruction by adding an advanced course in agricultural chemistry and "special courses of lectures upon the relation of forests to agriculture, of insects to vegetation, of geology to soils, and upon economic botany."

In spite of the uncertainties which it faced, the college took on new life from the very beginning of its career of independence, and even before its permanent location had been fixed, its enrollment began gradually to increase. Wide publicity was given to the fact that it was now a state institution, free of any suspicion of sectarian control, as well as to the many inducements offered to prospective students. The age for admission was lowered from sixteen to fourteen years, and tutors were provided for those who were not prepared for work on the college level. Expenses were held to a minimum. Fees included $12.50 for tuition and $10 for matriculation, figures which after one session were changed to $15 and $5 respectively. If a student wished to live on the campus, for $5 he could rent a room which he then had to furnish at an average cost of $12.50. He might obtain board in private homes for three or four dollars a week, or by participating in the club system he could exist for $1.50 to $2 a week.

Although the custom of paying for student labor had proved unprofitable to the college in the past and such labor was not needed by it to any great extent at that time, the school retained the principle of providing work, at rates of pay ranging from six to eight cents an hour, for a limited number of "meritorious young men in straightened [*sic*] circumstances" in order to assist them in defraying expenses. The matter of tuition was not allowed to debar anyone who wished to enroll in the school. In addition to the beneficiaries of free tuition from each representative district, the Board of Visitors offered a number of free scholarships, and in fact no "meritorious" young man who found himself unable to pay the required fees was turned away.

The success of the first session of the independent college was gratifying to the officials of the institution. One hundred and eighteen students, representing an increase of more than 50 per cent over the enrollment of the previous year, matriculated and more would have entered if there had been greater opportunity for obtaining work.

The first crop on the one hundred acres chosen by the Board of Visitors under the agreement with Kentucky University yielded a good return, and by exercising the most rigid economy the college managed to pay all expenses and to show a balance of more than one thousand dollars in the treasury at the close of the fiscal year. In spite of the limited number of courses offered, President Patterson was able to say that never before during his long connection with the college had he known another session so satisfactory in regard to "attendance, behavior, and application to study."[13]

During the second year of independence, in which 136 students were enrolled, operations continued on a restricted basis, but as the session drew to a close the legislative acts of 1880 opened to the State College an entirely new future. Acceptance of the bids offered by Lexington and Fayette County ended the disturbing problem of choosing a permanent location, although it made necessary a renewal and a continuation of the existing agreement with Kentucky University until buildings could be erected on the old city park. The new tax promised relief from financial worry and made possible a reorganization and an enlargement of the courses of study. The old Board of Visitors was replaced by a Board of Trustees, which in the spring and summer of 1880 began the work of establishing an institution that, if it fulfilled their hopes, would be a credit to the commonwealth.

One of the first and most important tasks which faced the trustees was reorganizing the school in accordance with its

[13] Agricultural and Mechanical College of Kentucky, *Annual Report,* 1878-1879, pp. 5-7; Kentucky *Documents,* 1879, I, No. 3, pp. 5-6.

charter and the acts of 1880. During the immediate past, the Agricultural and Mechanical College, despite its name, had in reality offered little more than a classical course. Now, however, the Board of Trustees, guided by plans that had already been formulated by the Agricultural and Mechanical College Commission, the Board of Visitors, and James K. Patterson, were able to expand the curriculum and to lay the foundation upon which a university would eventually be built. The classical department was retained and enlarged. President Patterson continued to serve as professor of metaphysics, civil history, and political economy; Robert Peter as professor of chemistry and physics; John Shackelford, English; James G. White, mathematics; A. R. Crandall, natural history; and F. M. Helveti, who had succeeded J. D. Pickett in 1879, French and German. John H. Neville, formerly of Kentucky University, became professor of Latin and Greek. R. G. Howell was succeeded during the next year by Second Lieutenant W. C. McFarland as head of the military department and as professor of civil engineering.

By providing for the first time for theoretical and practical instruction in scientific agriculture, the school endeavored to comply more closely than ever before with the terms of the Morrill Act. In the newly instituted Department of Botany, Agriculture, and Horticulture, the forerunner of the present College of Agriculture, each student was required to select "some special experiment in Horticulture or Agriculture" in which he might apply and test the knowledge gained through lectures, recitations, and demonstrations. In choosing a head for this department, the trustees were fortunate to secure the services of an able scholar, W. A. Kellerman, who had devoted many years to the study of plants.

Instruction in mechanics was revived by the establishment of a Department of Practical Mechanics in which the student could apply the principles of physics learned in the classroom and at the same time learn "mechanical drawing, the study and care of tools, work in wood and metals at the bench, the lathe and the forge." David A. King was placed in charge of this department. A Commercial Department was organized under T. C. H. Vance, who also served as traveling agent for the college when needed. The scarcity of good high schools in the state made necessary the establishment of a Preparatory Department, which was placed under the supervision of the President's brother Walter Kennedy Patterson.

The array of departments was completed by the creation of a Normal School, provided for by the legislative act of April 23, 1880, which constituted the forerunner of the present College of Education. Maurice Kirby became its first Principal. The Normal School began with a small attendance, but it attracted more students as the session progressed and became one of the most popular divisions of the college. Its course of study, extending over three years, included the theory and practice of teaching as well as instruction in the subjects to be taught. This program was designed to accomplish the dual purpose of "supplying the immediate necessities of the common schools, and of raising the standard of scholarship among teachers by inducing them whenever possible to aim at something higher than proficiency in the branches required for the lower grade certificate." Each year was to be complete in itself: the first course prepared a student to teach a common school, the second fitted him for the higher grades, and the third enabled him to conduct an academy or a high school. Appropriate certificates were issued at the completion of each year's study.

Graduates of the Normal School and of the Commercial Department received diplomas attesting to their attainments, but no degrees were conferred upon them. Students who completed the courses offered by the Normal School could, if they chose, continue to work for one of the degrees offered in other fields of the college. These awards included the Bachelor of Science as well as the older Bachelor of Arts, both of which required a minimum of one year's residence and a satisfactory examination on the entire course of scientific or of classical study as the case might be. Two years of graduate work in courses prescribed by the faculty entitled a student to a higher degree, either the Master of Arts or the Master of Science.

The establishment of the Normal Department paved the way for the admission of women as students in the college, a revolutionary step for which President Patterson claimed the credit. Backed by Judge W. B. Kinkead, he succeeded in convincing a rather reluctant Board of Trustees that under a fair interpretation of the law women, who comprised a large portion of the teachers of the state, could not be excluded from the Normal School. Before the session of 1880-1881 had ended, forty-three women entered this department. Once the ice had been broken, it was easy to open other classes to them, and soon they were allowed to pursue any course of study upon the same basis as men.[14]

The session of 1880-1881, the first under the new organization, proved to be the most successful in ten years. The addition of new courses and the stability which had been attained through the action of the legislature attracted 234 students, the increase in enrollment being due in part to the return of good times to Kentucky after several years of depression. In only one respect was there cause for dissatisfaction: the accommodations were painfully inadequate. Every room on the Woodlands estate, from cellar to attic, was pressed into service, and still more space was needed to house the various departments. In an effort to alleviate this crowded condition the school rented a part of the Masonic building in Lexington, in which the Chemical, Commercial,

[14] James K. Patterson, "State University of Kentucky" (Commencement Address, June 4, 1908), in Pollitt, *Patterson,* 363.

and Normal departments were established temporarily, but even this expedient worked none too well. The distance between the Masonic Hall and the Woodlands estate necessitated the duplication of some classes, increased the labors of a few professors, and caused officials of the college impatiently to look forward to the time when, upon the completion of its new buildings, the school could move into its own quarters. It was hoped that the buildings would be ready for occupancy at the beginning of the next session, but unforeseen delays in construction caused the college to remain at Woodlands nearly a half year longer than had been anticipated.

While working out the details of reorganization, the Board of Trustees at the same time took steps toward inaugurating the school's first building program, which had been made possible by the donations from Lexington and Fayette County. At its first meeting the board directed its Executive Committee to prepare "plans, specifications and estimates for the building of suitable college buildings, dormitories, etc." On June 8, 1880, the board approved a contract with H. P. McDonald, an architect who had been employed by the building committee for a stipend of sixty dollars to make plans and estimates for a more limited program of construction which should include one "College Building" and a dormitory. On the next day McDonald's plans, enlarged by the addition of a proposal for a home for the President of the college, were accepted. McDonald was employed as architect for the erection of the buildings "at a compensation not exceeding four per cent on $52,000," and the trustees adjourned, well pleased with their accomplishments.

Their complacency vanished, however, in the face of unexpected developments which necessitated changes of plans and caused repeated postponements of the completion of the building program. The first of a succession of rude shocks came in July, 1880, when the building committee opened sealed bids for various phases of work on the buildings, only to find that all of them were too high, the lowest being ten thousand dollars more than the funds available. The Executive Committee then began eliminating some of the features of the original plans (including steam heat for the dormitory) and within the week awarded contracts for the necessary excavations, the brick and concrete work, and the carpenter's work. Soon the new campus was bustling with activity. Its soil was found to be "of a superior quality" for brickmaking, and by August about fifty hands, using "appliances . . . of the latest and most approved patterns," were engaged in manufacturing brick.[15]

After a brief delay, the cornerstone was laid on October 28, 1880, "with the ceremonies usual on such occasions." A large audience, braving the dreariness of a rainy day, assembled to be entertained by Wolf and Trost's Band, to listen to speeches by various dignitaries, and to watch the Masonic Fraternity pour upon the stone "the corn, the wine, and the oil, the emblems of plenty, of gladness and of peace." Under the stone was placed a box, twelve inches by nine by twelve, which was packed with an array of mementos ranging from the acts of incorporation of the college to "a piece of stone brought by Prof. Pickett from Jerusalem," all neatly wrapped in tin foil.[16] The outstanding address of the day was delivered by Governor Blackburn, already a demonstrated friend of the college, who now declared that "for one, I shall ever feel the liveliest interest in its progress and success, and consider its substantial organization the most important measure which has transpired during my administration."[17]

According to the original schedule, the buildings were to be under cover by the winter of 1880 and completed during

[15] Lexington *Daily Press,* August 18, 1880.
[16] *Ibid.,* October 23, 27, 29, 1880.
[17] Frankfort *Weekly Yeoman,* November 2, 1880.

the following February. Construction had not progressed far, however, when the contractor for the stone work refused to continue, necessitating the appointment of a foreman to direct the work under the supervision of the Executive Committee of the Board of Trustees. The brick contractor also virtually abandoned his contract, and other unforeseen delays causing the college considerable expense postponed the completion of the buildings for approximately a year. Meanwhile, instruction continued at Woodlands, where every building was crowded beyond its capacity, where conditions were tolerable only because of the expectation that the college would move to new quarters within a short time.

In February, 1882, the buildings were at last completed, and during the second week of the month the Agricultural and Mechanical College was transferred to its new campus. February 15 had already been set as the date for the dedication ceremonies, a committee on arrangements had been feverishly at work, and a gala celebration had been planned. The appointed day dawned warm and fair, and Lexington, donning holiday attire, welcomed hundreds of guests for the occasion. "All the morning," wrote a reporter, "came the sturdy yeomanry of our country with their wives, their sisters, their cousins, and their aunts, to do honor to our worthy Governor and the Legislature who had come as representatives of the Commonwealth to receive the stately buildings erected for the people's use, and dedicate them to the service of the State."[18]

The occasion was marked by great formality. Toward midmorning a reception committee met the legislators and state officials as they disembarked from their train, and headed by a brass band imported from Cincinnati, the dignitaries marched in procession to the Phoenix Hotel. After lunch as guests of the Chamber of Commerce, the visitors joined

[18] Lexington *Daily Press,* February 16, 1882; Louisville *Courier-Journal,* February 16, 1882.

a parade which wended its way to the college campus. There an immense throng quickly gathered, filling the Main Building and overflowing to the grounds outside. Inside the Chapel, President Charles Louis Loos of Kentucky University opened the exercises with prayer, after which Judge Kinkead introduced the orator of the day, Henry Watterson, "who on behalf of the trustees of the A. and M. College formally delivered the college over to the State."

With his usual wit and common sense, and with occasional flights of higher oratory, "Marse Henry" tried to impress upon his hearers the need for such an institution as was now being dedicated. He recalled the great men of Kentucky's past and contrasted their period with his own day:

> Magnificent Commonwealth! Shrine of the beautiful and godlike! How have the mighty fallen! Tell it not in Boston; proclaim it not in the streets of Cincinnati; the chief among Kentuckians today—the one Kentuckian having a world-wide fame—is a race-horse by the name of Foxhall! I say it with emotion and not without a feeling of gratitude and gratulation that even so much is left us of our ancient prestige and distinction. Nay, I am the last among Kentuckians to sneer at and undervalue the exploits of thoroughbreds, which have not only kept Kentucky in some sort at the front, but have done more to establish a rational conception of America in Europe than all the other diplomatists we ever sent there. I salute, therefore, this first of living Kentuckians with a thrill of exultation; and, if we are not to have a system, let us by all means stand by our stable. That which moves me to protest is that we have no system. I contend, simply, that, if we devote half the patient thought and care to our children that we bestow upon our horses, we shall not only do our duty as citizens, and retain our old place among the States, but may fairly hope in the coming years to bring forth men and women before whose deeds and names even Foxhall will have to bend his proud and maned head!

He appealed to Kentucky to abandon complacency and to

join the march of progress, to learn the value of its soil and climate and natural resources, and to erect and support a system of education "suited to the needs of the time and adequate to our own peculiar wants."

Governor Blackburn, in the speech by which he formally accepted the buildings and grounds on behalf of the state, declared his belief that a new era had dawned for Kentucky. He predicted a great future for the institution, praised those whose work and liberality had aided its progress, commended it to the care of future legislatures, and promised that "as long as I am the Executive of this Commonwealth, I will use every effort in extending the influence, in promoting the efficiency, and in building up the institution which you deliver to the State this day." Other, but briefer, speeches were made by representatives of the two houses of the General Assembly, all of whom pledged their support to the college. A banquet in the evening brought to a close the greatest day which the Agricultural and Mechanical College had ever known.

Chapter Seven

James K. Patterson, Benevolent Despot

THE FOUNDER OF THE AGRICULTURAL AND MECHANICAL College of Kentucky and, consequently, of the present University of Kentucky was John B. Bowman. Paradoxically, failure brought Bowman this claim to honor, for if he had overcome his sectarian opposition and the difficulties arising from depression, the State College would probably have remained merely a part of a quasi-denominational institution. As it happened, he witnessed the breakup of the university which his energy and self-sacrifice had erected, and his career as an educator ended in bitterness. More fortunate was another educator who also became connected with the State College in the year of its birth, who also suffered disappointments and tribulations, but who as President of the institution militantly overcame obstacles for forty-one lean years to build a university whose stability and soundness of scholarship were his chief sources of pride. Bowman had been forgotten until the dedication of Bowman Hall (a men's dormitory) in 1948 rescued him from obscurity, but James Kennedy Patterson is honored as the father and builder of the University of Kentucky.

The memory of Patterson still is green. His long association with the school left an imprint which will never entirely disappear, and the man himself has become almost a legendary figure. An imposing statue near the center of the campus introduces him to the wandering freshman, who may also chance to see the plaque which announces that the present Faculty Club building was once the President's home. The scholarly upperclassman may meet him in the Patterson Literary Society or in the jealously guarded Patterson Collection of the university library. His desk, his chair, and other mementos are carefully preserved. Of all the monuments to his memory, however, the greatest is the university itself.

Those who knew him recall his kindness and his wisdom, as well as his tyranny and his many idiosyncracies. They remember his striking appearance, his bright, intelligent eyes, his straggling whiskers, the tilt of his head, his falsetto voice, and the ever-present crutch with which he swung along at a brisk pace. No one could forget his forceful personality. He was a man of wide interests; the scope and thoroughness of his intellectual activities were limited only by the exacting nature of his position as head of a struggling college. He was a scholar, although he achieved greatness in no field of scholarship. His writings show him to have been an acute observer of world affairs, as well as a devout Presbyterian and a proud son of old Scotland. He was devoted to his family and, above all, to the school which he looked upon almost as his own child. Perhaps not a great man, at least he approached greatness, for no puny figure could have matched his accomplishments. To him the University of Kentucky owes more than to any other individual, and it is unfortunate that he is remembered chiefly as an old, jealous man, made bitter by forced severance from the school he had built.

James Kennedy Patterson was born in the Parish of Gorbals, Glasgow, Scotland, on March 26, 1833, the first of a brood of six children of Andrew and Janet Kennedy Patterson. When he was four, an accident crippled him for life, but his lameness came at such an early age that he was able to accept it almost as a natural condition, with no complaint or mental sensitiveness. It is said that later in life he sometimes pointed to his withered limb with the remark, "the little lame leg was the architect of my fortunes."[1] Learning

[1] The material for this sketch of Patterson's life was taken largely from Pollitt, *Patterson,* and William B. Smith, "James Kennedy Patterson, Pater Universitatis Kentuckiensis, His Career, His Achievements, His Personality" (manuscript in Bureau of Source Materials).

to walk again with the aid of a crutch, the lad at the age of six was able to attend the parish school where he "learned to read and to write and to work with numbers."

Meanwhile, the stress of the times brought to his father, a calico printer, frequent periods of unemployment and led to a decision to emigrate to America in 1842. In the next year Andrew Patterson, who had not found work in New England, moved his family westward to Bartholomew County, Indiana, where with the help of his brother-in-law, a South Carolina planter, he purchased a farm. There the whole family, including the cripple, labored long and hard under unfamiliar conditions to wrest a meager living from the soil. No schools were available, and for six years none of the children received any formal education. The mother, however, endeavored to give them private instruction, and James soon became a voracious reader, repeatedly perusing the few books owned by the family and borrowing as many as possible from the neighbors.

In 1849 James was apprenticed to a tailor in Madison, Indiana, but before he had hardly begun his new work he was enabled through the kindness of fellow Scots to enter an academy. Poverty compelled him to leave this institution in 1850, and at the age of seventeen he began his long career as a teacher, conducting four brief terms of school in neighboring communities within one year.

Convinced that his destiny lay beyond the ranks of underpaid itinerant teachers, he entered Hanover College in 1851 and graduated in 1856, the intervening time being occupied alternately with study at Hanover and teaching at New Castle, Kentucky, where he first appeared in 1854. Immediately after his graduation, he became Principal of a Presbyterian Academy in Greenville, Kentucky, where he remained for three years. There he met Lucelia, daughter of Captain Charles Fox Wing, and he married her in 1859. Patterson's thriftiness, which enabled him to accumulate a small fortune during his life as a poorly paid educator, was evinced at this early date when he saved enough money to buy with his brother William more than eight hundred acres of western land, which they were able to sell much later for a sizable profit.

Shortly before his marriage, Patterson secured a position as Principal of the Preparatory Department of Stewart College, Clarksville, Tennessee, where he was promoted in 1860 to the professorship of Latin and Greek in the college proper. During his spare time he plunged into a study of the classics with the local Presbyterian minister, who had been educated at King's College, Belfast, Ireland. The association with Dr. Wardlaw encouraged Patterson to begin the fulfillment of a long-cherished desire to enter the Presbyterian ministry. He placed himself under the care of the Nashville Presbytery, undertook the study of theological literature, and began preparing himself for theological school and eventually for a pulpit. He probably would have attained his objective if the Civil War had not interfered and changed the direction of his aim.

In 1861, within a few days after the fall of Fort Sumter, Stewart College closed its doors, leaving Patterson without employment and with no plans for the immediate future. Upon returning to the home of his father-in-law, however, he found that fate was more kind than had first been apparent. Awaiting his arrival was the Rev. R. G. Brank of Lexington, who advised the troubled young man to apply for the principalship of the high school to which the once proud Transylvania University had degenerated. Patterson went to Lexington to submit his application in person, and the Board of Trustees employed him almost immediately. He chose his two brothers William and Andrew as his assistants, and in the fall of 1861 he began a struggle to maintain the school during the chaotic war years. In addition to his administrative troubles, he was saddened by the deaths, within the space of two years, of his father and the two brothers whom he had brought to Lexington. Ever mindful of family ties, in 1864 he made a younger brother Walter his assistant.

With the return of peace and the educational revival which was certain to follow, Patterson was in a logical position to become the head of a reorganized Transylvania College, but his opportunity faded when the school was united with Kentucky University. Instead, upon the recommendation of the Transylvania Board of Trustees he was appointed to a lesser position as professor of Latin, political economy, and civil history in the new university at a smaller salary than he had been receiving. When the Agricultural and Mechanical College opened its doors in 1866, he became a member of its first faculty as professor of history. At the same time he continued to teach in the College of Arts, conducted one class each day in Sayre Institute, and gave instruction to a number of private pupils. His duties were manifold, and yet he found time for self-instruction, which made these years the most satisfying intellectually and perhaps the most important, from a personal standpoint, of his whole life. He busied himself with Latin, Greek, philosophy, philogy, history, and science, and he waded without guidance into Sanskrit, a language which always thereafter seemed to hold a special fascination for him.

After 1868 his attention was diverted somewhat by a series of events which turned his thoughts into less scholarly channels, although he did not entirely abandon his studies. In that year he became the father of a boy, whom he named William Andrew, of whom he was inordinately proud and whose training and intellectual development became his chief concern. (Another child, a daughter born in 1870, died at the age of six months.) In addition, he was once again saddled with the burden of administrative duties when in August, 1869, he was elected head of the Agricultural and Mechanical College, a post which he retained until his resignation in 1910. From 1871 to 1875 he also contributed regularly to the Louisville *Courier-Journal,* presenting scholarly articles on foreign affairs and domestic politics. In 1875 he went to Europe as the official representative of Kentucky at the International Geographic Congress held in Paris, a journey which brought him new acquaintances and new experiences, broadened his outlook, and strengthened his conviction that one of the greatest needs of his adopted state was "a first-class university adequately endowed, where all her youth may obtain as good an education as can be had anywhere in America."

Well might he feel concern for the future of higher education in Kentucky, for by 1875 the university which had been enthusiastically launched ten years earlier had lost its pristine vigor and was carrying the Agricultural and Mechanical College downward with it. Patterson enjoyed the confidence and respect of John B. Bowman, and the relations between the two men were entirely friendly. In the struggle between the Regent and the Christian Church, Patterson sympathized with the former, although he remained as much as possible out of the conflict. He did, however, appear before the legislature in 1874 to oppose the attempt by the Christians to revise the charter of the university, and his statement contributed to the defeat of their scheme. He was also quick to defend himself against insinuations published in February of the same year by the *Apostolic Times.* Occasionally during the fight between Bowman and the Christians over control of the university, Patterson's forbearance must have been sorely tried, but as presiding officer of the state institution he refused to participate in a sectarian quarrel.

His lofty and correct position was rewarded in 1878 when, after the legislature had dissolved the connection between the state school and Kentucky University, he was elected immediately and unanimously to the presidency of the independent Agricultural and Mechanical College. At the request of the Agricultural and Mechanical College Commission he prepared the bill which established the college on a temporary basis in 1878, and his advice was followed in the reorganization of the institution. He was instrumental in drawing up the petition by which the donors to Kentucky University from Lexington and Fayette County unsuccessfully asked the Board of Curators to concede to the State College an equitable share of the Ashland and Woodlands estates, and "he assailed Bowman as being guilty of a culpable oversight" in vesting the title to this property in the university rather than in the college. He worked to retain the institution in Lexington, appealing to the City Council and to the Fayette County Court for aid shortly before these bodies decided officially to bid for the location of the school permanently in Lexington.

His experience, his study of agricultural colleges in general, his familiarity with the needs of his own institution, and his sound judgment made Patterson the most important figure in the events attending the erection of the independent Agricultural and Mechanical College. He was consulted by the Governor, the college commission, and the Board of Trustees, and to a very great extent the legislation of 1878 and 1880 reflected his ideas and advice. His was the responsibility for carrying on the work of the school, and whatever successes were attained were in a real sense his own triumphs. In fact, from 1878 to the day of his retirement, his life and the life of the college were so intertwined as to be inseparable; the biography of Patterson is during those years a history of the University of Kentucky.

It is no great exaggeration to state that the University of Kentucky owes its very existence to Patterson, for on at least two occasions he snatched it from imminent destruction. The first instance occurred in connection with the school's initial building program, which was threatened with disruption within a few months after its auspicious beginning. As work on the buildings progressed, it became painfully apparent that the actual costs of construction would far exceed the original estimates as the result of expensive delays and the necessity of reletting at higher figures some of the contracts which were abandoned by the original contractors. Late in 1881, when the buildings were only half completed, all available funds were exhausted, and construction came to a halt. Without additional money nothing more could be done.

The situation was highly dangerous, and only by treading warily could an explosion be averted. The trustees could not appeal to the legislature, nor could they even make their troubles known, because the school was already under attack by the denominational colleges, whose representatives would gleefully have seized the opportunity to make accusations of wastefulness and to proclaim a scandal. Other opponents of the half-cent tax would have joined the clamor, and the fate of the college would have been placed in jeopardy. Under these conditions the wisest course seemed to be to maintain silence, to borrow funds with which to continue construction, and to depend on future income to liquidate the indebtedness. Patterson's dramatic account of the difficulty may be taken as substantially correct:

> Major Bullock and I were appointed a committee to effect a loan from one of the banks. His bank refused to touch it. So did the First National, D. A. Sayre & Co., and the old Northern. They said: "You have no security to offer; you cannot hypothecate the income from the congressional fund; you have only a contingent usufruct of your grounds, and if the half-cent tax be knocked off, as it is likely to be, the whole will collapse like an egg-shell." In this emergency I took the desperate chance. I led the forlorn hope. I borrowed the money from the Northern Bank on my own securities, took the notes of

> the college and placed the necessary funds for carrying on the buildings to completion in the hands of the Executive Committee. When we finished building, and before the motion to repeal the tax was defeated, the college was $35,000 in debt. But it was all paid within a few years. No one outside the Executive Committee and the Board knew anything of the crisis until it was all over. I bore the burden and the risk alone. Not one of the members of the Board would share the risk with me. In justice to myself, I make this a matter of record.[2]

The risk was great, for if the half-cent tax had been repealed, the school would have been bankrupt, and Patterson's small fortune would probably have been irretrievably gone. Nevertheless, he had saved the day. His timely act made possible the resumption of construction, and the buildings were pushed toward completion. The dedication ceremonies in 1882 were more than a marker along the road of educational progress in Kentucky; they celebrated a personal triumph for the President of the college.

Even while this difficulty was being resolved, another, more fundamental struggle arose to endanger the life of the sorely troubled institution, and Patterson again was obliged to come to the rescue. The storm had been brewing since the passage of the half-cent tax in 1880, a measure which was considered by the denominational colleges in Kentucky as a great injustice to themselves. Murmurs of discontent during the following months led the Lexington *Daily Transcript* on November 19, 1881, to observe bitterly that "some denominational colleges are private institutions of learning, and are afraid the A. & M. College will cut into the patronage they receive, and consequently are trying to make war upon it. The masses must go uneducated if it hurts them. This is a vital strike at the poor, and base pandering to the rich for lucre's sake." Seeing in the Agricultural and Me-

2 Address made at a banquet in honor of Judge Henry Stites Barker, January 5, 1911 (manuscript in University of Kentucky Library).

chanical College and in the tax levied to support it a common danger, the sectarian schools were able temporarily to drop their own differences and to organize against the State College an opposition which emerged aggressively into the open late in 1881.

At a meeting in Lexington in November of that year representatives of six denominational colleges prepared for publication an appeal to the people of Kentucky which constituted a strong presentation of their case. They first declared their friendship toward the principle of an Agricultural and Mechanical College, "pure and simple," but they strongly opposed inclusion in its curriculum of courses other than those directly related to mechanics and agriculture. In their opinion the institution should be merely a limited technological school, for whose support the income from the federal endowment would be sufficient. They declared it wrong in principle for the state to tax the many for the benefit of the few, "the few" in this case being the small number of people who wished to attend a college. The legislation, according to their argument, catered to the wealthy, since "it is only as a poor boy, here and there, desires to enter the learned professions that he ever tries to get a college education." Apparently they did not consider an extension of educational opportunities desirable, since they maintained that there were already "almost too many" colleges in Kentucky. From their viewpoint it was "unjust to use the power and wealth of the State to injure the existing colleges," for "what encouragement can there be for the citizens of Kentucky to perform generous deeds and build magnificent monuments if the State comes on afterwards and even taxes herself to sweep them all away?"[3]

The attack, selfish and illogical though it may have been, was well timed; it was designed to launch a surprise offensive against the tax shortly before the legislators departed from

[3] Lexington *Daily Transcript*, November 22, 1881.

their homes to attend the next regular meeting of the General Assembly. Solely by chance it was answered immediately. On November 18 Patterson happened to be in Louisville for a conference with Henry Watterson, and he discovered the attack in the columns of the *Courier-Journal* of that date. Greatly troubled by its appearance, he devoted most of the night to framing a reply, which was carried by the same newspaper on the next day. Patterson's alertness enabled the legislators and the general public to consider both sides of the dispute at the same time and nullified the element of surprise which would have been advantageous to the denominationalists.

This swift exchange was but a preliminary skirmish to the real fight which developed after the legislature began its deliberations. Both factions lobbied manfully to attain their respective ends, and the newspapers, both editorially and through reader contributions, joined vigorously in the debate. To a slight degree the effectiveness of the denominationalists was hampered by a disagreement among the officials of Kentucky University. The president of the Board of Curators of that institution, Elder J. S. Sweeney, had signed the appeal against the state tax, but the Executive Committee, the faculty, and the President disclaimed any responsibility for or connection with the attack. Yet the organization among the sectarian college leaders was strong, and President R. M. Dudley of Georgetown College and Chancellor L. H. Blanton of Central University appeared in Frankfort with the avowed intention to "fight the A. & M. College as now organized and equipped to the bitter end."[4]

President Patterson was also on the scene, diligently buttonholing legislators and professing confidence in a victorious culmination of the struggle. His confidence was not without justification, for none of the arguments thus far advanced

[4] Louisville *Courier-Journal,* December 1, 1881.

seemed to carry great weight with the majority of the senators and representatives. In January, 1882, President Ormond Beatty of Centre College appeared before a joint committee of the Senate and House to denounce the half-cent tax and the Agricultural and Mechanical College in the most elaborate and the strongest statement which had yet been uttered. His was thought to be a telling blow, but it was successfully parried by Patterson, whose two-and-a-half hour speech before the same committee has been characterized as "a masterly address, perhaps the most distinctive that he ever delivered."[5] He was frequently applauded by the large audience which had assembled to hear him, and it was evident that he had convinced his hearers of the need for state-supported higher education.

The opposition was by no means ready to admit defeat, however, and it now launched a new assault that had been held in reserve, which proved the most difficult of all to withstand. Previous argument had centered about public policy in regard to the wisdom and justice of levying a general tax for the support of an institution of higher education, but now the attack was directed along purely legalistic lines. An imposing array of legal talent had been employed by the denominationalists, and on the evening of January 25, 1882, William Lindsey, formerly Chief Justice of the Court of Appeals, appeared before the legislative joint committee with the intention of proving the half-cent tax unconstitutional. He appeared to have a good case, for the constitution of Kentucky included a provision which stated that "The capital of the fund called and known as the 'Common School Fund,' . . . together with any sum which may be hereafter raised by the State, by taxation or otherwise, for purposes of education, shall be held inviolate, for the purpose of sustaining a system of Common Schools. The interest and divi-

[5] Smith, "James Kennedy Patterson," 111.

dends of said funds, together with any sum which may be produced for that purpose, by taxation or otherwise, may be appropriated in aid of Common Schools, but for no other purpose." Judge Lindsey declared these words to mean that no tax could be levied for the support of any educational institution above the common school level, and his interpretation was quite convincing. When he finished speaking, the State College seemed doomed.[6]

The Board of Trustees of the Agricultural and Mechanical College had no funds with which to employ legal talent, and at any rate it was doubtful that any prominent member of the bar would have undertaken the defense. John G. Carlisle, who was consulted by Judge Kinkead in behalf of the State College, declared emphatically: "You have no case. Article II of the constitution is plainly and decisively against you."[7] Again it was Patterson who came to the rescue. Impelled by a chance remark made by J. P. Metcalfe, clerk of the Court of Appeals, he investigated the debates held prior to the adoption of the constitution in 1850, and there he found the basis for his reply. His opportunity came on the evening of January 30, when he addressed the joint committee in the presence of an audience which included legislators and a large delegation of visitors from Lexington. He was preceded by J. S. Simrall, who attempted from a legal standpoint to refute the arguments of Judge Lindsey, but the real event of the evening was Patterson's speech.

It was a masterpiece. Patterson disputed Lindsey's interpretation of the purpose of the Agricultural and Mechanical College, corrected the Judge's lofty references to history, and showed how denominational control had ruined old Transylvania. Turning to the heart of the issue, he used the principle of contemporaneous construction, citing the

[6] Lexington *Daily Transcript,* January 26, 1882.

[7] Patterson, Address in honor of Judge Barker, January 5, 1911.

debates in the constitutional convention of 1849, to prove that the framers of the constitution had sought merely to protect the Common School Fund, not to debar state aid to institutions of higher learning. He appealed to the legislature, in view of his findings, to "brush away the flimsy web of technicalities woven by an ingenious advocate, and stand upon the solid substratum of fact and common sense," and he approached the close of his argument with a fiery challenge:

> If, gentlemen of the Legislature of Kentucky, you desire to apply to the purposes of a liberal and practical education the fund received from the General Government by the State, to supplement its deficiency in order to render it effective; to carry out in a liberal and magnanimous spirit the trust accepted in 1865; to realize the expectation created in 1879; to go on in the good work begun in 1880; to fill the halls which await your sons with a vigorous, hardy, self-reliant youth, and to provide them with such facilities and opportunities as the geographical position of Kentucky, her agricultural and mineral wealth, her traditions and influence and dignity demand for those to whom you will ere long hand over the administration of the affairs of this Commonwealth, and to do this in a spirit generous, comprehensive, catholic, then stand by your College. Nurture it, cherish it, build it up, and make it your glory and your pride.
>
> But if you care little for the present, and less for the future—if you are indifferent to your trusts, preferring stagnation to activity, ignorance to culture, denominational vassalage to progress, expansion, vitality, freedom, then withdraw the aid which now vitalizes your scant income from the Congressional fund, cut down the emoluments of your College to meet the demands of the clergy, write upon your statute books that Kentucky is too miserly or too obsequious to clerical menace to maintain the education which the Church will not allow you to give them at home. This is the alternative placed before you today.

> Let Kentucky rouse from her slumber, shake off her lethargy, and in the provision which she makes for the education of her sons dare to be free.[8]

At that moment there was no doubt about his triumph. He carried his audience with him, and frequent roars of applause testified to the skill and effectiveness with which he drove home point after point. The majority of the members of the legislature, one of whom characterized the speech as "the ablest constitutional argument he had ever heard," was convinced.[9] Patterson had won a victory in the face of almost certain defeat, and he thereby rendered to the school and to the state a service granted to few college Presidents. He had insured the continuation of his school upon a broad and liberal basis, had successfully defended the cause of the many against the attack by the few, and incidentally, had saved his own fortune, which would have been lost if the tax had been nullified.

The denominationalists had not yet exhausted their attack, but the remainder of the struggle was anticlimactic. Judge Lindsey had the opportunity of uttering the last word before the joint committee, but he could not destroy the impression that Patterson had made. Late in February the House of Representatives began consideration of the repeal of the half-cent tax, but the bill was soon tabled, much to the relief of supporters of the college.

Defeated in the General Assembly, the opposition now showed its determination and versatility by an appeal to the courts. Almost simultaneously in April, 1882, suits to test the constitutionality of the act of 1880 were brought in the Circuit Court of Magoffin County and in the Louisville Chancery Court, and in both cases the college emerged

[8] James K. Patterson, *Constitutionality of the Tax for the State College. Reply of James K. Patterson . . . to the Argument of Judge Lindsey before the A. & M. College Committee, in the Hall of the House of Representatives, Monday Evening, January 30, 1882* (Frankfort, 1882), 29.

[9] Lexington *Daily Press,* February 2, 1882.

victorious. The hotter of the two fights developed in Louisville, where each side was represented by able counsel whose arguments lasted two full days. In this instance W. C. P. Breckinridge rendered yeoman service in defense of the college, for his presentation of the case was so "remarkably clear, forcible and logical" that a member of the opposing counsel later admitted that it "shook my confidence in our case to the foundation."[10]

As a last resort the losers now submitted the question to the Court of Appeals, where it was argued in the spring of 1883. W. C. P. Breckinridge, Temple Bodley, and Henry Stites Barker represented the college, and Patterson, though not an attorney, was also permitted to file a brief. Credit for the victorious outcome was claimed by Patterson, who declared that "it was generally understood by all concerned, by the court, and by the attorneys that my brief won the case," but according to opposing counsel, Breckinridge's argument was at least equally important.[11] At any rate, the decision was not soon reached, and the case dragged along for nearly a decade. Finally, in 1890 the Court of Appeals, admitting that "its consideration has been delayed because of repeated legislative agitation upon the subject," declared that "as a convention is now in session, framing a proposed organic law for the State, it is proper that it should be decided." Accordingly, on December 9 the court handed down a decision upholding the constitutionality of the half-cent tax, and the question was finally laid to rest.[12]

The ruling on the constitutionality of the tax did not mean that the opposition to the State College was ended, for the fight dragged through many long years before it gasped its last, although its strength declined with the passage of time. For years nearly every mention of the school in the

[10] Alex P. Humphrey to Desha Breckinridge, December 23, 1905, in Lexington *Herald*, December 25, 1905.

[11] *Ibid.*, December 25, 26, 1905.

[12] 91 *Kentucky Reports* 6 (1890).

legislature "produced a shindy," in which someone was certain to rehash old arguments in an effort "to stir up a war against the great institution that is doing so much for the cause of education in Kentucky."[13] Investigations were conducted, and debate often waxed hot, but in every instance the college was upheld. The constitutional convention of 1890 caused some apprehension when attempts were made to erect a constitutional barrier to future aid to the institution, yet the document which emerged from the convention declared specifically that "the tax now imposed for educational purposes, and for the endowment and maintenance of the Agricultural and Mechanical College, shall remain until changed by law."[14]

After 1890 President Patterson could breathe somewhat easier. He could turn his back on the troublesome period just past in which he "never sat down to a meal without apprehension, nor enjoyed a night's rest without the dread of impending calamity upon the morrow,"[15] and he could face the future with a new confidence. There would still be days of gloom and discouragement, when available finances did not meet pressing needs or caused progress to be excruciatingly slow, but at least the college came to be generally accepted as a part of the educational system of the state. Public opinion became more favorable toward the principle of state support, and in the course of time even the denominationalists forgot their animosity toward the institution. The great victories of the eighties proved conclusive, and to a large degree they were Patterson's own.

Having won for State College its very existence, Patterson became its protector and its despot. Wherever danger arose—

[13] Lexington *Daily Press,* February 25, 1890.

[14] *Constitution of the Commonwealth of Kentucky, Adopted by the Constitutional Convention, April 11, 1891, and Submitted to a Vote of the People at the August Election, 1891* (Frankfort, n. d.), 38.

[15] Patterson, Address in honor of Judge Barker, January 5, 1911.

in the legislature, in the courts, or in public opinion—he was on hand to defend his school. He represented it abroad and became well known to Presidents of other agricultural colleges. After the death of his son in 1895, the institution became his chief interest, and he looked upon it with an air of possession almost as if it were his child. He rejoiced in its growth and sought to keep it growing in a healthy manner. He enjoyed his dominance, and doubtless he accepted as his just due the birthday celebrations staged in his honor by students and faculty. Sometimes he showed an unnecessary jealousy of his prerogatives, as in 1901 when as a friendly gesture President Burris Jenkins of Kentucky University issued in the name of his own students and those of State College an invitation to the Governor to attend a football game between the two schools. Patterson was absent at the time, and upon his return he showed his resentment toward the manner in which the invitation had been extended without authorization from officials or students of his own institution. Addressing his assembled subjects, he declared loftily: "I think that I am amply able to attend to our own business without invoking the aid of President Jenkins or any one else."[16] Even in small matters he intended being the master of his own domain.

In his role as administrator Patterson was as nearly an absolute monarch as the President of the state institution could well be. No one could have labored more assiduously at the tasks which confronted him, and no one could have been more devoted to the welfare and progress of the school. In recognition of his ability, his sincerity, and the difficulties of the situation, the Board of Trustees for the most part accepted Patterson's advice and endeavored to aid him in carrying out his program. For a time around 1900 the trustees broke away from his dominance to pursue an independent course of which he did not approve, but with the

[16] Lexington *Democrat,* November 20, 1901.

exception of that brief period of rebellion they followed his leadership and gave him virtually a free hand in the management of the college.

The faculty was likewise under his sway. Division of authority was at a minimum, since until the last years of his reign the school was not large enough to necessitate the erection of semiautonomous colleges, each under its own Dean, and since the heads of the various departments were responsible directly to the President. Some form of democracy was, however, observed from the beginning, for the faculty, sitting as a Senate, was an integral part of the administrative organization. It met regularly, and Patterson regularly sought its advice, but its powers were extremely limited. It discussed such weighty problems as regulations and requirements for degrees, and it often defended the school against adverse criticism. Apparently, investigations into student misconduct and decisions on disciplinary problems were its chief duties, whereas larger considerations of policy were left to the President. In fact, Patterson's relationship to his staff was that of a high school principal to his teachers, rather than that of a college President to a Senate of professors.

The faculty, especially during the uncertain period of the nineteenth century, usually showed a commendable loyalty to its leader, and only on rare occasions was opposition to his policies openly voiced. When friction did occur, moreover, the solution was simple: the subordinate who could not work in harmony with the administration soon found himself no longer connected with the college. One of the most regrettable incidents of this nature, which were fortunately few in number, involved the venerable Dr. Robert Peter, whose honored career as a scientist and teacher had begun in 1833, far back in the dim reaches of Transylvania's past. After the erection of the independent Agricultural and Mechanical College, Patterson urged Dr. Peter to expand his courses in chemistry, to which the latter agreed on condition that an assistant be allotted to him. This aid the Board of Trustees refused to grant on the ground that Dr. Peter should devote less time to the State Geological Survey and more to the duties for which he had been employed by the college.

During the course of the dispute, Professor A. E. Menke was appointed to the chair of agriculture and immediately organized under his own instruction classes in chemistry, zoology, botany, and veterinary science. According to Patterson, Dr. Peter disliked Menke from the beginning, regarding him "as a rival and a possible successor. He said to me that he considered Prof. Menke's introduction into a department in the College as a reflection upon himself. I replied that his refusal to expand his chemical course rendered the addition of Agricultural and organic Chemistry under another man imperative, and that the scientific necessities of the college could not be subordinated to his prejudices."[17]

As the relations between the two old friends grew more bitter, Patterson charged that Dr. Peter had not kept abreast of the new developments in chemistry, that his lectures had not changed in fifty years, and that because of impaired vision and hearing, he could not keep order in his classroom. The trustees, greatly embarrassed by the whole affair, hoped that Dr. Peter might resign, but the venerable chemist, like Patterson at a later date, was reluctant to give up his work in spite of his advanced age. The problem was finally solved in June, 1887, when the Board of Trustees consolidated the departments headed by Menke and Peter, declared the new post vacant, and stated the necessity "to dispense regretfully with the services of Professor Peter who as a

[17] Patterson to W. M. Cravens (not dated, but apparently written in 1890 during an investigation of the college by a legislative joint committee of which Cravens was chairman), in Patterson Papers, University of Kentucky Library.

chemist in various important positions has had a long and distinguished career not often equaled in honor and usefulness." In order to soften the blow, the trustees ordered that the title and dignity of "Emeritus Professor" be conferred on Dr. Peter, that his name be continued in the catalogue during his lifetime, and that he be allowed to use his old laboratory as long as he wished. Dr. Peter never forgave Patterson for his ouster, and until his death he remained extremely critical of the administration of the college.

In 1889 A. R. Crandall, described as "one of our older and more dignified professors,"[18] who for more than a decade had taught natural science in the college and for a time had been director of the Mechanical Department, committed an indiscretion which led to his immediate resignation. For some time he had been harboring certain grievances against the President, and when a Winchester paper published an article lauding Patterson and the college, Crandall could no longer keep his own counsel. He unburdened himself to a newspaper reporter, Charles C. Moore, who published an account of the interview. "Professor Crandall, of the A. and M. College, meeting a newspaper man on the street in the city this afternoon, said that the article printed in a Winchester paper stating the College was in excellent condition and well managed was anything but correct; that the college was badly managed, and conducted in a very unsatisfactory manner, and that the president was incapable of properly managing the scientific department, and moreover was in the habit of exhibiting partiality toward some of the professors."[19]

During the resulting excitement Crandall declared that he had given out nothing for publication and that Moore had reported inaccurately views which had been expressed in

[18] John W. Gunn, written statement (undated) in Bureau of Source Materials in Higher Education.

[19] Article from Cincinnati *Commercial Gazette,* reprinted in Lexington *Leader,* February 21, 1889.

a private conversation. Nevertheless, he added that "while sorry that he had been tripped up, he was ready to take the consequences." The reporter, however, stated that he had understood that Crandall wished his statement to be published, and that the professor had further remarked that "He [President Patterson] puts out anybody that does not agree with him, and I expect he will put me out, but it won't make any difference, because I am going to resign the first of June anyway."[20] Whatever the truth of the matter, Crandall had placed himself in a position from which there was only one exit, and he accordingly submitted his resignation.

But the affair was not yet ended, for the former professor now proceeded to wage an aggressive campaign against the President. When the Board of Trustees assembled for its next regular meeting, Crandall placed in the hands of each member a communication which reflected "in terms of great severity upon the President of the College." Both Crandall and Dr. Robert Peter appeared before an investigating committee of the legislature during the next year and bitterly criticized the organization and management of the college. In both cases the adverse testimony was futile, for the trustees resolved "that the Administration of President Patterson has been obedient to the Board and harmonious with the law and its purposes," and that "his official acts have been either authorized by the Board or reported to it by him and received its approval, and that he is entitled to and receives the full confidence of the Board."[21] The majority report of the legislative committee before which the two former professors testified stated that the objections raised by Peter and Crandall "were not corroborated by any of the trustees or by any member of the Faculty."[22]

20 Lexington *Daily Press,* February 23, 24, 1889.

21 Agricultural and Mechanical College, Minutes of the Board of Trustees, June 5, 1889.

22 Kentucky *Documents,* 1889-1890, V, 13-14.

Crandall's activities aroused Patterson's ire to a pitch seldom reached and led the President to express himself in words singularly lacking in benevolence. The following extracts from a penciled manuscript illustrate a little-publicized side of Patterson's nature and indicate that the usually reserved and dignified scholar could on occasion give voice to his passion:

> Prof. Crandall is in a very unamiable mood, "The winter of his discontent is upon him." For months past he has been brooding over his fancied wrongs and those of the general public.
>
> With the arrogance of the half-educated Yankee he convinced himself that he had a mission for reforming and righting things generally. The educated New Yankee [*sic*] or New Englander descended from reputable ancestry is generally a man of good breeding as well as good education, but the half educated are among the most pestilent and disagreeable of men. Cynical captious, ill-balanced to such a degree that his best friends pronounce him a crank I do not hesitate to say that notwithstanding his good qualities as a teacher, the College and his own department would have been better off had he never been a member of its faculty. But he has an impression or wishes the public to believe that he . . . is indispensible. Since his frantic efforts have failed to procure his own reinstatement he now announces his determination never to desist until he has compassed my overthrow. If he cannot induce the present Board to dispense with me, he will move the Legislature to displace the present Board, if this Legislature prove refractory he will elect another. Should this fail no one can foretell the consequences! Well, I am satisfied of one thing that the people of this Commonwealth whom I have served for twenty years and more are not going to throw me overboard at the behest of a pestilent Yankee unless on reasons of much more gravity than are within the compass of his proof. To the series of charges now formulated I at present make no reply further than this, that from beginning to end they are a mass of exaggerations

> of fictions and falsehoods, vindictive malicious and libellous.[23]

The complaints lodged against Patterson were not wholly without justification, and in the last years of his regime dissatisfaction became more widespread among the faculty. Crandall had charged that Patterson was not a scientist, that he emphasized the literary and classical courses of study while neglecting the sciences, and that he was therefore unfit for the presidency of the Agricultural and Mechanical College. On the other hand, Patterson believed that a well-rounded education was desirable, and he accused Crandall of wishing to push his own department to the detriment of the college as a whole. No doubt the sciences could have, and should have, been more rapidly expanded, but Patterson firmly believed in his own ideas, he was in control, and he received the backing of the Board of Trustees. Nevertheless, the feeling persisted in some quarters that the college was not performing entirely its proper functions.

Another persistent basis for criticism of the President lay in the relationship between him and his brother Walter Kennedy Patterson, Principal of the Academy, which led to charges of favoritism. As stated by one who had occasion to observe the situation for many years, "the President nearly always seemed easily, and often unduly, influenced by suggestions and claims made by the Principal of the Academy, even when these mainly affected departments of the College proper. This ready, and well known, responsiveness furnished additional grounds for accusations that the preparatory school 'overshadowed' the College, and that it 'wagged' the College."[24] Students as well as faculty grumbled at the favored position of the younger Patterson, whom they irreverently dubbed "She Pat" because he had once held the position of assistant matron of the girl's dormitory. They

23 In Patterson Papers. 24 Pence, "University of Kentucky," part 2, p. 53.

believed "She Pat" to be something of a secret intelligence agent for his brother "He Pat," the President. One of their number in 1902 mildly expressed their opinion in a parody which brought the displeasure of the administration upon its author:

> Walter K's the overseer
> At State College.
> He reports whatever's queer
> At State College.
> Into the "Prep" he doth cajole us,
> Then like that wind-god Aeolus
> In his prison ever hold us,
> At State College.[25]

As the faculty grew in numbers, it tended to become more independent, especially during the period of general unrest in the college early in the twentieth century. Petty regulations were ignored, causing the Board of Trustees in 1904 to censure the professors for not attending strictly to their duties. The board blamed the prevalent laxness of discipline upon the failure of the teaching staff to attend chapel, to "admonish and rebuke idle students," and to observe other rules laid down for the conduct of the faculty. Low salaries constituted a grievance which was expressed more and more frequently and vigorously during the latter part of the Patterson era. Little complaint on this score was voiced earlier, for the sad economic plight of the college was generally recognized. Even later it was known that money was not too plentiful, and yet the appearance of new buildings led to a belief on the part of the faculty that the administration could always find funds "to do what it *wanted* to do!" The President's own salary was never large, yet he was able to amass from it a small fortune, and consequently he was none too sympathetic towards his subordinates' demands for higher pay. His management of the

[25] Lexington *Leader,* April 1, 1902.

school was economical, almost parsimonious, for "above all he was heart-set on enlarging and improving the College into a University by every possible means, and hence unwilling to divert its meager income and heap it up needlessly on the teaching staff." The "starveling Faculty" sometimes failed to appreciate his point of view, and there resulted an increasing estrangement between the staff and the President.[26]

Yet Patterson remained the master of his domain, although his dominance was threatened in 1904 and 1905 when serious friction developed between him and a part of his faculty. In spite of the fact that the Board of Trustees was willing then to listen to complaints against the ancient warrior, again his triumph was complete. Two professors were not re-elected as a measure "to curtail expenses," and Professor Ruric N. Roark, head of the Normal Department, who had become involved in a controversy with Patterson over the latter's alleged slighting of that department, was constrained to offer his resignation. The tempest gradually quieted, and in the next few years "strangely enough he [Patterson] found himself once more successful all round; the Board and Executive Committee staunch and one-minded at his side and the murmurs outside hushed if not forgot. . . . An era of good feeling now seemed to set in," and in this peaceful atmosphere the monarch at long last decided to lay down his scepter.[27]

[26] Smith, "James Kennedy Patterson," 155-56.
[27] *Ibid.,* 170-71.

Chapter Eight

Student Life

IN HIS RELATIONS WITH THE STUDENTS PATTERSON was again the benevolent despot. On the campus his word was law, and there he attempted to enforce obedience and diligence upon his people; some of whom, it must be said, were none too docile nor too respectful of the rules which governed them. Some students saw only the tyrant in him, but many found him human and even lovable. He was especially appreciated by poor boys who wanted an education, for he usually contrived to find work for them, and he often made in their favor exceptions to regulations such as the requirement that all cadets purchase full uniforms. No one was "ever . . . turned from this institution on account of lack of ability to pay the tuition fee."[1]

Alumni often recall minor incidents which reflect a kindly side to the personality of the sometimes dour Scot. One hard-working student found that he had no time for the required military drill, and yet he was allowed to continue his studies. Another remembers being asked to go to the second floor of the Main Building to bring down the presidential hat. The lad reluctantly reported his inability to find it, and then Patterson "went up that stairway, two steps at a hop, on his usual means of locomotion, with his ease and my pain, and got his hat. Then he molified [*sic*] my spirits by cheerfully explaining it all: 'It takes a man without a hat to find a hat.'" He sometimes showed an uncanny ability for detecting offenders, who often found, however, that "after all it was not so bad to have him know." He disapproved of breaches of discipline and was considered a

[1] Kentucky *House Journal,* 1904, p. 649.

President Patterson conducting Chapel exercises, 1907

hard taskmaster, yet when students ran afoul of the law, he was on hand to secure their release from jail. No matter what troubles might arise on the campus, the President always insisted that his boys were the finest to be found in Kentucky.[2]

Nevertheless, Patterson was cordially disliked by many who considered him unduly tyrannical. Dissatisfaction among the students was based on many grievances, both real and fancied, and was perhaps summarized by the "Grumbler" of the class of 1905 in an essay which was supposed to be humorous but in which the author, Karl L. Dietrich, unwisely expressed his honest convictions:

> For four long years have I been obliged to express my opinion in private, but at last the opportunity is given me to voice in public the grievances of myself and my fellow students. The task is of such stupendous proportions as to be most appalling, and, in the short space of time at my disposal, it will be impossible to more than sketch rapidly the main causes of discontent. . . .
>
> Perhaps it is best to start with the most conspicuous person in the faculty, who is, as well, one of the chief causes of this discontent, President James K. Patterson, Ph. D. L. L. D. F. S. A., Old Pat, He Pat. This withered specimen of the antediluvian fauna, handed down to us as a relic of prehistoric ages is so very busy hunting new jobs for Walter K., and seeing that the end doors of the main building remain closed, that he had to give up his single class a day to another professor who was only engaged in teaching, and therefore had plenty of leisure time.
>
> But let us not forget the arduous labor he performs in chasing the skippers from the hall. This is a noble task most nobly done. Many a time has he caused the hearts of these recalcitrants to fly to their throats in fear of the impending wrath to come. The fearful ones are, however, the Freshmen. After a month or so, they find that

[2] Coleman C. Cartwright, statement in Bureau of Source Materials in Higher Education; Rufus L. Weaver to Ezra L. Gillis, November 4, 1940, *ibid.*

the threats are empty ones and they merely move slowly away to another resting place where they will not be disturbed. The rapping upon the floor, and the exhortation to "get out" might prove awe-inspiring, were it not so ludicrous and utterly ineffective.

He also reads prayers, communications from the Civil Service Department, guaranteeing as the result of a life-time work $1,500 per annum and emoluments, and delivers yearly one lecture upon "Keep off the Turf," and one upon Senator Morrill, and frowns daily upon the dignified seniors.

. . . It is to be feared that no one will ever be required to take his place, for, like Tennyson's Brook it seems that he may say, "Men may come and men may go, but I go on forever." The descendants of the present generation who will attend State College will probably see the same old fur coat, hear the same old prayers, and listen to the same old discourses warmed over.

Another one of his tasks is to oppose everything that any one proposes, and to make life miserable for every instructor who is popular with the students. He does condescend to honor with his presence those athletic events to which he receives a complimentary ticket, but, as far as giving any encouragement, pecuniary or otherwise, to athletics, he not only gives none, but in fact casts a figurative wet blanket on every branch of manly sports. It is true that, in public, after a great victory, he has been heard to raise his feeble voice in praise of the "foot-ball nine" or "Base ball eleven," but this, you know, pleases the students. As for the discipline he maintains and the respect in which he is held by the students, these are subjects of which, out of respect for the good name of our College, small mention will be made.

When use is made of spies and informers, taken from the student body, to inform on other students, small credit redounds to either the employer of these or the institution of which they are unworthy members. Spies are employed and will probably continue to be employed as long as the present regime exists. From past painful experiences I know whereof I speak. When he dies he is going to present the College with a most magnificent library worth several thousands of dollars, but it has been made a matter of conjecture as to why he waits until these books

> become out of date and ancient before he places them where they will do the most good. Some irreverent persons have been known to insinuate that he holds his place by this means, fearing to give up the library before he resigns voluntarily lest he should be involuntarily removed. Nevertheless, when the institution becomes the recipient of this magnificent gift, all the shortcomings and small faults of this great man will undoubtedly be wiped from the slate of memory, and his name will be handed down to posterity as the greatest benefactor of our institution in presenting it with one of the greatest collections of ancient literature in existence.[3]

This paper, which included references to other members of the faculty, was prepared for presentation on Class Day but was not delivered. A horrified Senate charged the author with "preparing with the purpose of delivering on class day a paper containing disrespectful, scurrilous, and defamatory statements, allusions, and references to members of the faculty with the intention of holding them up before the public to ridicule, opprobrium and scorn; and this contrary to regulation 76." He was then suspended from the college and was denied the privilege of graduating with his class. The lad's father, both in person and through attorneys, attempted to intercede, but in vain. The senior class petitioned for a reconsideration of the case, and even went so far as to resolve to "refuse to take part in any exercises upon Class Day or Commencement Day, or to accept any degree from this institution until a diploma is given Mr. Dietrich." The faculty stood firm, however. One year later the Board of Trustees voted to confer the degree of Mechanical Engineer on Dietrich and directed President Patterson to deliver to him his diploma.

The appearance of tyranny could hardly be avoided if the administration tried sincerely to enforce the many regulations formulated for the governance of the students. Upon

[3] Karl L. Dietrich, "The Grumbler," copy of the original manuscript in Bureau of Source Materials in Higher Education.

the removal of the college to its present location, the Board of Trustees drew up a list of 189 rules relating to virtually every phase of the management of the school and conduct of the cadets, provided further that additional laws might be established by the faculty, and even then found it necessary to promulgate others in the course of time. In view of the many restrictions and the punishments provided for their violations, one may question the efficacy of the pronouncement that "no one is to be admitted in to the College whose moral character is not satisfactorily attested, and no one will be allowed to remain whose behaviour is not that of a gentleman."

Demerits according to a scheduled system, arrest and confinement to quarters, public or private admonition, suspension, dismissal, or some combination of these various punishments awaited the erring youth whose guilt could be established. Conviction was often difficult because of the usual reluctance of students to testify against one another, and yet violations of the regulations were common. In fact, only an angel could have lived four years on the campus without breaking a few rules, and at State College the boys were after all mere humans. It is doubtful if any lad adhered so closely to the narrow path marked out for him by authority that he did not at some time commit a breach of laws whose tenor may be illustrated by the following samples:

> 75. All deliberations or discussions among students having the object of conveying praise or censure, or any mark of approbation or disapprobation toward the College authorities, are strictly forbidden.
>
> 79. No student shall play at cards, or any other game of chance, within the College limits, or bring or cause to be brought within the limits, or have in his room, cards or other articles used in games of chance. All games and amusements of every kind are forbidden during study hours.

81. The use of tobacco for smoking or chewing on any duty, or in the College building, dormitories, or dining-rooms, and all profanity and obscenity, are forbidden.

99. Every student will be expected to attend divine services in some church at least once every Sunday.

100. All permits to be absent from any duty, or from quarters during study hours, must have the approval of the President.

123. No student shall be absent from his room between taps and reveille without permission from the Commandant.

129. Students are forbidden to take or have in their quarters any newspapers or other periodical publications without special permission from the President. They are also forbidden to keep in their rooms any books except textbooks, without special permission from the President.

156. Students are forbidden to have in their possession any description of firearms or other deadly weapons not issued to them by proper authority.

164. Each Cadet shall have a particular place at table, which shall not be changed without permission from the Inspector of the Mess.

Moreover, the student was expected to conform to a rigid schedule which was designed to govern his movements during virtually every minute of the day. He arose at the sound of reveille at 5:30 in the morning and stood by for inspection of quarters thirty minutes later. At 6:30 he marched to breakfast, and at 7:30 he was called to quarters for an hour's study before the chapel services. Recitations followed until noon, and after eating he was again called to quarters for study from one to four, unless he had further classes or other duties. At four, except on Saturday and Sunday, he reported for an hour of "military exercise," after which he hastened to prepare for supper. Another study period began at 6:30 and continued until tattoo at 9:30. The sound of taps at ten o'clock signaled the end of the day, and if he had faithfully observed the schedule, the cadet was ready for sleep.

Even a nominal enforcement of this detailed regimentation was beyond the capacity of any one man and necessitated the establishment of a large hierarchy of officials under the President. Every member of the faculty was, of course, expected to see that regulations were obeyed and might arrest any offender, but the military system constituted the main reliance for maintaining order. The Commandant was especially charged with "the details of discipline and police," with the help of various cadet officers who were expected to exact obedience from their subordinates and to report in writing any infraction of the rules. Minor disciplinary problems were handled by the Commandant, or by the Board of Discipline, composed of the Commandant and two professors elected monthly by the faculty. Disciplinary offenses of a graver nature were referred to the Senate for decision. Patterson, however, wielded final authority in all such matters.

Despite all rules and all precautions, complete preservation of order proved to be an impossibility, a fact that led Patterson to mourn "that the young men of Kentucky found it so difficult to accept discipline."[4] With monotonous regularity the Board of Discipline, the Senate, and the President conducted investigations into misconduct, accorded hearings to the accused, and imposed punishments which were usually as lenient as possible under the regulations. Occasionally even the Fayette County Grand Jury felt itself constrained to take a hand after student outbursts of particularly serious nature, but its efforts were usually futile. The police, often called upon to aid in maintaining order on the campus at times conducive to rowdyism, sometimes merely served as additional subjects for student pranks.

[4] Lexington *Leader,* March 6, 1900.

Punishment was not always meted in accordance with the letter of the law, because in many cases culprits could not be tracked down. In 1900 pranksters dismantled the old cart used for hauling various objects about the grounds, and the joke backfired when the authorities made no effort to recover it. At the end of the year, the boys, who had always used the cart for hauling their trunks, were forced to patronize the city transfer companies with a resulting expenditure of money. Again, at the close of the school year in 1909 the students of the State University, as the institution was then known, were reminded of the removal of an iron gate from the Transylvania campus when each was assessed thirty cents from his damage fee of ten dollars, deposited at the beginning of the term. The rules themselves were found deficient in 1904 when Herman Scholtz of Louisville attired himself in woman's clothing and accompanied the State College coeds to Georgetown to witness a basketball game from which all male spectators were barred. Discovered by the authorities when the game was half over, he was ordered from the scene and was later brought before the faculty. The professors were at a loss as to the specific charge to register against the masquerader, and they finally contented themselves by reprimanding him on general principles.

Not until the last years of his reign did Patterson seem to realize that there might be means of maintaining order other than through attempted suppression. The Hallowe'en riot of 1906 proved conclusively, if proof was needed, that even a squad of policemen was powerless to control the students once they had taken the bits in their teeth and started a rampage. As a beginning, a group of cadets captured Patrolman Meyers, who had been detailed to guard duty at Patterson Hall, stripped him of his badge, hat, and club, and took a flashlight picture of his humiliating condition. Next, they rolled a huge stone upon the nearby streetcar line and placed before it a red torchlight. The motorman of an approaching car, blinded by the light, attempted to dash by with extra speed and, of course, crashed into the boulder with injuries to himself and his vehicle. Meanwhile, the indignant Patrolman Meyers had called for reinforcements, who arrived in time to interrupt the rioters in their sport of breaking street lamps. Retreating to the campus, the students protected their rear by volleys of eggs and stones, and when one of the latter struck Police Captain Ford in the mouth, the situation became more serious. The police charged; sticks, stones, fists, and revolvers were brought into use; and when the melee ended, four policemen lay injured and seven boys were under arrest.

Patterson moved on another tack, and with better results, in the next year. On the eve of Hallowe'en in 1907 he addressed the students, explaining the origin of the festival and appealing to the boys to "conduct themselves in a dignified manner." He promised that no policemen would be stationed on the campus, and he declared that the college authorities "would commit the entire layout to the hands of the students, believing that when placed on their honor they would prove themselves equal to the occasion." In addition, an entertainment was staged at Patterson Hall, and as a result of this new policy, the usual destructive rowdyism was significantly absent.[5]

During the greater part of Patterson's regime, however, as the enrollment increased and the dormitories became crowded, discipline was a major problem for which no satisfactory solution could be found. Enforcement of severely restrictive regulations proved beyond the capacity of even a benevolent despot, and tales of student misconduct are legion.

Students who followed with some degree of conscientiousness the program of study, work, and drill at the Agricultural

[5] *Ibid.*, November 1, 1906, October 31, November 2, 1907.

and Mechanical College still had need of extracurricular activities to help fill any time which they might have free, to provide entertainment, and to enable them to acquire training which was not available in the regular college routine. Athletics and more or less harmless mischief offered outlets for the energy of some of Patterson's charges, but literary societies provided a popular and more sober method of self-expression, answered a social need, and gave experience which was considered valuable preparation for a career. Moreover, these organizations were encouraged by officials of the institution, and on occasion faculty members participated in their meetings. Through the Patterson regime, the students worked to make their societies successful.

The oldest group of this type, the Union Literary Society, was formed in 1872, while the Agricultural and Mechanical College was still a part of Kentucky University, as the result of a combination of two earlier organizations, the Yost Club and the Ashland Institute, which had failed to prosper in accordance with the expectations of their founders. Early in 1873 the state gave its blessing in the form of an act incorporating the society. One of its charter members was Henry Stites Barker, who later recalled that the name "Union" was adopted only after a warm debate among the membership which was "composed mostly of Southerners, in whom the spark of rebellion was not yet dead."[6] In the latter part of Patterson's administration the society had a "commodious and well-furnished hall in the Gymnasium" for its weekly meetings, owned a library which had in part been donated by the state, and held yearly an oratorical contest in which speakers competed for a gold medal.

The second oldest literary society for men was founded in 1887 and was incorporated by the legislature early in 1890. This organization, bearing the name "Patterson Literary Society," was near to the heart of the President, who

[6] *Ibid.*, February 12, 1911.

kept in close touch with its affairs. He sometimes attended its sessions, and he presented a gold medal each year to the winner of the society's oratorical contest. Another medal, also of gold, was for years given as a second prize by George Crum of Louisville. The annual "open sessions" of the society were elaborately staged. In 1888 the celebration, held in the college chapel, featured the music of the Saxton and Trost band as well as speeches by members and guests. In addition to the serious orations at these events, it became customary to have some member of the group present the "Spectator," a humorous paper which was well received even if sometimes "there was [*sic*] enough chestnuts in it to plant a grove."[7]

The Patterson Society, like the Union, had a library of its own and a room for its meetings. From the beginning of its existence its history was noteworthy, and through the early years of the present century it "exercised a tremendous influence for the advancement of literary and forensic attainment in the institution. Having a liberal endowment for prizes and medals, its contests for oratorical, declamatory and debating excellence . . . always aroused vigorous and spirited competition." It took pride in the fact that most of the State College representatives in intercollegiate oratorical contests were Patterson men and that at least two Rhodes scholars, Clark Tandy and W. B. Branham, were at one time "honored members" of the society. The president of the group in 1907 was Leo Brewer, who was not only a "brilliant student in the senior class of the classical department," but also was a member of the varsity basketball team and a candidate for the position of quarterback on the football squad.[8]

A keen rivalry existed between the Union and Patterson societies, especially for the honor of representing the college

[7] Lexington *Daily Press,* May 31, 1888, June 1, 1889.
[8] Lexington *Leader,* October 12, 1906, September 15, 1907.

in debates or oratorical contests with other institutions. Intercollegiate oratorical contests evoked among students of the schools involved much the same spirit reserved for athletic competition at a later day. The Agricultural and Mechanical College was a member of the Intercollegiate Oratorical Association, which was founded in 1887, for a number of years included also Kentucky University, Georgetown College, Centre College, and Central University, and staged an annual contest to determine the best orator in the league. Apparently the representatives of State College were unsuccessful in this competition until 1896, when John T. Geary won with an oration entitled "The Evolution of the Republic." Five years later Leonidas Ragan again brought the prize to the college. Clark Tandy distinguished himself by winning in 1901 and again two years later.

The enthusiasm of Kentucky college students over oratory seems to have reached its peak in the last decade of the nineteenth century. In 1891 interest in the approaching intercollegiate contest was so great that a large number of outsiders appeared in Georgetown to witness the selection of an orator to represent Georgetown College in the event. About forty State College students, several from Kentucky University, and many people who were not connected with a college took an afternoon train from Lexington to the neighboring city to be on hand for the contest, which was staged in the Scott County Courthouse. According to the press, the visitors made their presence known, "for they literally took the town for the next twelve hours, leaving there at 1:40 A. M." Because of the excitement, it was decided that the winner would not be announced until the next day, "to prevent the awful yelling that the admirers of the contending speakers indulge in while waiting for the judges to bring in their verdict." The successful contestant on that occasion went on triumphantly to win the fourth annual intercollegiate contest with a speech entitled "Conservatism and Reform in Government." The decision on the latter occasion was "received with yells of joy," and it was said that the contest of that year was "an Event Long to be Remembered in College Annals."[9]

So noteworthy indeed was this contest that there was danger that it might be the last of its kind. It was rumored that in most if not all the member institutions, officials were concerned about the evils attending overemphasis of the oratorical contests. The faculty of Kentucky University took the lead, announcing withdrawal of the institution from the association. The reasons for the decision were said to be "First, interference with regular studies; second, tendency to dissipation and drunkenness; third, gambling on the result."[10] The contests continued, however, and in 1893 Kentucky University again took a stand against them as well as against intercollegiate athletics. The faculty considered both the oratorical and athletic contests harmful, and pointed out that "the excitement which attends them, sometimes for weeks before the affair comes off, distracts the attention of the students from their studies," renders them unfit for college work, encourages gambling and dissipation, and causes "occasional disputes between students of rival colleges that are apt to result seriously."[11] When the students petitioned to be allowed to participate in the oratorical contest in 1893, the faculty relented once again.

Within the decade student interest in oratory began to decline. At a faculty meeting in the Agricultural and Mechanical College in 1903 President Patterson called attention to the lack of interest in the literary societies and expressed concern that the activities of these groups were decreasing. Nevertheless, intercollegiate oratorical contests continued from year to year, and as late as 1907 a debate between representatives of Kentucky University and the

9 Lexington *Daily Press,* March 25, April 11, 1891.
10 *Ibid.,* April 11, 1891.
11 *Ibid.,* February 22, 1893.

State College attracted much attention. Held in Morrison Chapel, the debate "was attended with the roars and yells of college students trying to cheer their teams to victory." The Agricultural and Mechanical College debaters, defending the negative of the question, "Resolved, that the United States Would Be Justified in Establishing Her Permanent Rule in Cuba," won over their rivals and received gold medals in testimony of their triumph.

Interest in things oratorical was not confined to the masculine sex, and the women students of State College not only cheered the male representatives of their school in the intercollegiate contests but also had literary societies of their own, patterned after those of their brothers. The oldest of the feminine groups, the Philosophian Society, was established in 1882 "for literary improvement and social pleasure." Like the men's organizations, it held regular weekly meetings and offered periodically a program, to which the public was invited, "consisting of declamations, essays, criticisms, and orations." The open sessions were said to provide "delightful entertainment" for the large audiences in attendance. At the session in 1893 "the stage was prettily decorated," and "the occasion was presided over very gracefully by Miss Nettie Reynolds." After Alice Shelby, "the accomplished young secretary," had called the roll, Elizabeth King read an essay on "a very live" subject, "Foot Ball." Logie Warner gave a recitation, Mamie Didlake read an essay on joking, and a Miss Gunn recited "a piece," entitled "the Apple." At the end came the humorous paper, "the Star," which was "always anticipated as the event of the evening, and, like dessert, . . . saved for the last." If it was similar to the same paper of the previous session, it was "full of true wit and humor, and interspersed here and there with 'hot shots' for the boys."[12]

[12] Lexington *Transcript,* March 18, 1893; Lexington *Daily Press,* December 10, 1893.

The Philosophian Society was without a rival at the college until 1904, when a group of girls formed the Neville Literary Society. Professor J. H. Neville, for whom the organization was named, showed his appreciation of the honor by providing prizes for the winners of the declamatory contests staged by the group. Members of the girls' societies were active outside their own groups. A coed sometimes presided over sessions at which representatives of the Union and Patterson societies competed in oratory, on occasion a girl read an essay at such a meeting, and the women joined in the oratory accompanying the annual Washington's Birthday celebration. The high point of the year for the Philosophian and Neville societies came when a representative from each met to determine the women's declamatory championship of the college.

Besides the literary societies, numerous other organizations appeared on the campus, some of which existed only briefly while others played a role in the life of the college for long periods of time. When Ruric N. Roark became head of the Normal Department in 1901, he organized clubs there similar to the literary societies of the college. The Biological Society, the first scientific association organized at the college, included in its membership at first mainly faculty members and the staff of the Experiment Station. Dedicating itself to "the stimulation of a spirit of original research," the group held regular monthly meetings at which the reading of essays was followed by discussion. Shortly before 1900 the society was reorganized and placed under the management of students, retaining at the same time many of its original members. On the third Friday of each month students from the engineering departments held a meeting of the Engineering Society. Ordinarily a paper would be read by some member of the group, after which a general discussion would be held. Occasionally the routine was varied by the appearance of experienced engineers who lectured to the society.

The Linguistic Society, organized in 1898, met twice a month "for improvement in languages." In 1902 the Agricultural Society was established, and in 1907 the Ashland Grange 1655, a branch of the National Grange, was set up with headquarters on the campus and with a membership which included students, faculty members, Experiment Station staff, and farmers of Fayette and adjoining counties.

The Young Men's Christian Association began its work on the campus in 1890, and a unit of the Y.W.C.A. was organized in 1904. Neither had a very large membership during the Patterson era, and neither employed a full-time secretary during that period. In 1910 the men's group, composed of 50 members, had the use of a room in the gymnasium for meetings, religious services, reading, and "harmless games." In addition to its religious work, the organization had control of the tennis courts on the campus and offered "an interesting social life to its members." An advisory committee, composed of one representative of the local ministry, another from the city "Y," five from the faculty, and three from the student body, co-operated with the association in its work. The girls' association had two rooms in Patterson Hall, one for religious meetings and the other for a reading room. The membership of 35 young women held services each Sunday evening and a Bible class which met on another evening each week.

Greek letter fraternities were slow to appear on the Agricultural and Mechanical College campus, partly because of opposition by the faculty to their establishment. In October, 1887, the faculty received a request from students for permission to organize a "Greek Society," described as a "secret society for promotion of morality, high class standing, etc.," but "on the ground that secret societies are not desirable," the petition was rejected.[13] The question of admission of

[13] Agricultural and Mechanical College, Minutes of the Senate, October 28, 1887.

fraternities was not settled by this case, however, and it continued to arise at irregular intervals. Early in 1893 President Patterson himself presented to the faculty a petition from "some of the students" who asked permission to establish a fraternity. On this occasion the faculty appointed a committee to study the question, and at the next regular meeting the committee recommended, Professor J. H. Neville dissenting, that the petition be granted. The report of this group was then adopted by a margin of 14 to 3, the negative votes being cast by Neville, Walter K. Patterson, and C. W. Mathews.

Even after the way had been opened, there was no rush of fraternities to the school. In 1893 Kappa Alpha and Sigma Chi established chapters on the campus, but seven years passed before others followed them. Then, in rapid succession five additional groups appeared: Sigma Alpha Epsilon in 1900; Kappa Sigma, Phi Delta Theta, and Pi Kappa Alpha in 1901; and Sigma Nu in 1902. After another seven years Alpha Tau Omega established a chapter at the State University. The women students were even slower than the men in establishing Greek letter societies. Several local organizations came into existence shortly after 1900, but not until 1907, when Alpha Xi Delta came to the campus, did a group have national affiliations. A chapter of Alpha Gamma Delta received a charter in 1908, and in the year of Patterson's retirement, a third national sorority, Kappa Kappa Gamma, established a chapter.

Honorary societies included Lamp and Cross, Mystic 13, and Tau Beta Pi, and toward the end of Patterson's administration a fourth, Key Roll, was established. The Agricultural and Mechanical College chapter of Tau Beta Pi, an honorary engineering fraternity, was established in 1902. Membership was based on scholarship, and only students in the last two years of engineering were eligible to join. Lamp and Cross was patterned after Skull and Bones and other organizations of like nature at Yale, and tried to copy their procedures, including observance of "tap day" when new members were chosen. The Mystic 13 was a society for juniors, which was conducted upon much the same order as Lamp and Cross.

Social life at the college seems to have been somewhat dull during most of the Patterson era. Shortly after the school moved to its present location occasional "grand balls," given by the "State College Hop Club," were reported to be the outstanding affairs of the season. During the next decade, however, the authorities frowned upon such pleasures, and according to one graduate who in 1899 severed five years' connection with the school, "it could scarcely be said that there was any social life in the College at that time."[14]

In December, 1901, a committee of students presented to the Board of Trustees a petition bearing a large number of signatures and requesting permission to use the gymnasium two Saturdays each month "for the purpose of giving a cadet hop." Upon motion of H. S. Barker, the petition was granted, and social life at the school "took on a brighter hue." The faculty was not pleased with the frequency of the entertainments, although a committee reported after mature consideration that the dances were "no more responsible for bad class work . . . than other forms of amusement." The trustees agreed that the dances should not be held more often than once each month and at the same time turned over to the faculty all power "to take full control of such dances" and to see that they were conducted properly.[15] Other social gatherings became more common as time passed. A Junior Prom was held intermittently, receptions helped

[14] Notes of interview with Judge Joseph H. Bullock, in Bureau of Source Materials in Higher Education.

[15] Agricultural and Mechanical College, Minutes of the Board of Trustees, December 10, 1901, June 5, 1902; Agricultural and Mechanical College, Minutes of the Senate, March 7, May 1, 1902.

vary the routine, and commencement seasons caused social life to move at a faster pace as the college year came to a close.

The rougher aspects of student life included hazing and class fights. The juniors sometimes resented the traditional paddling at the hands of the seniors as new cadet officers were appointed, and on occasion "a real pitched battle occurred." The hardest fought contests took place between the freshman and sophomore classes during their annual flag rushes, and blood was often shed. The rush of 1907, in spite of an agreement that no weapons or missiles were to be used, was notable for the fierceness with which the freshmen defended their flag, for the strategy with which the smaller number of sophomores equalized matters by picking off their enemies one at a time and locking them in the armory, and especially for the unscheduled fight that developed between the girls of the two classes. College officials condoned such class fights, if they did not approve them. On the day of the flag rush in 1907 classes were dismissed and the campus was crowded with spectators, who included not only students and faculty but also "hundreds of people from the city . . . out to see the fun." No doubt an opinion expressed several years earlier still prevailed: "this class feeling is in no way detrimental to the boys, but rather shows that attribute, which will in after life make them good business or professional men."[16]

The students did not have a paper of their own for approximately ten years after the college left Woodlands. Beginning in 1889 the Union and Patterson Literary societies co-operated for a time in publishing the *Bayonet,* a magazine. In November, 1890, the faculty gave permission to four students "to establish and continue the publication of a college paper until notified by the Faculty that it must be dis-

[16] Lexington *Democrat,* December 6, 1902; Lexington *Leader,* October 9, 1907.

continued." Established early in the next year, the *State College Cadet* continued to appear through most of the decade, though its form was changed in 1896. The faculty in 1900 again gave its permission for the publication of a paper, and the *K. S. C. Record* appeared on a weekly basis for a brief period. A longer life was enjoyed by the *Idea,* founded in 1908, which was the immediate forerunner of the present student newspaper. The present annual, the *Kentuckian,* first published in 1906, was preceded by *Echoes* in 1904 and by souvenir editions of a monthly magazine called the *Kentuckian,* which suspended publication shortly after 1900. Beginning in 1904 the students of the College of Civil Engineering published the *Transit,* and for a time after 1907 the *Mechanical and Electrical Engineering Record* was issued by students in the other branches of engineering.

Intercollegiate athletics played no part in the life of the college until late in the nineteenth century, and they were never as important during the Patterson regime as they became later. The first contest with another college took place in 1881 when three games of football were played with Kentucky University under rules quite unlike those now in effect. A few other games were played at intervals, but it was not until the fall of 1892 that organized athletics began at the State College. The most successful football season in the history of the school in some respects was that of 1898, when the "Immortals" won seven games without a loss and, moreover, scored 181 points while yielding none to their opponents. Baseball, which was being played at least as early as 1892, and basketball, in which a schedule was played in 1904-1905, attracted much attention among the students, but football was the major interest. Track contests were of relatively more importance early in the Patterson regime than later. The girls' basketball teams engaged in intercollegiate competition, though not as extensively as the boys' groups.

College officials were almost continuously troubled by problems arising from the increasing emphasis on intercollegiate athletics. The question of eligibility rules required frequent attention, and the use of "ringers" by other schools was often deplored. Under the best of conditions sports did not receive the approval of President Patterson, who in 1906 expressed freely to the trustees his opinions:

> Twenty years ago, the whole time of the Collegiate year from September to June, with the exception of legal holidays was given to study and class-room work. This, however, cannot now be said. Almost as soon as college work begins, football teams are organized and begin training. Twenty or thirty men are withdrawn for athletic exercise almost every afternoon. This interferes with the preparation of lessons, with military requirements, gymnastic training and laboratory work to a very serious degree, journeys long and short, involving absences, are undertaken to play match games. The whole student body is frequently detained after chapel in order to work up an artificial interest for contributing money to meet expenses. Games are preceded and accompanied by an excitement sometimes stimulated by reprehensible indulgences and money . . . is lost and won. I think that you can readily see that this is an atmosphere uncongenial to study and tends to defeat the purpose for which the college is organized and to disappoint the expectations of those who send their sons hither.
>
> From the end of November till about the middle of March, when the base-ball season begins, there is a comparative lull and during the interval the serious work of the year is done. I do not speak of broken noses, legs and arms, but of the time wasted, idleness encouraged and a heritage of demoralization carried over to the succeeding year. This is a serious matter and deserves your careful consideration.[17]

The trustees and many members of the faculty were more sympathetic than the President toward athletics, and in spite

[17] Agricultural and Mechanical College, Minutes of the Board of Trustees, December 11, 1906.

Spectators at a football game early in Barker's administration. President Barker is looking directly into the camera

of his protests intercollegiate sports played an ever-larger role on the college scene during the last years of his administration.

During an age more boisterous than the present, an age before the time of organized athletic programs and diversified social activity, it is not surprising that students sometimes broke their usually rather monotonous routine and conducted themselves in a manner not approved by the good President Patterson. No doubt the behavior of the majority was generally irreproachable, but a few bold spirits found difficulty in refraining from mischief, and on occasion the pent-up exuberance of even the average individual was likely to explode into action which flaunted all the rules and regulations designed to keep him in submission. Such occurrences often found their way into the local and state-wide press, much to the embarrassment of the college authorities who feared an unfavorable reaction from public opinion. Headline writers were hard put to avoid repetition in describing these happenings and sought variation by the use of synonymous phrases, such as: "The State College Trouble," "State College, Another Ruction," "On a Tear," "Student Racket," "State College Rumpus," and "Cadets on Rampage." Most often repeated were the words, "Midnight Artillery," which alone spoke volumes to those who knew State College.

Liquor and firearms were banned from the campus by faculty regulations, but they nevertheless frequently appeared. The combination, fortunately rare, of whisky, arms, and a vindictive disposition was certain to mean trouble. Early in 1883 a student from Logan County, already under arrest for violation of regulations, went to the city, "came back intoxicated about noon and discharged pistols from his room in the dormitory with promiscuous threats." At the direction of the faculty, Colonel McFarland, the Commanddant, disarmed the lad and cited him to appear before the college authorities. Failing to conform to the order, he was immediately expelled, and a policeman was summoned to remove him. He then promised to leave quietly, and the policeman was told that his services were not needed after all. When the representative of the law walked from the Main Building, however, he was probably nearer death than he had ever been before, for the student procured a loaded rifle which he trained on the man from a window and did not fire probably only because his target turned toward the street instead of toward the dormitory. No doubt the feeling of relief was general when the recalcitrant became sober enough to depart peacefully.

Collecting past-due board bills seems to have been a hazardous task in the 1890's. On one occasion a Mr. Wilson accosted a student outside the mess hall and requested him to pay his account. An argument ensued, becoming more and more heated until the student drew a knife and stabbed his adversary. Wilson died within a few days, and his murderer disappeared, not to be apprehended for months. A similar altercation at about the same time resulted in the shooting of another collector for the mess hall, John O'Bannion, who, however, was not seriously wounded. President Patterson upon hearing the shot appeared on the scene and courageously took the gun from the culprit, who ran and was never brought to justice.

Drunkenness, hazing, and rowdyism of various kinds, of which scores of examples might be cited, tended to injure the good name of the college among the people of the state in spite of the President's efforts to curb these evils and to minimize the extent to which they prevailed. During Patterson's administration the reputation of the school suffered most, however, from an incident which turned out to be something in the nature of an unpremeditated hoax, but which was serious enough for several months. Occurring at a time when the public was apparently willing to believe the worst in regard to hazing on the campus, the "Disappearance of Willis Smith" became a subject of public interest and conjecture.

The case was shrouded in mystery from its very beginning. On the night of September 22, 1908, W. E. Smith, a freshman, left his room to attend a meeting of his class at the Old Dormitory, but he never reached his destination. When he had not appeared by the next day, his brother became alarmed and appealed to university and city authorities. Having been the victims of so many pranks on the part of the students, the police at first refused to take the matter seriously. Likewise, the faculty for a brief time faced the situation calmly. Accepting the general opinion that the boy was being held prisoner by hazers, university officials appealed to the students to release him. When Willis still did not appear, the case became a state-wide sensation. There was no scarcity of theories and clues, most of which proved false, and as usual the cranks who delight in muddying the waters on such occasions made their appearance. Early in October the brother, L. E. Smith, found in his box a penciled note signed, "Black Hand," which warned that he "had better stop this investigation." Detective Chief Malcolm Brown took this as virtual proof that the missing youth, perhaps injured by hazers, was being kept in confinement by students; yet the most energetic efforts failed to discover him.

Meanwhile, other clues had to be investigated. A report that a body had been discovered burning on the city dump caused a momentary furor until the story was laid to rest as the product of wild imagination. The search was widened after a small boy told an astonishing story of overhearing a conversation among university students, from which he gathered that Smith had been bound, gagged, and locked in a freight car. Although railroad officials attempted to discount the story, it received wide credence, and Smith was "discovered" at widely separated points. A man found in a boxcar in Pennsylvania attracted some attention until he established his identity as a foreigner who had never heard of State University, Lexington, Kentucky. A strange young man who turned up in Decatur, Illinois, where a letter to Willis Smith was also found, caused much speculation. A stranger at Wyandotte Station near Lexington brought attention closer home, but again the trail was false. A picture which was thought to resemble the missing freshman was discovered in the band of a hat found floating down the Ohio River near Louisville, and this discovery convinced many people that at last the lad's fate had been brought to light.

The failure to find a solution of the mystery after weeks of investigation led to a widespread conclusion that the youth had met with foul play. The gravity of the affair had reached such proportions by late December that the school was in actual danger of disruption, since there was a possibility that parents would not allow their children to return after the Christmas recess to an institution over which hung this black cloud of suspicion. To make matters worse, the Fayette County Grand Jury, which had undertaken its own investigation, concluded from the evidence before it that Smith had been murdered and that his body had been concealed in a newly-constructed sewer on Winslow Street (now Euclid Avenue). This theory was substantiated by a letter written by an anonymous woman, who painted a gory picture of the crime. Further confirmation was afforded by a hat which was found near the open end of the sewer.

The question could have been settled by digging up a part of the sewer, but it developed that no funds were available for this work. A professor suggested that the newspapers, since they had exploited the story to the utmost and had kept it continuously before the public, should bear the expense of excavation. The Lexington *Herald* retaliated by declaring that the college, whose interests demanded a solution of the mystery, should do the work itself. While this squabble was in progress, the supernatural world provided another angle to the case. Smith's cousin, an Indiana woman, while participating in a seance summoned the "spirit" of Willis Smith and from this shade learned that the boy had been killed as the result of hazing on the campus and that his body had been thrown in an abandoned well. At this point, while the spiritualist made preparations to come to Lexington to locate the well, while means for probing the sewer were being sought, and while Patterson worried for fear many students would fail to return after Christmas, Willis Smith calmly walked into his sister's home at Owensboro!

His reappearance could not have been better timed, and great was the relief felt by all friends of the university. The ridiculous affair was not yet closed, however, for the errant youth now told a hair-raising tale of being kidnaped, drugged, transported over a long distance by freight car and horse, and held for days in an isolated mountain cave in Wisconsin from which he had finally managed to escape. His sunburned face and work-hardened hands gave the lie to this story, however, and after consultation with his brother he concocted another. According to "The Second Series of Wandering Weary Willie's Novels," as the student newspaper phrased it, he had left Lexington when a fraternity threatened to haze him, knowing that "if they tried that somebody would get killed." The students branded this story as a fake, and Smith's veracity was generally doubted.

Each year until their graduation, the members of Smith's class observed with appropriate ceremonies the anniversary of his disappearance, flying the flag at half-mast and constructing in front of the Main Building a grave over which was shed many a mocking tear. Although the students were able to make merry over the affair after its denouement, without doubt the incident injured the reputation of the school. Despite the exploding of the wild theories broadcast during Smith's absence, there remained more than a faint suspicion that all was not well on the campus—that discipline was deplorably lax. While rejecting the wanderer's statement of the reasons for his disappearance, the public was still willing to believe that hazing and rowdyism were prevalent and that the situation demanded an investigation. This attitude was well expressed by the Lexington *Herald,* which declared that "If discipline is not enforced, those responsible for its non-enforcement should be got rid of. If it is enforced, the fact should be established beyond the possibility of further question. . . . State University can make no more effective answer to the criticism to which it has been subjected within the past few months than to remove all possible occasion for criticism. Had no supposed occasion for criticism existed, the Smith incident would never have assumed the proportions to which it attained."[18]

During the Patterson era the "Midnight Artillery" became notorious for its pranks and its breaches of discipline. Supposedly, the order was composed of dormitory boys and received its intriguing title from its practice of firing on various occasions in the dead of night the cannon used by the artillery battalion of the Military Department and, later, the old Spanish American War relic which still stands in front of the Administration Building. The name came to be applied, however, to any group of students involved in mischief.

The resourcefulness of the students in finding occasion for pranks and the labor which they often expended on their schemes merit sincere admiration. Apparently nothing was overlooked, no man nor thing was immune. In 1893 the President had considerable difficulty in building a fence on the campus because the boys at night meticulously filled every posthole which had been dug during the day. Finally,

[18] Lexington *Herald,* January 2, 1909.

Old Spanish-American War cannon

Left rear, the first Experiment Station building

it was said, Patterson threatened to set a watch to catch some of the offenders and to plant them for posts. Sometimes the activities of the midnight band were directed by real or imagined grievances, as when two trees, which blocked the view of spectators at the athletic field but which Patterson sought to preserve, mysteriously disappeared.

Patterson and the entire faculty were fair game for the practical jokers. In 1893 some mischievous boys obtained a quantity of green paint which they applied liberally to the cannon and to some of the floors, after which they climaxed their sins by painting green stripes on the President's horse. The poor horse also suffered another indignity when he was placed in the Chapel one dark night, a feat which required a tremendous amount of labor, quietly performed. About two hundred crossties, stacked in front of the campus for use on a southward extension of the streetcar line, were borrowed to make steps up which the horse could be led to the second floor of the Main Building, where the Chapel was located. Then the ties were returned to their original location and neatly stacked. Great was the surprise occasioned by the presence of the animal when the college assembled for chapel the next morning. The most calm individuals in the hall were the horse, which seemed only mildly interested in the proceedings, and the President, who went ahead with the services as if nothing unusual had happened.[19]

Even so august a body as a special committee of the legislature was not safe from the pranksters. Early in 1904 the House of Representatives sent a committee to Lexington to investigate the affairs of the college. At the invitation of the faculty, the probers drove out to the campus one night at about ten o'clock to examine at first hand the living conditions in the men's dormitory. Leaving their carriages at the main entrance, the legislators devoted over an hour to in-

[19] R. T. Gunn, written statement, May 26, 1940, in Bureau of Source Materials in Higher Education.

specting the rooms, where they found nothing but peace and quiet. Upon returning to the street, however, they discovered that the outward appearance of quietness had been illusory. While the committee was in the dormitory, some unknown students slipped out, chased away the drivers, unhitched the horses and scattered them, took the wheels off the carriages, rolled them away, and left the bodies of the vehicles resting on the ground. Some of the legislators were inclined to be angry, but a philosophical reflection that "boys will be boys" helped restore their good humor. Without audible complaint, but with a better understanding of life at State College, they walked back to the Phoenix Hotel, where they were registered.

Shearing the locks of the freshmen was an annual practice, and by more drastic means the newcomers were further introduced to college life. In these initiations the Midnight Artillery performed with exceptional brilliance. Year after year one particular joke, with occasional variations, was repeated. Relying on the victim's ignorance of the school's military system, the hazers chose a likely prospect and, representing themselves as officers, ordered him to stand guard at some specified post. One innocent youth in 1895 was ordered, as his first task as a cadet, to perform all night sentry duty in the frog pond below the hill to keep the "enemy" from taking the fort unawares. The eager young soldier obeyed without question, and at the end of each hour all through the night he could be heard calling, "All is well at the frog pond!" Perhaps understanding began to dawn on him when he returned half-frozen to his room at daybreak to find it bare of furniture and flooded with water.

The Midnight Artillery was famous for its observance of all occasions which gave any excuse for celebration. Sometimes its efforts were sadly misunderstood, as when a newspaper announced that "Young Nihilists At the State College Explode a Bomb Under the Window of Col. Swigert's Quarters On Saturday Night and Follow This Up With Another Active Bomb On Sunday Night. Matters Pretty Lively."[20] It is true that matters were "pretty lively" and that explosions had been heard, but not for the reasons hinted at by the press. No "Young Nihilists" were attempting to overthrow authority, for the Midnight Artillery was simply rejoicing with time-honored noise over a newly-won football championship of the Inter-Collegiate League.

Hallowe'en was an occasion much dreaded by townsmen, college authorities, and policemen, for on that night the boys gave free rein to their talents. Cannon, revolvers, drums, horns, and raucous voices made the welkin ring; stolen gates, broken street lamps, barricaded car tracks, and streets piled high with debris bore mute testimony to the cadets' idea of fun. The boys serenaded the girls in Patterson Hall, and sometimes they were even more attentive. In 1904 a large group marched noisily to this dormitory pulling a heavy horse-drawn lawnmower, which they dragged up the steps to the veranda over the protests of the policeman who had been detailed to protect the young ladies. While the attention of the harassed guard was thus distracted, twelve or fifteen boys climbed to the roof of the veranda to talk to a number of girls who crawled out of the windows to meet them. Needless to say, such conduct did nothing to add luster to the good name of the college.

Campus troubles lost nothing in the telling when described by the local newspapers, and students often resented the adverse comment concerning their exploits. The faculty, too, deplored such bad publicity, and around 1900 something of a feud developed between the college and the Lexington *Herald,* edited by Desha Breckinridge. Ordinarily the school defended itself by public statements signed by professors or students, but in 1902 bitter feeling against the newspaper led to a regrettable incident.

[20] Lexington *Daily Press,* December 4, 1894.

At that time discipline on the campus was poorly enforced, for the boys had little respect for their Commandant, Major McKee, because of his alleged intemperance and profanity. One night in April, after completing his regular inspection of the Old Dormitory, McKee turned back at the sound of exploding firecrackers and was deluged with a pail of water from above. Rushing to the second floor, he ordered the students to fall in line and was further angered by the reluctance and lack of decorum with which his command was obeyed. When he raised his hand, either as a commanding gesture or to strike a particularly perverse cadet, he was knocked flat, the lights went out, and he was rather severely beaten. In chapel the next morning President Patterson announced that he had temporarily suspended the major from his duties and that he himself would take command. He also expressed a desire, in which the students heartily concurred, to avoid publicity.

Such an occurrence could not, of course, remain a secret. The Lexington *Herald* heard of the incident and sent a reporter, Denny B. Goode, to investigate. After receiving on his head the customary pail of water as he passed the dormitory, Goode obtained an interview with the President, and then he called upon McKee. When walking to the home of the latter he prudently avoided the dormitory, which caused the boys to shout "coward"; and while he talked to the major, a mob whose number was variously estimated at from fifty to two hundred and fifty assembled outside to await the reporter's exit. When he finally emerged, a few eggs and stones fell harmlessly near him, and after a brief parley, he was ordered to leave the campus and never to return. When Goode hesitated, a barrage of missiles fell about him, and to prevent further harm a few of his friends among the students grasped him by the arms and rushed him to the entrance, where he was released.

Instead of avoiding publicity by ejecting the reporter, the

students brought a veritable hornet's nest upon themselves, for seldom had an incident created such an uproar among the local press. Punishment for the guilty parties was demanded, and when Patterson issued a statement explaining the cause of the trouble, he was accused of condoning the "cowardly assault." The faculty carried on a lengthy probe, found itself unable to fix responsibility for the affair, and finally issued a statement censuring the unknown students but at the same time intimating that Goode's conduct in the past had provided sufficient provocation for the act. The attitude of the faculty was perhaps expressed by the adoption of a facetious resolution introduced at one of its meetings by Professor Neville: "In view of our protracted suffering in the sweat box, we most earnestly hope that no unpopular reporter will ever appear on these grounds, whether he be Goode, bad or indifferent." The Board of Trustees, prodded by an angry letter from Desha Breckinridge, also conducted an investigation with approximately the same result.

Though dissatisfied with the outcome of the case, the papers could do nothing beyond continuing a policy of criticism of the administration and the students and continuing to call for a more rigid enforcement of discipline. In view of the many disturbances on the campus and the wide publicity they received, an unknown rhymer no doubt expressed, in a parody upon a more famous poem, a generally prevalent opinion:

> Some jokes are the roughest
> At State College
> With ideas of fun the toughest
> At State College
> Rude jests they think is [*sic*] witty
> Discourtesy is pretty,
> Rank impudence is gritty
> At State College.[21]

21 Lexington *Leader,* April 9, 1902.

Chapter Nine

The Noncollegiate Divisions

According to President Patterson, immediately after separation from Kentucky University in 1878 the Agricultural and Mechanical College of Kentucky began an uninterrupted growth "in patronage and public confidence," even during the time in which it was housed temporarily in buildings owned by the denominational school. Removal in 1882 to the present campus gave the institution greater independence than it had ever possessed before. In addition, from that date forward there was about it an air of permanence which previously had been lacking. Policies, programs, and traditions could now be expected to endure and to influence the development of the institution far into the future.

That the college was not yet free from danger, however, was demonstrated by the fury of the assault launched upon it by the denominational colleges in 1882. Fortunately, the attackers did not achieve their objective, and Patterson used the widespread knowledge of the onslaught and its failure as publicity favorable to the school. His public explanation of the fight and its results was expressed in the newspaper press and in the college catalog for 1881-1882:

> The effect of the unprovoked assault made last winter upon the State College before the Legislature by the various denominational colleges of the State was to increase, rather than to diminish its attendance. The plea which the aggrieved colleges made, that education was made too cheap, too many advantages offered, and too wide a range of instruction provided, failed to convince the Legislature that State aid should be withdrawn from an institution to which, by accepting the trust from the

> General Government the Commonwealth had pledged her support. Should the State College be let alone and allowed to devote itself to its own work and to operate on its own lines, work which in no proper sense interferes with that of the denominational colleges, and in no proper sense traverses the lines on which they are laid down, five years will not elapse until it has six hundred students within its walls. Then we may hope that the reproach which has hitherto attached to Kentucky, that she had no institution worthy of her, may in some degree be removed.

Whether or not this view assigned the real reason for the increase, the enrollment of that year, 318 students in all departments, far surpassed any number previously attained. Approximately the same figure was reached in the next year, but the session of 1883-1884 witnessed a disheartening drop to only 211 matriculates, the smallest enrollment in the history of the independent college. During the next four years a steady but not spectacular growth took place, and with the addition of a summer normal, the total enrollment mushroomed from 391 in 1888-1889 to 549 in the next year. The discontinuation of summer classes and the depression of the 1890's dropped the figure to only 367 in 1896-1897, after which an almost constant increase was recorded. The revival of the summer school, together with the addition of short courses, raised attendance for the first time to more than 700 students in 1903-1904, and during the year in which the college became a university the enrollment reached 1,064, including 895 men and 169 women.

The exact number of bona fide college students in the institution at any given time during the early period is difficult to determine, since it was Patterson's custom to stress the total enrollment rather than the number of matriculates in the various divisions, some of which did work below college level. For example, not until 1893 were the enrollees in the Academy (or Preparatory Department) listed separately in the college catalogs, but by a large margin this department overshadowed all others combined. It has been said that "on purpose, these numbers were not published on account of being large,"[1] and under the circumstances perhaps an admission that after all the besieged and struggling State College was but little more than a high school would have been unwise. In 1907, after the dangerous years were safely behind, Patterson could confess that "for years the percentage of students in the preparatory department was about 75 to 80, and in the college proper between 20 and 25. In the later years of its history," he continued, "these proportions are reversed, the matriculation in the preparatory department during the last biennial period [1905-1907] was less than 20 per cent of the whole; of the college proper, more than 80 per cent."[2] In addition, for many years neither the Commercial Department nor the Normal School did work on the college level, although their students were of course always included in the total college enrollment.

President Patterson once said that "no fact more distinctly marks the growth of the College than the increase in the number of its graduates."[3] If that statement is true, the growth of the school was extremely slow almost to the end of the nineteenth century. The Agricultural and Mechanical College of Kentucky, during the whole time it was a part of Kentucky University, granted only two graduate and twelve bachelor degrees; four was the largest number given in any one year. In all three of the commencements held from 1878 to the removal of the institution from Woodlands to the present campus, the school could boast of no more than nine graduates. Supporters of the college in 1882, pleased with the prospect of a new era in its history, could find additional encouragement and cause for rejoicing in the

1 Pence, "University of Kentucky," part 2, p. 53.

2 Kentucky, Department of Public Education, *Biennial Report of the Superintendent of Public Instruction of Kentucky*, 1905-1907, p. 186.

3 *Ibid.*, 1899-1901, p. 75.

THE CAMPUS ABOUT 1900, FROM SITE OF THE PRESENT COLLEGE OF EDUCATION

fact that six degrees, the largest number ever given in one year prior to that time, were granted at the first spring commencement exercises held in the new college building. That number, repeated twice during the next seven years, was not surpassed until 1890, if graduate and honorary degrees are excluded. In 1890 eight degrees were given, and beginning in 1892, the annual number of graduates never dropped below ten. An almost constant increase was recorded from year to year until in 1908 the number of bachelor degrees reached eighty-five, the highest point attained during Patterson's administration.

Besides those who had earned degrees, there were other students who "graduated" from the college upon completing certain courses in departments which gave only subbaccalaureate certificates. Among these divisions was the Normal Department, which in 1884 granted a diploma to Leonora Hoeing of Lexington, thereby causing her to be termed "the First Scholastic Maiden Graduated by Kentucky State College." The Lexington newspapers applauded her achievement and pleaded for a more general admission of girls to the school. "Falcon," a contributor to one of the papers, indulged in an outburst of rhyme to the "maiden ripe and roseate and fair:"

> The seasons glide
> Toward the end of time, and thou with them
> Shalt float like some fairy lily on its stem,
> Borne on the ocean waves, away from me;
> But I shall not forget how unto thee
> Today I looked, and thought how fair the first
> Sweet fruit of this collegiate tree that burst
> Into fresh maiden blossom here today
> Among these awkward boys, like smiling May,
> Making the cold earth glorious. I hail
> With joy the first most fair, most learned female.[4]

Actually, not until 1888 did the college first grant a de-

[4] Lexington *Daily Press,* June 3, 5, 1884.

gree to a woman, Belle Clement Gunn of Lexington. When at the commencement exercises she read her essay on "work," according to the *Daily Press,* she gave "to the merit of the effort the added charm of the grace and beauty of a perfect womanhood, for she is a strikingly handsome young lady, and, offset by a background of somber boyhood, seemed like a bright flower in a soberly hued meadow."

Originally the degrees offered by the college were the Bachelor of Science and the Bachelor of Arts. As the various departments matured, the institution offered new degrees: Civil Engineer (C. E.) in 1887, changed to Bachelor of Civil Engineering (B. C. E.) in 1895; Bachelor of Agriculture (B. Agr.) and Master of Agriculture (M. Agr.) in 1889, transformed respectively to Bachelor and Master of Science in Agriculture (B. S. Agr. and M. S. Agr.) in 1907; Bachelor of Pedagogy (B. Ped.) in 1891, replaced in 1907 by two degrees, Bachelor of Arts and Bachelor of Science in Pedagogy (A. B. Ped. and B. S. Ped.); Mechanical Engineer (M. E.) in 1892, changed in the next year to Bachelor of Mechanical Engineering (B. M. E.); Master of Civil Engineering (C. E.) and Master of Mechanical Engineering (M. E.) in 1895; and Bachelor and Master of Mining Engineering (B. E. M. and E. M.) in 1902. After the reorganization in 1908 the pedagogical degrees became the Bachelor of Arts, Bachelor of Science, Master of Arts, and Master of Science in Education (A. B. Educ., B. S. Educ., A. M. Educ., and M. S. Educ.). The new College of Law made possible the addition of the LL. B., and for the first time the school ventured to list among its offerings the Ph. D., a degree which actually was not conferred until 1930.

Honorary degrees to a limited extent were conferred upon successful alumni, upon outstanding state and national figures, and on occasion even upon members of the school's own teaching staff. Honorary master's degrees were granted in 1888 to James G. White, head of the Department of

Mathematics, and to Francois M. Helveti of the Department of Modern Languages; in 1896 to Walter K. Patterson, brother of the President and Principal of the Preparatory Department; in 1906 to C. J. Norwood, professor of mining engineering; and in 1908 to Judge W. T. Lafferty, Dean of the College of Law. In 1899 the LL. D. degree was conferred upon J. H. Neville, professor of Greek and Latin, and upon John Shackelford, resigning from his posts as head of the Department of English and as Vice-President of the college; in 1908 upon Judge Henry Stites Barker, who was to become Patterson's successor.

During the thirty years which elapsed between the establishment of the independent Agricultural and Mechanical College and its transformation into a university, the State College evolved along slowly expanding lines, increasing its offerings when possible in an effort to afford college training to more and more Kentuckians of divergent interests. Limited resources and facilities restricted the usefulness of the school, especially during the early years, but Patterson and the Board of Trustees never ceased striving to make the institution more attractive to the sons and daughters of the state and more useful to the commonwealth as a whole. Because of necessity and because of the educational philosophy of President Patterson and most of his faculty, the main emphasis for years was upon the type of instruction found in virtually all colleges of the day, but the obligation to teach agriculture and the mechanical arts was not entirely forgotten. Though limited at best, instruction in these two fields became more important as the condition of the college improved.

Not only were the energies of the school channeled largely into the operation of Classical and Scientific departments, but great emphasis was placed on preparatory work. Perhaps it would be more accurate to state that this emphasis was placed on work in departments below the college level, for the Preparatory Department was not the sole noncollegiate division of the institution. The Normal Department, the Commercial Department, and short courses in agriculture helped build up the total enrollment, although in none of these divisions was college credit given. Nevertheless, they helped to spread the influence of the school through the state and to extend the services which Patterson and his colleagues sought to render to Kentucky.

For years the Preparatory Department was one of the most useful divisions of the institution, since it bridged the gap between college and secondary school at a time when the curricula of the latter left much to be desired and were not uniform over the state. A legislative investigating committee reported in 1888 that nearly all the state appointees were enrolled in the Academy, since they "came only prepared to enter" that department.[5] Two years later, Hugh P. Cooper, drawing up a minority report after an investigation of the college, could complain:

> The relation of the preparatory school to the College is such as to prevent good work where otherwise more might be expected. The fact is that the College is overshadowed by the preparatory school, which, if separated from the College as it should be so far as instruction is concerned, would carry with it seventy-five to eighty per cent. of the students whose names appear in the catalogue as college students, and this after deducting the names of those who attend the normal school. It has always been a very common thing for students in the preparatory course to be also assigned to the college classes. In other words, there is no class organization, and the consequent clashing of studies has been the cause of very serious complaint and of discouragement, for which the only remedy is a reorganization and a complete separation of the College and preparatory courses.
>
> The preparatory school also burdens the College by

[5] Kentucky *Senate Journal,* 1887-1888, p. 1656.

> demanding the time of the College professors for instruction of preparatory classes as such, time which should be given to College classes and to practical investigation.
>
> This comes from the fact that numbers have been made the criterion of success to the breaking down of standards of scholarship, thus multiplying the classes down even to primary work. In other words as astutely remarked by one of the professors, the grade of college work has been lowered to relieve the stress in the nursery.[6]

Notwithstanding any dissatisfaction with its manner of operation, the necessity of the work of the Preparatory Department could not be denied. For more than a decade after 1880 all new students who desired admission to the freshman class were required to take an entrance examination which was based on the material covered in the Academy's classes. Since few schools in Kentucky gave training of such high caliber, most of the applicants were placed in the Preparatory Department to prepare for work on the college level. Not until 1896 did the State College catalog indicate that students might be admitted to the freshman class from certain "accredited" schools without an entrance examination. At that time twenty-four schools, both public and private, had fulfilled the conditions specified in a faculty resolution concerning entrance requirements. Of these institutions the Ashland, the three Louisville, and the Nicholasville high schools were accredited even to the sophomore class, but for only a year. The list of accredited schools was extended from time to time, and in 1907 it included fifty-nine public and thirty-nine private high schools. Of the total number, five were located in states other than Kentucky.

Certain entrance requirements existed also for those who wished to enter the Preparatory Department. The conditions of admission in 1880 included "a good knowledge of

[6] Kentucky *Documents,* 1889-1890, V, No. 6, p. 25.

Arithmetic as far as fractions ["as far as percentage" in 1886], English Grammar, and Geography." Beginning with the session of 1888-1889 all applicants were required to show evidence that they had "completed the common school course prescribed by the State Board of Education." In addition, the entrance examination was a hurdle which all had to pass, and after 1893 questions on the history of the United States were added to that test.

The minimum age for admission into the Preparatory Department varied. At the beginning of the existence of the independent Agricultural and Mechanical College the General Assembly provided that the age of the applicants for legislative scholarships lie between twelve and twenty-five years. In its regulations adopted in 1882 the Board of Trustees ruled that except for scholarship holders, no one under fourteen would be admitted. A decade later the minimum age was set at fourteen for legislative appointees and fifteen for all others. Exceptions to the rule were sometimes made, as is illustrated by the case of Warren L. Eubank of Lexington. Called by a Lexington paper "perhaps the youngest matriculate" ever to enter the college, he was only eleven years old when he was first admitted to the Academy, at which time he expressed a determination to remain at the school until he earned a degree.[7]

In its whole existence the Preparatory Department of the Agricultural and Mechanical College had only one Principal, Walter Kennedy Patterson, brother of the President. Never popular among the students, he probably held his post mainly because of the loyal support and protection of his elder brother. In later years, one of his former students said of him: "I found Prof. Patterson, despite generally received opinion to the contrary, a good careful instructor. I had only one study, Algebra under him, and he taught that well. He was much inferior to his brilliant brother the

[7] Lexington *Leader,* June 4, 1908.

President, and consequently suffered in comparison. However he was successful financially and like his brother left quite a large fortune when he died."[8]

Patterson's assistants in the department changed frequently, and sometimes he relied in part upon students in the college as teachers. Some of his staff later made reputations for themselves in the university, as in the case of Merry Lewis Pence, who became head of the Physics Department; Mrs. Lucy B. Blackburn, who served as "Monitress" before the office of Dean of Women was created; Victor E. Muncy, who held briefly the post of business agent of the college at the turn of the century; and Joseph Morton Davis, who became a professor in the Mathematics Department. One instructor in the Academy, L. N. Taylor, in 1905 took time from his scholastic duties to engage in a successful political campaign as Republican nominee for the office of Superintendent of Common Schools of Pulaski County. Another, John Leslie Purdom, in 1907 caused a momentary flurry of excitement on the campus by challenging one of his students "to fight a duel with boxing gloves to settle a dispute between them," but the student chose to apologize rather than accept the challenge to settle the argument "in a gentlemanly way."[9]

The Preparatory Department offered the student a choice of two courses—classical, and agricultural and scientific—each of which covered a period of two years' study. No revision was made until the general reorganization of the college in 1889, when the "Preparatory Department" became the "Academy," and even at that time the changes were slight. The next year an elementary course, which existed for only two years, was added; the agricultural and scientific course became the "Agricultural, Scientific and Engineering Courses" with no change in the offerings; and students in

[8] John W. Gunn, statement in Bureau of Source Materials in Higher Education.

[9] Lexington *Leader,* January 22, 1907.

the classical course were required to attend classes in elementary sciences. A reorganization took place in 1907: the Academy then offered only one program of study, covering three years.

Except for the level of his studies, the student in the Preparatory Department was indistinguishable from his fellows in the college. All were subject to the same rules and regulations, and the preparatory student was required to attend the college "only during the hours of recitation and other college exercises, such as chapel, drill, etc., the preparation of their lessons being made elsewhere." He dressed as did the other students, he drilled with them, he lived with them, and if chosen a county appointee, he was eligible to receive the benefits accorded all who entered the school with that assistance. His classes met in various rooms of the Main Building, and as Hugh Cooper complained, he might even be a member of one or more college classes while enrolled in the Academy, although after 1890 the school proclaimed through its catalog that no preparatory student would be allowed to take any work outside his regular course except on the recommendation of the Principal, a permission often given. When he had completed the courses in the Academy, the student found it easy to move into the freshman class. Since he was already familiar with the college routine, and since his preparation was superior to that received in most of the schools of the state, he possessed many advantages over the stranger who enrolled as a freshman.

Also below college level was the commercial training which was a part of the program of the Agricultural and Mechanical College during a large part of its early history. Expanding trade and industry, the quickening of business tempo, and the increased use of modern office machines opened to thousands of young men and women careers for which they needed specialized training. Commercial schools appeared in growing numbers to transform eager students into secretaries, "typewriters," and "phonographers," and many colleges, swept along by the trend in that direction, endeavored to make themselves more serviceable to society by offering training in business methods and administration. When the State College was first put in operation, its courses included "those branches essential to commercial and business education," but the difficulties experienced by the school soon caused the abandonment of that phase of its program.

After its separation from Kentucky University the college revived its business training feature. In 1880 a Commercial Department was inaugurated under the supervision of T. C. H. Vance, who was not only Principal of that department but also adjunct professor in the Normal School and traveling agent of the college. The department sought to attract three groups of students: those who wished to work toward a diploma in business training, those who wished to learn bookkeeping alone, and those who, while regularly enrolled in the Classical and Scientific departments of the college, wished to avail "themselves of the opportunity of familiarizing themselves with the principles and practice of a business education." The course of study for the diploma covered a period of three years and, according to Patterson, went far beyond the requirements "of most of the Commercial Colleges of the country."[10] An examination of the schedule indicates that the school endeavored to give the student as much of a general education as possible, with comparatively little emphasis on basic business training.

Upon the departure of Vance in 1883 the versatile Merry L. Pence became professor of bookkeeping, as well as assistant in the Preparatory Department, and held the post for the next five years. Shortly after Pence took charge of the commercial classes, the college Executive Committee under-

10 Agricultural and Mechanical College, *Annual Register,* 1880-1881, p. 9.

took to expand the training program, not by adding classes to those already established, but by an agreement with a business school in Lexington. Beginning early in 1885 State College students were permitted during their free time to attend the Williams School for training in telegraphy, stenography, and typewriting.

In 1889 a further expansion occurred through the expedient of annexing to the college another Lexington business school, with which the existing Commercial Department was merged. The Commercial and Shorthand Institute, located at 50 North Broadway, gave up its independence in this union, but its Principal, J. C. Orcutt, became the head of the new school, the Commercial and Shorthand (or Phonographic) Department of State College. The new department was self-sustaining, depending for its income upon fees paid by its matriculates. Students were charged ten dollars for a course in merchant bookkeeping, fifteen dollars for shorthand and typewriting, ten dollars for typewriting alone, twenty-five dollars for a complete course in bookkeeping, and for a "life scholarship" which included all courses, fifty dollars. The complete course in plain and ornamental penmanship cost the student five dollars, and it was announced that special terms were available to those who wished to take Fancy Flourishing and Pen Sketching. One of the special features of the department was the series of lectures on commercial law given by Judge Matt. Walton of Lexington, and another was the lack of a rigid schedule. No specified time was required for the completion of any of the courses, and each student was advanced "as rapidly as his ability and industry" would allow.

In return for the prestige acquired as a department of the state-supported college, Orcutt's school agreed to give free instruction in bookkeeping to all regularly enrolled students in the college who wished to take advantage of the offer. In addition, college students might have access to the classes in shorthand, typewriting, and penmanship upon the payment of two thirds of the fees regularly required by the Commercial Department. Students in the department likewise were permitted access to classes in other departments upon the payment of two thirds of the college tuition.

After one year as head of the Commercial Department, Orcutt left the college. His successor, C. C. Calhoun, proved to be an aggressive administrator. He added telegraphy to the courses offered, and in November, 1890, he undertook to attract more students by establishing night classes in shorthand and typewriting "for the benefit of the young ladies and gentlemen in the city who are employed during the day, and who wish to take up this very interesting and beneficial study."[11] His efforts bolstered the annual enrollment of the department, then at 135-137 East Main Street, from slightly more than one hundred to a peak of 261 during the six years in which he was connected with the State College.

Unfortunately for the peace of mind of Calhoun and for the continued connection of the Commercial Department with the Agricultural and Mechanical College, the success of his business school inspired a spirited rivalry between it and another operated by Wilbur R. Smith. To make the competition even more intense than it might otherwise have been, Smith's institution enjoyed a connection with Kentucky University somewhat like that between Calhoun's school and the State College. Both business schools advertised aggressively for students. Smith boasted of the hundreds of men and women who allegedly had attained success in the business world as a result of the superior training they had received under his direction; Calhoun, who claimed to have opened through his institution "a sure avenue to success for young men and women," referred with a not inconsiderable evidence of satisfaction to the fact that "This

[11] Lexington *Daily Transcript,* November 9, 1890.

school received the Highest Official endorsement of any similar Institution in the United States, its diplomas being granted under seal and signed by the Governor of the Commonwealth."[12]

The antipathy of the two educators for each other led them to excesses which could hardly have had the approval of the State College and the sectarian university, especially after Calhoun in 1891 began a suit for damages against Smith, alleging that his character had been injured by "false, defamatory and libelous" circulars published by the defendant. President Patterson, in his statements to the public, was careful to point out that the Commercial Department was "only an annex" to the Agricultural and Mechanical College.

Nevertheless, when Calhoun in 1892 incorporated his school as the Lexington Business College, newspaper accounts of the event revealed that Patterson was himself a stockholder in the venture and that he was a member of its Board of Directors.[13] His connection with the school became the object of severe criticism which resulted in the appointment of a committee by the trustees of the Agricultural and Mechanical College to investigate the matter. The report submitted by this group in June, 1894, showed that Patterson owned only two shares of stock in the business school and that these shares were obtained only for the purpose of allowing the President of State College some voice in the management of its Commercial Department. In 1895, however, the Board of Trustees ended the contract between the college and the business school. During the remainder of the Patterson regime, the college operated without a Commercial Department.

One of the avowed purposes behind the establishment of the Normal Department of the college was to improve the

12 See, for example, Lexington *Daily Press,* February 1, 17, June 28, 1891.
13 Lexington *Daily Transcript,* July 31, 1892.

common schools of Kentucky by giving the proper training to individuals who planned to enter the teaching profession. Attainment of that high objective was difficult because of the poor preparation many prospective and active teachers had before enrolling in the department, the reluctance of the college to depart appreciably from the traditional classical course of study in any division of the school, the lack of facilities, and the lack of aggressiveness in the leadership of the department during its first decade.

In 1880, as Patterson later admitted, no more than a rudimentary course in teacher training was offered, and in the main those who enrolled in the Normal Department received instruction in elementary subjects and in the classics, a situation which the President felt called on to defend before the General Assembly in 1882.[14] Maurice Kirby, professor of theory and practice of teaching and Principal of the Normal School, whose duties as head of the department were so light that in 1882 he served also as professor of moral and political philosophy, announced in 1880 a three-year program for teacher training. Among the requirements for a diploma in the Normal School, the theory and practice of teaching was overshadowed by the long list of nonprofessional subjects offered. All other departments in the college were open to the normal students, who, if they preferred not to work toward a diploma, could earn "certificates of qualification to teach . . . those branches in which the required degree of proficiency is attained."[15]

Little change in the operation of the department occurred under Kirby, although during his last year as Principal he set down a list of aims for the school which, if attained, would have produced well-rounded, scientifically prepared

14 See Patterson's speech, "State Aid to Higher Education," delivered in the Kentucky House of Representatives, January 20, 1882. Pollitt, *Patterson*, 288-89.

15 Agricultural and Mechanical College, *Annual Report of the Board of Trustees*, 1879-1880, p. 15.

teachers for the public schools of the state. J. R. Potter, Kirby's successor and former assistant, reorganized the curriculum to offer four courses of study: the common school normal course, covered in one year's work; the advanced course, two years; the intermediate course, three years; and the collegiate course, four years. Potter's brief regime was no more successful than that of Kirby, and a legislative investigating committee reported in the spring of 1888 that it found "the Normal Department doing but little because of lack of pupils." Explaining that county appointees seeking teacher training came to the college unprepared to enter classes above the Preparatory Department, that when they had there prepared themselves to enter the Normal Department they were also eligible to teach county schools, and that they left to teach and rarely returned, the committee flatly declared that the "Normal Department is not a success." With a somewhat mournful accent, the legislators then confessed that "We could discover no way to remedy this."[16]

The trustees, apparently more confident in their judgment of the situation than the legislative committee, took a simple and direct step in their search for a remedy. On June 6, 1888, they ordered their secretary to notify Potter that his services were no longer required. To put new life into the department, which in the words of a Lexington newspaper "up to this year has not amounted to much," the Board of Trustees then offered the vacancy on a one-year basis to a popular educator and politician, A. L. Peterman of Monroe County. The appointment of Peterman, who was said to be "not only invincible on the hustings, but . . . a Horace Mann as well," caused one optimist to exclaim that "the future of the State College is as 'Bright as the star that melts afar, Into the morning's gold.' "[17]

With the assistance of J. W. Newman, professor of theory

[16] Kentucky *Senate Journal,* 1887-1888, p. 1656.
[17] Lexington *Daily Press,* January 23, 1889.

and practice of teaching, Peterman reorganized the offering of his department into two courses of study. The first, a one-year course, permitted the student to review elementary subjects and thereby prepare himself to teach in the common schools. The second, which required four years' work, was designed to give "a thorough preparation for higher professional work as teachers." The department recommended that advanced students should also receive a degree, and in 1891 the Bachelor of Pedagogy was added to the list of degrees granted by the college. Peterman introduced briefly a summer term in his department, he attended teachers' institutes over the state, he carried on an extensive correspondence, and he sent out numerous circulars. His efforts brought students in such numbers that an additional assistant was employed, but at the same time a legislative investigating committee, while praising his "energy and industry and ability," frowned on his expenditures and on his frequent absences. Politics seems to have been Peterman's chief interest, and in January, 1890, he took his seat in the Kentucky legislature, turning the management of the Normal School over to Newman.

Newman's tenure as acting head of the department lasted only until September, when Ruric N. Roark became Principal. Roark, who had begun his connection with the institution as a professor in the Normal Department in the session of 1889-1890, possessed more than any other individual who filled the headship of the department the viewpoint of the professional teacher of teachers. Educated at an Ohio normal school, he had several years' teaching experience in that and other similar institutions before coming to Lexington. He possessed in large measure self-confidence and determination, qualities which sometimes irked Patterson and members of the Board of Trustees but which made him one of the outstanding leaders in the field of education in Kentucky.

According to Roark, "The teacher must be possessed of three things, in addition to an upright and sterling character, and a healthy body. These three things are (1), An adequate knowledge of what he proposes to teach; (2), Skill in teaching—knowledge of how to teach; (3), Some broad and liberal culture, wherewith to illuminate his work and increase its value. These three things it is the business of the Teachers' Training School to give."[18] He made no drastic changes in the courses offered by his department, though after a few years arrangements were made to provide instruction suitable to teachers who wished to earn one of several certificates or diplomas, which ranged from the county certificate to the professional degree. In spite of an increasing enrollment, the staff of the department remained small, owing to an 1892 ruling by the Board of Trustees that the department "be confined to strictly technical instruction in the art of teaching and all other named instruction be given in the Academic Depts."

Even the student who received the B. Ped. degree did most of his work outside his major department. He had no education courses whatever during his freshman and sophomore years. As a junior he enrolled in Educational Psychology, the first of the very small number of professional courses available to him. Before graduation he added Normal Methods, School Management, and History of Education. For the junior course the textbook, *Psychology in Education,* was written by Roark himself. According to one reviewer its style was "pervaded by a strong and pleasing personality which cannot fail to hold the attention of the reader."[19]

There is no doubt that Roark's personality was strong and pleasing to Kentucky public school teachers, among whom the head of the State College Normal Department was most active. His services were in demand at teachers' institutes,

[18] Kentucky *Documents,* 1891-1892, V, 228.
[19] Lexington *Leader,* January 13, 1896.

he took a leading role in the Kentucky Educational Association, he obtained from the trustees permission to revive the summer normal, and by letter, circular, and personal contact he convinced teachers of the benefits to be derived from training given by the department. He became known to and respected by hundreds of public school teachers throughout the state, and the enrollment in his division grew until it presented a housing problem to the college authorities. In 1898 Roark informed the Board of Trustees by letter that the publicity he had given to the free room, fuel, and light offered to county appointees was about to result in an overflow of applicants for those services. He stated frankly that he would be "greatly chagrined" if appointees arrived only to find that the promises could not be kept. The board, stating that it had "neither money nor time to erect additional buildings," dumped the problem in the lap of President Patterson by authorizing him "to make the best arrangement possible to meet the necessity."[20]

At length a clash occurred between the ambitious Roark and the Board of Trustees, dominated by the strong-willed James K. Patterson. Perhaps an undercurrent of feeling existed long before it came to the surface, for as early as 1897 Roark had been called before the board to explain his failure to abide by regulations concerning faculty meetings. His greatest error in the eyes of administrative officials was to act on his own initiative in lobbying at the meeting of the state legislature in 1904 for additional money for his own department. At the next session of the Board of Trustees, the chairman of the Special Committee on Legislation introduced a resolution expressing "regret and displeasure" at the action of Roark, declaring it to be "an officious intervention in matters outside of his province," accusing him of "a want of delicacy and a lack of the proper sense of pro-

20 Agricultural and Mechanical College, Minutes of Board of Trustees, December 14, 1898.

priety," and stating that he had shown "a spirit of insubordination and disloyalty wholly incompatible with the duties of a professor." In spite of the harsh tone of the resolution, the board did not demand the culprit's resignation, but the trustees did "rebuke and condemn his action as wholly gratuitous and unjustifiable action which they believe resulted in the practical failure of important legislation much needed by the State College." After Roark had been permitted to appear in his own defense, the resolution was adopted by a vote of 8 to 2, Patterson siding with the majority.

Almost immediately the college was attacked by "the Normal School men," as Patterson called them, who prevailed on the State Teachers Association to adopt "resolutions reflecting in very uncomplimentary terms upon the School . . . for its alleged inadequate support of the Normal School." Patterson later claimed that he prevented similar action in certain county teachers institutes, and at his insistence a special committee of the Board of Trustees was created to study the situation and prepare "to meet any action adverse to the interest of the College in the next Legislature." Roark denied a rumor that he intended presenting his case to the legislature, but Patterson on May 30, 1905, warned the trustees that the State Teachers Association, "inspired by hostility outside our own organization, and by disaffected persons within," was organizing an effort to separate the Normal Department from the college and establish it as an independent institution. The President was doubtless somewhat relieved when on the next day Roark presented his resignation, which was accepted immediately by the Board of Trustees.[21]

Milford White, who had served since 1898 as Roark's assistant, now became Dean of the Normal Department, with James Thomas Cotton Noe and Joseph Evans Warren

[21] *Ibid.*, June 9, December 13, 1904, May 30, 31, 1905.

as his assistants. Their department faced an uncertain future for a time, owing to an effort, in which Roark was one of the leaders, to separate it from the State College. Failing in that endeavor, the dissatisfied element then pursued successfully a plan to establish two new normal schools, one of which was located at Richmond, the other at Bowling Green. Roark became the first President of the Eastern Normal School, which later became the Eastern Kentucky State College.

Patterson and other college officials were pleased that the Normal Department continued to flourish after Roark's departure. In a report to the trustees the President, referring to a fear expressed by some that the recent resignation would injure the department, stated malevolently that "Instead of a loss we have gotten rid of an *incubus* which retarded its development and hindered its growth."[22] Further cause for gratification came with the passage of an act by the legislature in March, 1906, which authorized graduates of the Normal Department of the Agricultural and Mechanical College to teach without certificate for life in the public schools of the state, and permitted the Board of Trustees to award certificates to students who had completed certain courses of study in the department. In the same year long-sought relief was promised in the form of plans for a new building to house the Normal School, which moved into its new quarters (now Frazee Hall) in 1907.

Apparently Patterson was taken by surprise when the legislative act which transformed the institution into a university eliminated the Normal School and created in its place a Department of Education. He expressed to the trustees his regret and humiliation at the disappearance of the Normal Department and charged that the action reflected not the will of the people but "the persistent jealousy and hostility of the Normal Schools established under the Act of

[22] *Ibid.*, June 5, 1906.

1906." He paid tribute to the department, stating that during its twenty-eight years of existence it had trained more than 3,000 teachers economically and well. He predicted that the change would cause a drop of from three to four hundred students in the college during the next year, and he doubtless regretted the loss of this means of spreading the influence of the State University through Kentucky.

Chapter Ten

The Academic Stature of the College

PERHAPS THE WORST FAILURE OF THE AGRICULTURAL and Mechanical College during its whole period of independence before evolving into the State University lay in its lack of success in the teaching of agriculture. The obligation to provide courses in that field was clear enough, although President Patterson might quibble and try to maintain that a distinction existed between "those branches of learning which are related to agriculture and mechanic arts" and "agriculture and mechanic arts" themselves; that legally the related branches must be taught and that no obligation existed to teach the specific subjects.[1] Less extreme but along the same line of thought was his argument at a meeting in Colorado that agricultural colleges were supposed to do more than merely teach farming. According to his idea, the Morrill Act did not confine the work of land-grant colleges "to farming pure and simple, but to branches of it," and the schools while preparing their students to become successful agriculturists at the same time equipped them "for other walks of life."[2]

Time and again Patterson remarked on the school's lack of success in creating among students interest in taking agricultural courses. At one time he explained the difficulty in obtaining students by saying that "Farmers do not want their sons to be farmers, neither do clergymen, lawyers or other professional people, particularly since the agricultural interests have become depressed."[3] Somewhat later he remarked that "in former years" the college found it impossible

1 Kentucky *Documents,* 1889-1890, V, 9.
2 Denver (Colorado) *Republican,* July 16, 1895.
3 *Ibid.*

to awaken interest in agricultural courses, and he claimed that because of this fact the institution devoted its energies to building up "those other courses of study into which students desired to enter."[4] Whatever the reason, it is true that the Department of Agriculture lagged behind the remainder of the institution until it rather suddenly took on new life around 1904 and 1905.

For several years after moving to its present location, the college had little evidence to substantiate its claim that instruction in agriculture was given at the institution. Most of the courses offered under Kellerman and his successor, Albert A. Menke, dealt with botany, some instruction was given in agricultural chemistry, and very brief attention was given to stock breeding and to veterinary science. Shop work was soon added to the schedule, as were specific courses in agriculture and horticulture. Nevertheless, as expressed by the Board of Trustees in 1883, "the means of carrying out the idea of Congress in regard to scientific practical agriculture" were "conspicuously deficient." The crying need, in the opinion of college officials, was for a farm. Some land had been rented, but the impossibility of doing much in the nature of experimentation on rented land was recognized.[5] Not until 1887, two years after the establishment of the Experiment Station, did the college acquire a farm—48.5 acres for a price of $17,000.

Even after a farm had been purchased, agricultural education lagged. Trying to attract more students in this field, the college in 1886 established a "partial" course, permitting those who enrolled in it to leave at the end of two years with training which was "practically valuable in Agricultural occupations." The desired results were still not obtained, and after an investigation in 1888, a legislative joint

[4] Agricultural and Mechanical College, Minutes of the Board of Trustees, December 13, 1904.

[5] See report of the Board of Trustees in Kentucky *Documents,* 1883, III, 4.

THE FACULTY IN 1886

ottom row: W. D. Lambuth, Latin and Greek; President Patterson; James G. White, athematics; John Shackelford, English

econd row: Dr. Robert Peter, chemistry and experimental physics; Alfred M. Peter, ssistant in chemistry in the Experiment Station; J. C. McClelland, assistant in Preparaory Department; A. T. Parker (with dark beard), microscopist, Experiment Station; rancois M. Helveti, French and German; Lieutenant F. E. Phelps (in straw hat), engieering and military science; and Walter K. Patterson, principal of the Preparatory epartment

op row: Albert A. Menke, agriculture and horticulture; J. R. Potter (side whiskers), eory and practice of teaching, Normal School; A. R. Crandall, natural history; John H. eville (hatless), Latin and Greek; and Maurice Kirby (top right), principal of Noral Department

committee was constrained to report that at the college "nothing has been done towards teaching Horticulture or Veterinary Surgery, and but little towards teaching Agriculture and the Mechanical Arts."[6] A somewhat drastic move took place in 1890 when the school made obligatory on all male students attendance at a so-called "popular course" of lectures relating to agriculture. The trustees were highly pleased at the large number in attendance at these lectures, although several years later the student newspaper *Idea* probably pictured the situation with a fair degree of accuracy when it recalled that "the students were herded in the chapel and only a few took the lectures, while many slept."[7]

The trustees relieved Menke of his duties in connection with the Agricultural Department in 1887 and transferred them to M. A. Scovell, Director of the Experiment Station, hoping by this move to bring about a closer relationship between the two divisions now headed by Scovell. The union was ended in the next year when J. H. Connell took charge of the Department of Agriculture and Horticulture. After one year Connell was succeeded by W. B. Stark, who two years later was followed by C. W. Mathews. Mathews, who became Dean of the College of Agriculture in 1908, enjoyed a tenure of eighteen years as the director of agricultural education in the state's highest institution of learning.

Meanwhile, in the reorganization of the college in 1889 the agricultural course, with a Dean and a faculty, was set up on an equal basis with other, more successful departments. Though the degrees of Bachelor and Master of Agriculture were offered, the schedule included relatively few courses purely agricultural in nature. Few students were tempted to enroll, and fewer still completed the work outlined for them. Not until the session of 1899-1900 did the annual enrollment in agriculture exceed five, and three more years passed before that number was doubled. The first B.

[6] Kentucky *Senate Journal,* 1887-1888, p. 1656.

[7] January 5, 1911.

Agr. degree was conferred in 1898, and the second in 1901. The title "Dean" as applied to the head of the department was dropped when Stark left the position, and Mathews served as professor of agriculture, horticulture and botany until by action of the Board of Trustees in 1897 he was designated as Dean.

A Department of Veterinary Science was created by the Board of Trustees in 1891, but it was even less successful than the regular Department of Agriculture, and after five years it was discontinued because of insufficient patronage to justify its existence. A ten weeks' short course in agriculture, established in 1895, was at that time almost as great a failure, although in later years it became much more popular.

Early in the present century the Department of Agriculture began to show some signs of life. President Patterson reported to the Board of Trustees in 1902 that the growing demand for instruction in that field required the exclusive attention of Professor Mathews, who had to that time given part of his services to the Experiment Station. By 1904, when, according to the catalog, the enrollment reached 18, Patterson informed the trustees that more students had entered the agricultural course than ever before and that he and Mathews were in agreement that "a critical stage in the development of that course of study" had been reached. Now, however, when a demand for instruction in "critical and practical Agriculture and Horticulture" was being made, the college found itself without the necessary equipment and instructors to meet the need. Emphasizing the seriousness of the matter, the President pointed out that "We are bound to keep faith with the Federal Government and with our own people even at the expense, if need be, of curtailment in other directions."[8]

[8] Agricultural and Mechanical College, Minutes of the Board of Trustees, December 13, 1904.

No doubt the main reason for Patterson's concern for the welfare of the Agricultural Department was that farmers over the state were beginning to accuse the college of building up certain other departments and neglecting the one which concerned them most. Patterson claimed that by appearing and speaking at the Shelby County Farmers Institute in 1905 he had prevented the launching of an attack on the college, and he warned that the danger still existed. He pointed out to the trustees that "its recrudescence before the Legislature would seriously embarrass us," and he confessed that "the fact is we have not provided adequately for Agricultural education." With a note of insistence in his voice, he told the board that "The Agriculture side of State College claims your attention and urgently claims it. If you ignore or neglect it, you fail in your duty and the interest of the Institution will suffer. The farmers will aid us if we do our duty by them. If we do not, we shall come to grief."[9]

When Professor Mathews in December, 1906, requested the trustees to appropriate $15,000 to erect a structure which was expected to be a wing of a future larger agricultural building, he received an unusually cordial response. Patterson himself moved that the appropriation be made, the motion carried, a committee was appointed to advertise for plans and specifications, and the chairman of the board was authorized to borrow a sum of money sufficient to pay the appropriation, which was increased in the next year. Work on the building was started in 1907 and was completed in the next year, after the Department of Agriculture had become the College of Agriculture in the new State University.

The sudden concern for the welfare of the Department of Agriculture was reflected in the addition of courses and instructors to care for the increasing enrollment. Most of the courses had been taught through the years by the head of the department, with assistance when required from mem-

[9] *Ibid.*, May 30, 1905.

bers of the Experiment Station staff. In 1905 John J. Hooper, a graduate of the Texas agricultural college, became professor of animal husbandry, and for the first time the college devoted more than passing attention to that phase of agricultural education. Hooper was an energetic advocate of improved breeds of livestock, and his activities received much favorable publicity in the Lexington newspaper press. Mathews, Hooper, and Alfred H. Gilbert, an assistant in botany, in 1907 were able to provide more extensive offerings in subjects pertaining to agriculture than the college had afforded prior to that time. Besides courses in general agriculture, students could undertake study in the specialized fields of animal husbandry and horticulture. In addition the two-year course and the winter short course were offered to those who desired instruction in agriculture but did not wish to work toward a degree.

A far more creditable record was made by the college in regard to its courses in engineering, although, unfortunately, each of the three which in time were established developed independently of the others with the result that three separate, unco-ordinated engineering departments arose. As in the case of agriculture, the offerings in the fields of engineering were extremely limited in 1882 and for several years afterward. According to the annual catalogs, students who enrolled in the scientific course might receive instruction in practical mechanics and in civil, mechanical, and mining engineering, but the school did not profess to offer anything like a real course in any one of these fields. In fact, only an extremely superficial type of instruction could have been possible, since until 1888 the Commandant, or head of the Military Department, was expected to include engineering among his courses in military art and science. At the same time, perhaps resulting from an effort to justify at least half the title of the school, the Department of Practical Mechanics established in 1882 offered students an opportunity to learn through actual experience "mechanical drawing, the study and care of tools, work in wood and metals at the bench, the lathe, and the forge."

The catalog of 1885-1886 outlined for the first time an engineering course, which included classes in civil engineering, military engineering, and drawing, as well as a considerable amount of shop work. The activities of the Mechanical Department, now directed by A. R. Crandall who was also professor of natural history, did not fall within the bounds of the engineering course. Lieutenant F. E. Phelps and Lieutenant Dillard H. Clark, his successor as Commandant after one year, each bore the title "professor of civil, mechanical and mining engineering and military science." As part of the changes made in the organization of the college in 1889 a Department of Engineering was established under William Newbrough as Dean. Newbrough held also the title "professor of civil engineering," and in fact the greater part of the work in the new department was in that branch of engineering, although mechanics, shop work, and mining engineering received slight attention.

Upon the resignation of Newbrough in November, 1889, Merry L. Pence was chosen to fill the chair of civil engineering, a post he held until he became associate professor of civil engineering two years later as a result of reorganization which established the Department of Mechanical Engineering under a newcomer, F. Paul Anderson, and added to the faculty James Poyntz Nelson as professor of civil engineering and physics. Nelson also served as Dean of the combined departments. Electrical as well as civil engineering was placed under the supervision of the Dean, who endeavored to give his students actual experience in their work, and who conducted a course of training of some real value. Within a short time, however, his department was overshadowed by the Department of Mechanical Engineering, whose head, Anderson, considered Nelson "not very well acquainted with engineering processes in modern schools of education for engineers" and told the Board of Trustees that he was not "willing to stay at this institution . . . and be handicapped by a man not competent to give orders."[10] By 1895 the trustees, while making new appropriations for Anderson's department, were expressing dissatisfaction at the "meager returns from the Department of Civil Engineering." Some members of the board wished to warn Nelson that he had to make a better record or resign, but Patterson won approval for a milder resolution which advised the Dean that his work was not satisfactory and that "his serious attention is invited . . . to the organization, management and instruction in his department."

Nelson's efforts to revitalize his course led merely to a rapid expenditure of operating funds and to further expressions of disapproval from the trustees. By 1897, when the enrollment in this department had dropped to seven students, the Board of Trustees reached the limit of its patience. After hearing its Committee on Internal Expansion report that, though Nelson was well qualified in his field and though the work of his students was excellent, the department had not made a satisfactory showing, and that "with, therefore, the kindest disposition toward Professor Nelson we feel constrained to recommend that his resignation be requested," the board called for the resignation of the Dean.[11] Pending the selection of Nelson's successor, the department was placed under the supervision of James G. White, professor of mathematics and astronomy. A few months later John P. Brooks, formerly of the faculty of Lehigh University, became professor of civil engineering.

10 "Testimony Heard by the Special Investigating Committee of the Board of Trustees of University of Kentucky" (3 vols., typewritten manuscript, 1916), I, 70.

11 Agricultural and Mechanical College, Minutes of the Board of Trustees, June 4, July 31, 1895, June 2, 3, 1897.

During the next decade the department gradually recovered from its ebb tide and grew much stronger in spite of the fact that it was practically "out of doors" as far as buildings were concerned. In 1899 a committee of the Board of Trustees "found everything in good shape in the department of Civil Engineering (Professor Brooks) and that the work in that department was well and efficiently done."[12] When Brooks resigned in 1906 to accept a position as head of the Department of Civil Engineering at the University of Illinois, his place in the State College was filled by Walter E. Rowe, a graduate of the University of Nebraska. By that time the department had progressed to such an extent that it had "a matriculation of over a hundred and much the largest percentage of the graduates in the class of 1907." Still it stood in such need of buildings and equipment that in this same year President Patterson in his report to the Board of Trustees referred to the "absolute destitution" of the courses in civil and mining engineering.

No other division of the Agricultural and Mechanical College achieved such instantaneous success as did the Department of Mechanical Engineering, which was established in 1891. If circumstances had permitted, this department would have emerged at an earlier date, since the work in practical mechanics constituted a foundation upon which to build. The basement of the Administration Building afforded insufficient room for expansion, however, not to mention the impossibility of securing additional equipment, and not until 1890 was the college able to make provision for the erection of a suitable structure. Completed in 1892, Mechanical Hall provided space for classrooms, drawing room, library, engine room, tool room, boiler house, wood shop, blacksmith shop, and foundry, and for the first time made possible the establishment of a course directed toward "one great end—the building up of educated mechanical engineers." At the

[12] *Ibid.*, May 31, 1899.

same time practical instruction in the shops remained open to students from other departments and to special students who might desire a year's vocational training in preparation for work as carpenters, blacksmiths, or mechanics.

At the time of its organization the Department of Mechanical Engineering was placed under the direction of F. Paul Anderson, a young engineer who had received his training at Purdue University. Anderson, who remained with the institution until 1934, became the first Dean of the consolidated College of Engineering in 1918. He was one of the most energetic individuals ever to serve on the faculty, and in addition to his regular duties he found time to design new buildings for the institution, to serve as consulting engineer for several railroads, and to engage in private business until asked by the trustees to quit his outside activities.

Under his astute and aggressive management the department quickly became one of the best known in the college. Frequent open houses to which the public was invited served to make known the work being done by the faculty and students, as did exhibitions presented in other parts of the state. A newspaper article published in 1895 described the successes achieved in the year since graduation by the four members of the department's first class, whose activities were characterized as "certainly a credit to the College."[13] Year after year the newspapers carried similar stories which illustrated the ease with which graduates of the Mechanical Engineering Department obtained jobs in private industry. Dean Anderson also demonstrated his concern with the necessity of giving practical training and of keeping abreast of the times, taking his advanced classes each year to visit manufacturing centers such as Cincinnati, Chicago, and Birmingham, where they might study in actual operation the machinery with which they had become acquainted in classroom and shop.

[13] Lexington *Press-Transcript,* August 1, 1895.

The Dean was always alert for opportunities to make the department more successful and to increase its prestige. After the resignation of James P. Nelson, Anderson with the approval of the Board of Trustees incorporated the course in electrical engineering into his own domain; and he inaugurated a summer school in engineering in 1903. Always he endeavored to choose as his assistants ambitious and promising young men. Never closefisted in regard to money, he showed no hesitancy in expending his appropriations and in asking for additional funds. Though his requests were not always granted, they brought results often enough to arouse frequently the jealousy of his colleagues. His success in obtaining new equipment and in expanding the buildings used by his department resulted from the favorable impression his activities made upon the Board of Trustees, who in 1897 declared that "We approve strongly of the development that has been given to the Department of Mechanical Engineering. It is doing more to bring the college into prominence and attract patronage, than could be accomplished in a very long period of mere formulary training in Science and Literature, where the competition is formidable in numbers and character." A few years later the Committee on Internal Expansion of the Board of Trustees, urging an enlargement of facilities for Anderson's department, used language which must have caused Patterson to wince: "We had better drop the classical Latin and Greek than the practical."[14]

According to the catalogs of the college the course in mechanical engineering established with the creation of the department was followed with few changes through 1907. Most of the work throughout the four years required for a degree was in technical and scientific subjects relating directly to the business of learning engineering. English was required of all students in the freshman year, as was Ger-

[14] Agricultural and Mechanical College, Minutes of the Board of Trustees, June 2, 1897, December 11, 1901.

man until it was dropped from the schedule after a few years. At first seniors enrolled in classes in mental philosophy and political economy, though the former was replaced by history before the end of the period under consideration. Every applicant for a degree had to present a thesis "on some new design of a machine, or an original investigation." There is no doubt that the department offered excellent training in its field, and the reputation which it established over the years enabled it to state with some complacency that "The growth in attendance has been healthy, and for some years it has had the largest attendance of all the four-year courses."[15]

The third member of the trio of engineering departments did not come into existence until 1901, although it had been a matter of interest to the college for several years before that date. Before leaving the school, James P. Nelson had vainly suggested that a study of mining be added to his own departments, while various experiments had been conducted by Dr. Robert Peter, by his son Alfred, and by the Department of Mechanical Engineering; but the impetus for the organization of a Department of Mining Engineering came not from the college but from the legislature. By an act which in 1898 became law without the signature of the Governor, the office of the State Inspector of Mines, "together with the property and effects of the Geological Survey," was removed from Frankfort to quarters provided on the campus of the State College; and at the same time the college was authorized to create a School of Mining Engineering. Unable to make provision for a new line of expansion immediately, the Board of Trustees delayed action until 1901, when it established the Department of Mining Engineering and chose C. J. Norwood as "Inspector of Mines and Dean of the Faculty of Mining Engineering."

The new department leaned heavily on courses in chem-

[15] Agricultural and Mechanical College, *Catalogue,* 1906-1907, pp. 44, 46-49.

istry, physics, and the two older engineering departments, consequently enabling students to attend many classes already in operation. Nevertheless, from the beginning the problem of housing was difficult. Mining proper was at first taught in the basement of the Natural Science Building, soon expanded to two temporary wooden structures, and still needed more room. Year after year President Patterson deplored the lack of buildings and equipment, complaining on one occasion that "the parsimony with which this department is expected to do work is a disgrace to the State." He pointed out that the incalculable store of mineral resources in the state was just beginning to be opened for exploitation, and he stressed the necessity for offering at the State College training which would enable Kentuckians to take advantage of the opportunities offered by these resources. Kentucky capital and Kentucky intellect, said he, should develop Kentucky mines, and "We ought to rise above the idea of being hewers of wood and drawers of water for the millionaires of the eastern and middle states."[16]

Norwood submitted a request for a new building in 1907. His blunt statement of conditions and of the possibilities in the field of mining seems to have aroused the trustees to the need for immediate action:

> At present he had no suitable quarters in which to conduct his work; that he was without quarters for a laboratory; that the need for such a department was great and urgent at the present time, owing to the extensive and growing mining interests in various parts of the State; that he already had various applications for admission into a shorter course in Mining Engineering which, with present equipment and assistance he was unable to give; that he believed if the Board would put this department upon its feet by giving the small building asked for, that he would be able through the various mining interests of the State, to obtain from the Legislature after the next

16 Agricultural and Mechanical College, Minutes of the Board of Trustees, June 1, December 12, 1905.

> one an appropriation to build a proposed building; and that unless something was done at this time there was danger of losing entirely the school of Mining Engineering.[17]

After examining the plans and drawing which Norwood had prepared in advance, the Board of Trustees appropriated $7,500 for use in erecting a structure which was intended as the wing of a larger building and which was to provide laboratory space for the departments of both mining and civil engineering. The building, completed late in 1907 and named the "Mining Laboratory," still did not afford all the space needed for classrooms, offices, and laboratories. It did, however, help insure the permanency of the department which became increasingly important to the state.

When the Agricultural and Mechanical College moved from Woodlands to its present location, most of its work was offered in courses which now are included in the curriculum of the College of Arts and Sciences. The departments of study were grouped in two main divisions, the scientific course and the classical course, and most of the departments appeared in both. Agricultural and engineering subjects were included only in the scientific course, while the classical course placed more emphasis on languages. The teaching staff which had been assembled two years earlier remained intact until the reorganization in 1889, with two exceptions: the head of the Military Department was changed frequently and the retirement of Dr. Peter in 1887 vacated a post which was not filled for about two years.

The scientific and the classical courses were among the major college divisions, each under its own Dean, established in 1889. The faculties of these two courses were almost identical, and their requirements were very similar. Among the professors, some of them new to the college, who

[17] *Ibid.*, June 4, 1907.

were listed in both divisions were James K. Patterson, President and professor of history and metaphysics; James G. White, Dean of the scientific course and professor of mathematics and astronomy; John Shackelford, Vice-President of the college and professor of English language and literature; J. H. Kastle, professor of chemistry; F. M. Helveti, professor of French and German languages and literature; Thomas Hunt Morgan, professor of natural history; and D. H. Clark, professor of military science. William Newbrough, professor of physics, was not listed as a member of the faculty of the classical course; John H. Neville, Dean of the classical course and professor of Latin and Greek languages and literature, and William C. Prewitt, instructor in Latin and Greek, were not included among the faculty of the scientific course. Until their junior and senior years students in both divisions attended the same classes with very few exceptions.

Somewhat the same general ideas regarding courses in the classical and scientific fields persisted until the college became a university, although many changes in details occurred. The school catalog of 1891-1892 introduced a new division, the biological course, whose faculty was identical to that of the scientific course, even to the deanship which was filled by J. G. White in both cases. The main difference in the schedules of the two courses was that the biological course offered more work in zoology and related fields. Two years later the classical and scientific courses were no longer listed. Instead, courses in biology, in chemistry, in ancient languages, and in science comprised what would now be termed the offerings in the arts and sciences. A more logical arrangement was instituted in 1895 with the grouping of the various courses according to degrees and major subjects: mathematics, chemistry, and biology for the B. S. degree; Greek and Latin for the A. B. degree.

In 1899 the school set up separate schedules, which however differed little from one another, for science students who wished to major in chemistry, zoology, geology, botany, or physics. In the schedules of work leading to the A. B. degree English was placed on a parity with Greek and Latin as a major subject in 1900. In 1902 a new major, anatomy and physiology, was added to those in the scientific field. On the eve of the changes in organization in 1908, the college adopted a program more in line with modern practice. Instead of the different schedules outlined for the B. S. degree, only one scientific course was offered. All freshmen were required to take the same courses, sophomores could take a few electives, and upperclassmen had a wider range of choice. After his freshman year the student was supposed to choose his major subject and to work out with the head of the department in which he had selected the major his schedule of courses for the remainder of his collegiate career. The classical course remained unchanged at that time.

Changes in the personnel of the faculty were infrequent during the two decades before 1908. President Patterson, of course, continued to dominate the scene in spite of advancing years. Deans White and Neville seemed to be as durable as Patterson. Neville, it is true, had at one time considered relinquishing his post, but he decided to remain after receiving a rare tribute from the trustees who resolved that out of regard for "his ability and his great value to the Institution," they desired "him to continue to hold his place, inasmuch as we consider that the college would suffer by his retirement."[18] When in 1899 John Shackelford gave up his connection with the college, Neville succeeded to the post of Vice-President, and Alexander St. Clair McKenzie, a graduate of the University of Glasgow and later an instructor at the University of Pennsylvania, became head of the Department of English.

Two members of the faculty in 1889 remained only one year, after which Merry Lewis Pence succeeded Newbrough

[18] *Ibid.,* June 3, 1884.

Classroom, about 1900

as professor of physics, and Morgan's position as head of the Department of Natural History was not filled. New courses in science were established, and the teachers of these courses in most cases became well-known figures in the institution. Mathews, professor of botany, and Harrison Garman, professor of zoology and entomology, were more closely connected with agriculture and the Experiment Station than with the classical and scientific courses. Joseph W. Pryor, professor of anatomy and physiology, and Arthur M. Miller, professor of geology and paleontology, enjoyed long careers with the school. The death of Professor Helveti on April 25, 1894, and of Professor Emeritus Robert Peter on the next day removed from the college scene two figures who were institutions in themselves. Paul Wernicke replaced Helveti, serving as professor of French and German until 1906, when he was succeeded by Alfred C. Zembrod. After approximately seventeen years as head of the Chemistry Department Joseph H. Kastle in 1905 resigned to become Chief of the Division of the Chemical and Hygienic Laboratory of the Public Health and Marine Service. His place at the Agricultural and Mechanical College was filled by Chase Palmer for one year, after which Franklin E. Tuttle began a long career as head of the Department of Chemistry. Early in the twentieth century three young men who later played important roles in the life of the university began their connection with the institution: Theodore Tolman Jones, assistant in Latin, Greek, and German; William Snyder Webb, assistant in physics and at one time acting Commandant; and Ralph Nelson Maxson, assistant in chemistry.

It is impossible to determine for most of the period under consideration the enrollment in the classical and scientific courses. All students doing work on the college level were members of these courses until the establishment of the professional departments. According to the college catalog the 99 classical and the 55 scientific students in 1901 made up less than half of the enrollees in the college proper. The number in these courses declined both actually and relatively until in 1907 the 48 scientific and the 88 classical students made together slightly less than one third the total student body. Most of the classes making up these two general courses were taught in the Main Building. In 1898 a new Natural Sciences Building gave needed relief to overcrowded conditions, and in 1902 the Board of Trustees agreed to devote the old Experiment Station Building to the Department of Chemistry when the station moved to its new quarters on South Limestone Street.

In addition to the long-established courses and departments, innovations in the academic life of the college appeared early in the present century. The completion of the gymnasium in 1902 permitted the creation of the School of Physical Culture, which was divided into two departments. Under the supervision of Mrs. Florence Offutt Stout, the first physical director for women, the Department of Scientific Physical Education for Women strove to attain for the young ladies of State College the following laudable aims: "1. To stimulate the functioning of all bodily organs. 2. To train the muscles so that curves may displace angles and grace banish awkwardness. 3. To arouse the mind to superior alertness. 4. To develop character." The department for young men, headed by W. Walter H. Mustaine and including H. H. Downing and J. S. Crosthwaite as assistants, had the much more commonplace objectives of health, strength and grace, correction of physical deformities and functional disorders, and "the fortification of the body against bad hereditary tendencies."[19]

The trustees in 1903 took an unprecedented step in the creation of a lectureship in English literature and the appointment of Miss Elizabeth Shelby Kinkead to fill the position. Strangely, the salary, $800 a year, was fixed before

[19] Agricultural and Mechanical College, *Catalogue,* 1906, pp. 87-88.

the duties of the lecturer were determined. The trustees apparently thought she might be of assistance in some manner to the English Department, but she did not become a member of the faculty, and her work consisted solely in delivering weekly lectures on English literature. At first sophomores and juniors were required to attend the lectures; later that privilege was given to the freshman and senior classes. It is somewhat doubtful that the objective, to give to the student "that polish and enlightenment of spirit which is derived from contact with what is fine and delicate," was attained even though the hearers had the opportunity to become acquainted with literature "through the medium of formulated criticism, and by means of recitation by the lecturer of the more beautiful passages of the composition discussed."[20] Whatever the value of these weekly sessions, they were continued even after the reorganization of the institution in 1908.

While the college administration and trustees after 1900 were busily trying to improve conditions in certain departments, they were subjected to pressure from various groups of women who demanded that the college establish a Department of Domestic Science, "with a dean at the head of said Department, on equal footing with the deans of other departments."[21] The trustees appointed a committee to examine ways and means of putting the proposal into effect. Another delegation of ladies convinced the board in 1905 that further delay was inadvisable, and in that year a Department of Domestic Science was established "as a branch of the College." A committee composed of two trustees was empowered to consult with the matron of the women's dormitory and a committee from the women's clubs of Lexington in regard to putting the new department in operation.

Other agricultural colleges were also concerned about this

[20] *Ibid.*, 1907, p. 90.

[21] Agricultural and Mechanical College, Minutes of the Board of Trustees, June 2, 1903, June 10, 1904.

matter, and at a meeting of the Association of Land-Grant Colleges in 1905 Patterson and Clarence W. Mathews heard much discussion on the subject. They came away from the session with the conclusion that "Domestic Science, whatever it may mean and whatever it may comprehend, is as yet ill-defined, and in what might be termed a formative state. No two persons agree upon what it should include or exclude." Patterson therefore recommended that a small beginning be made and that expansion be carried on in the light of experience. He also recommended that the department be connected with the Department of Agriculture, a suggestion which was not followed. The Board of Trustees authorized its committee on domestic science to select quarters, to spend not more than a thousand dollars for equipment, and to hire a teacher at a salary of not more than six hundred dollars a year. The committee established the new department in the basement of the girls' dormitory and hired Miss Isabella Marshall to teach domestic science at a salary of five hundred dollars per annum.[22] Instruction was devoted exclusively to the subject of foods. A course in practical cookery was conducted during the first two terms of the year, and during the third, lectures were given on food production, the students prepared balanced meals, and checks were made of the dietetic value of the foods thus prepared.

Even before the college acquired a farm and before agriculture occupied a position in the curriculum equal to the traditional courses, President Patterson and Chairman W. B. Kinkead of the Executive Committee proudly announced in a letter addressed "To the Farmers of Kentucky" that the school had established an "Experimental Agricultural Station, in close relationship with the Bureau of Agriculture at Washington."[23] The decision to create an Experiment

22 *Ibid.*, May 31, December 12, 1905.
23 Agricultural and Mechanical College, *Annual Register*, 1885-1886, p. 53.

Station in connection with the college was reached by the Executive Committee at a meeting in September, 1885. M. A. Scovell, a graduate of the University of Illinois and former Superintendent of the United States Experiment Station at Ottawa, Kansas, became the first Director.

College officials often called attention to the fact that the Kentucky Experiment Station was established two years before the passage of the Hatch Act, which began the flow of federal funds to and authorized the establishment of such an agricultural agency in every state. The idea was not new in 1885, however, and several stations had come into existence before that date. Their popularity led to a widespread clamor for federal aid in carrying out their work. As early as 1883 bills were introduced in Congress to provide funds for stations, but it was not until 1887 that the Hatch Act became law.

When the Kentucky station was first established the Executive Committee drew up no specific plans for its future because of the extremely limited financial resources of the college. Housed in one room in the basement of the Main Building, the station proposed "to analyze and test fertilizers, milks, waters, foods for stock, soils, etc., for the farmers of Kentucky *free of charge,*" to correspond with farmers about their problems, and to issue bulletins "in *language which the farmers can understand,*" detailing the results of experimentation. A few acres on the campus were set aside for an experimental plot, but this arrangement was not satisfactory because the surface had been removed from a portion of the ground for use in brickmaking when the college buildings were erected.[24] Scovell was in the beginning the only full-time member of the Experiment Station staff, and he was supposed to receive help from the professors of chemistry, agriculture, and botany if such assistance as they might give would not interfere with their regular college duties. Man-

24 *Ibid.*

agement of the station was placed in the hands of a Board of Control, composed of President Patterson, Director Scovell, and the Executive Committee of the Board of Trustees.

Beginning its life under adverse conditions, the Experiment Station enjoyed a rapid improvement in its prospects, until shortly it was the most prosperous part of the college. The first step in this improvement came in the form of "An Act to regulate the sale of Fertilizers in this Commonwealth, and to protect the Agriculturist in the purchase and use of same," which was passed by the legislature and signed by Governor J. Proctor Knott on April 13, 1886. Under the provisions of this act any person or company who offered for sale in Kentucky a commercial fertilizer whose retail price was more than ten dollars a ton was required to send a sample of the product to the Experiment Station. After analyzing the fertilizer, the station printed the results on a label, a copy of which had to be attached to every package of the material sold in the state. Fifteen dollars was charged for the analysis, and the labels were furnished to the retailer at one dollar a hundred. The fees received from this work, in 1894 estimated at from $3,000 to $4,000 a year, were turned over to the college, whose authorities were enjoined to expend the money in meeting the expenses of the station. Aid for Scovell in carrying out his new duties came when Alfred M. Peter was appointed assistant chemist in the Experiment Station in June, 1886.

Washington's Birthday, 1887, found President Patterson in the national capital lobbying for the passage of a bill which, with the signature of President Grover Cleveland in March of that year, became the Hatch Act. This law provided for the establishment of an Experiment Station in each state which would accept the conditions laid down by the act. Aided by an annual appropriation of $15,000, each station was to conduct experiments and research in the field of agriculture under the general supervision of the United States

Department of Agriculture and to disseminate the findings of this experimentation through bulletins which could be mailed free of postal charges.

With an assured annual income of $15,000 beginning the next year, in addition to fees collected under the fertilizer law, the Board of Control moved swiftly and confidently to improve the condition of the Kentucky Experiment Station. Scovell, who threatened to resign in May, 1887, received an increase in salary which made him one of the highest-paid employees of the college. Immediate steps were taken for the purchase of a farm, and plans were worked out for an Experiment Station Building (now the Health and Hygiene Building) which was completed in August, 1890. New members were added to the staff: H. E. Curtis became assistant chemist in 1887, the next year C. L. Curtis was appointed assistant agriculturist, and in 1889 Harrison Garman was employed as entomologist and botanist. By 1891 three circulars and thirty-three bulletins had been published by the station, and Scovell claimed that the demand for these publications was so great that more than ten thousand copies of each of the later bulletins had been distributed.

Under the capable direction of Scovell the station steadily expanded its activities. At the same time it was able to increase its staff, add approximately 186 acres to its farm by 1908, and erect on the farm an insectory, a dairy building, and barns to replace losses caused by fire. Additional income was provided by the Kentucky Pure Food Law of 1898 and by the Adams Act which was passed by Congress in 1906. The former made the sale of adulterated or misbranded food unlawful within the bounds of the state and authorized the Experiment Station to make analyses of foods and to report violations of the law to grand juries and prosecuting attorneys. For this service the station was paid "only actual travelling expenses and five dollars for each sample taken and analyzed," the expense not to exceed $2,500 in any one year. The Adams Act provided additional federal funds to be used only in original research; the first appropriation of $5,000 for each station was to be increased by $2,000 each year until the income from this source reached $15,000 per annum.

The Experiment Station Building, which provided quarters for the college Departments of Agriculture, Chemistry, and Natural History in addition to offices and laboratories for the station proper, soon became overcrowded. The questions then arose about the equity in the building held by the college and the station and about which of the two institutions should be left in full possession of the structure. President Patterson in 1899 offered resolutions, adopted by the Board of Trustees, that instructed the secretary to determine "the pecuniary interest which the A. and M. College, has in the Experiment Station Building," and that committed the board to consider selling to the station whatever interest the college might be found to have, using the proceeds to construct new quarters for the Departments of Physics and Chemistry. Eventually it was decided that the equity of the college in the building was three times as great as that of the station and that the station should erect a new building. The "Graham property" on Limestone Street south of the campus was chosen as the site of the structure, Professors Anderson and Faig were selected to draw up plans, and in 1903 work on the building began. In 1905 the station was able to move into its new home, which it still occupies.

Many of the staff members of the station during the period from 1885 to 1908 achieved distinction in their fields. Scovell held various offices in national organizations of agricultural colleges and experiment stations, he was in demand as a judge at state fairs over the country, and he was consulted occasionally by the federal government on agricultural matters. At least two men, David W. May and Joseph N. Harper, left Kentucky to become heads of experiment stations elsewhere—one in Puerto Rico and the other in South Carolina. Among others who gave long and distinguished service to the Kentucky Experiment Station were Alfred Peter, Garman, and H. E. Curtis, who were among its first employees, William H. Scherffius, Job D. Turner, Robert M. Allen, James O. La Bach, Miss Mary LeGrand Didlake, George Roberts, Saxe D. Averitt, Oliver M. Shedd, Erle C. Vaughn, Edwin S. Good, and Miss Oleva Louise Ginocchio. By 1907, according to the college catalog, the station employed nineteen staff members, not including two United States Weather Bureau observers who were attached to the station.

By 1908 the Experiment Station had become highly important to the social and economic life of Kentucky, benefiting not only the farmers but, through its work in connection with the Pure Food Law, all other citizens of the state as well. The constant experimentation carried on by experts in various fields brought many discoveries which, publicized through the medium of numerous bulletins, proved extremely valuable "to those of the people of Kentucky who seek profit from any one of those prime sources of wealth—the soil, the flock, and the herd." Enjoying a large income compared with that of the college, housed in a building constructed specifically for its use, possessing a large farm, and employing scientists of proven ability, the station was without doubt "extremely useful to the Commonwealth at large."[25] On occasion the station could render an unusual service as in 1900, when it furnished oxygen for the use of physicians in their futile effort to save the life of Governor William Goebel, who had been shot by an assassin a few days earlier.

The claim that the Experiment Station was "an important adjunct to the College" was not beyond question. As President Patterson pointed out to the Board of Trustees in 1908,

[25] Agricultural and Mechanical College, *Catalogue,* 1907, p. 3.

"the Experiment Station has become a self contained entity, having little or no connection with the Agricultural College," and he went so far as to say that the college received no more educational advantage from the existence of the station than if it was located in another part of the state.[26]

[26] Agricultural and Mechanical College, Minutes of the Board of Trustees, June 2, 1908.

Chapter Eleven

State University, Lexington, Kentucky

As THE AGRICULTURAL AND MECHANICAL COLLEGE, after having passed its first and leanest years as an independent institution, grew in physical size and in academic stature, its friends were led to think of greater things which might come to pass in its development. Spokesmen who continually emphasized the fact that the school was a state institution were aware that the commonwealth had no university, and they reasoned logically that the college should some day fill that void. At least as early as 1891 a self-anointed prophet foresaw that development. In February of that year a newspaperman, writing in a highly optimistic vein of conditions at the school, spoke for some of his fellow citizens (though doubtless not for all whom he claimed to represent) when he said: "The people of Kentucky are anxious to see this institution grow into a university which will not lose by comparison with the great universities of Michigan and Virginia. Before many years have elapsed, with proper support, the State College will have become a university worthy of the name."[1]

By late 1897 Patterson himself believed that "the time has come when we should drop the name of a College and assume that of a University." The Board of Trustees agreed and went on record as favoring the name, "The State University of Kentucky," but a note of caution prevailed. Patterson had suggested the possibility of assimilating certain schools of law and medicine which were already in existence, but the trustees considered the proposal "fraught with grave objections." Action was consequently delayed pending further

[1] Lexington *Daily Transcript,* February 8, 1891.

study. The President's suggestion must have reached ears outside the board meeting, for shortly afterward a Lexington newspaper, claiming that the school was already a university except in name, asked its readers the question: "Why should Kentucky not have a great State University?" In the state legislature Senator C. J. Bronston introduced a bill to change the name of the school to the State University of Kentucky. One striking feature of the bill, which was not passed, is that much of its language is identical with that of the longer measure which was enacted into law ten years later.[2]

After the rejection by the trustees of his proposal in 1897, Patterson did not again officially suggest a change in the name and organization of the school for almost ten years. On occasion, it is true, he asked the board to consider the advisability of forming some connection between the college and a medical school already in operation in Louisville, and in each instance he was gently rebuffed. In 1903 he urged the establishment of a law school, pointing out that it "could be constituted and conducted at comparatively little expense" to the State College. His arguments were so convincing that the board appointed a committee to "consider the feasibility and advisability" of creating not only a law school but a medical school as well.[3] Again, nothing came of the proposal.

After failing to obtain action from his Board of Trustees, Patterson adopted new tactics. Early in 1906 he appeared before the Lexington City Council with an appeal for funds with which to establish a medical college. Reminding his hearers that seventy years earlier, when the population of the town was only four or five thousand and hospital facilities were scarce, "there was maintained in this city a Medical College which was known far and wide, to which students

2 Agricultural and Mechanical College, Minutes of the Board of Trustees, December 15, 1897; Lexington *Press-Transcript,* January 22, February 12, 1898.

3 Agricultural and Mechanical College, Minutes of the Board of Trustees, June 2, 1903.

came from North and South, from East and West," he expressed confidence that a first-class medical school could be maintained by the city which had grown to 35,000 people, which had two hospitals, and which had "increased its wealth tenfold." He further reminded the council of the rich financial returns which the town had reaped from its contributions to the college in 1880, contending that "the students attending the A. and M. College have brought, both directly and indirectly, over $4,000,000 into this city." The day of such outright gifts by the town to the college were past, however, and the city fathers adopted a motion expressing regret "that the finances of the city will not permit favorable action on the request for $12,500 to aid and establish a medical college."[4]

By this time the President, encouraged by manifestations of interest in the Kentucky General Assembly, was glad to return to his original request: that the college be transformed into a university. He had not pressed the matter since 1897, possibly because unfavorable publicity had been given the college by a part of the local press and because the financial condition of the institution became embarrassing in spite of increased income. The initiative in 1906 seems to have come from members of the legislature, though Patterson may have been working behind the scenes. According to his report, when he was in Frankfort working for the passage of "legislation introduced by the College," he was asked repeatedly why the college did not become in name and in reality a university. A more tangible evidence of interest was a resolution adopted by the legislature setting up a special committee to work out and report to the next General Assembly "the best plan to make a university of the State College and harmonize it with the State Normal Schools."[5]

Patterson now believed that the legislature was willing to approve the change, and he urged the trustees to take up the

[4] Lexington *Herald,* January 5, 17, 1906.
[5] Lexington *Leader,* March 6, 1906.

initiative in bringing it about. The reasons presented in his argument to the board were:

> 1st. All the States in the Union, with one or two exceptions, have Universities, most of them liberally provided for by their respective States.
>
> 2nd. The State College of Kentucky is the only institution in the State doing anything like University work.
>
> 3rd. It is owned and administered exclusively by the State.
>
> 4th. The title and functions of a University would carry with them a dignity and prestige which do not attach to a college.
>
> 5th. The State would feel more pride in an institution bearing the name of University than it does in a college.
>
> 6th. With more pride felt and a greater interest attaching to a University, it would be less difficult to obtain the necessary appropriation for buildings and Revenue.
>
> 7th. The development and growth of the College during the period of forty years now completed.[6]

The trustees were not to be rushed, particularly in view of the fact that the legislature would not meet again for two years. They appointed Patterson a committee of one to investigate all aspects of the problem and in December of the same year they adopted, with one dissenting vote, his recommendation that the name be changed, provided a legislative act to that end could be obtained.

In a statement to the board, Patterson claimed that the conciliatory spirit manifested by the Agricultural and Mechanical College had quieted the feeling of animosity which once had been held by most of the denominational colleges in the state. His statement was true at least in the case of Kentucky University, which during the next few months demonstrated a magnanimous and friendly spirit toward the State College. It was patently necessary that these two institutions, located in the same city, come to an agreement. If

[6] Agricultural and Mechanical College, Minutes of the Board of Trustees, June 5, 1906.

the Agricultural and Mechanical College became the "University of Kentucky" or the "State University," the similarity between its name and that of Kentucky University would cause endless confusion. Fortunately, the denominational school showed itself willing to give up its own name as a means of avoiding that confusion. As a matter of fact a movement among alumni of Kentucky University to have their alma mater resume its original and hallowed name, "Transylvania University," was noted as early as 1897. Nothing came of that early proposal, and apparently the authorities of the institution did not seriously contemplate such a change until faced with a request to that end submitted by the trustees of the Agricultural and Mechanical College.

By 1907 a more widespread agitation for a change in the name of the State College became noticeable. The Alumni Association, headed by W. H. Scherffius of the Experiment Station staff, appointed a committee of graduates, one in each congressional district, to influence public opinion, and the student body undertook to propagandize in each county. At the same time efforts were made "to present the importance of the matter to the members of the Legislature all over the State."[7] To the State Superintendent of Public Instruction President Patterson complained that only Kentucky and Delaware enjoyed "the unenviable distinction of having no State University and no equivalent of one." He was able to report, however, that "While our State is discredited by her educational inferiority in this and other respects, and especially by her disgraceful illiteracy, it is yet encouraging to know that there is an earnest and apparently a growing demand for an institution of higher title, grander proportions and wider usefulness than the State College."[8]

At its June meeting in 1907 the Board of Trustees, after hearing another plea by Patterson, appointed a committee

[7] Lexington *Leader,* May 19, 1907.
[8] Kentucky *Documents,* 1906-1907, I, 191.

to confer with representatives of Kentucky University on the problems raised by the proposal to change the name of the college. In the next month representatives of the governing boards of the two schools assembled in a meeting whose prevailing spirit, in the words of one reporter, was "rife with good feeling."[9] After frank and friendly discussion the meeting adjourned, and the committee representing Kentucky University prepared a report for submission to the Board of Curators. Among the aspects of the problem considered were the following: that the state institution was "entitled to bear the name of the State," and that Kentucky University, which had borne its name honorably for half a century, would have to give up that name "or be placed in the attitude of opposing the aspirations of the State institution." Such opposition would work to the injury of both schools and to the cause of education in Kentucky. Consequently, the committee recommended acquiescence in the change desired by the State College and it further recommended that Kentucky University adopt once more the name "Transylvania University." The only conditions proposed were that the state should grant necessary legislation to keep the control and management of Transylvania in the hands of the existing Board of Curators of Kentucky University, that the state school would not use its new name until June 1, 1909, and that the college would turn over to Kentucky University $5,000 with which to pay all expenses suffered by the latter institution on account of the change.[10] The Board of Curators adopted unanimously the recommendations of its committee and thereby virtually insured the success of the movement to change the names of the two schools involved.

Further encouragement for the college came from the normal schools. The Executive Committee of the Kentucky

[9] Lexington *Leader,* July 11, 1907.

[10] Agricultural and Mechanical College, Minutes of the Board of Trustees, December 10, 1907.

Educational Improvement Commission, meeting in Frankfort in June, 1907, adopted a resolution proposed by President H. H. Cherry of Western Normal inviting the governing boards of State College and the two normal schools to send representatives to a conference to discuss "needed legislation looking to the unifying and uplifting of our entire educational system." Assembling in three sessions held consecutively at Louisville, Bowling Green, and Lexington, representatives of the three institutions reached agreement on several points, including "the establishment of a State University of standard grade by such legislative act or acts as may be necessary in order to transform the State College into such an institution," the elimination of both subfreshman work and the Normal Department at the State College, and the establishment at that institution of a Department of Education of collegiate grade.[11]

In an atmosphere of good will all around the campaign for a new name for the Agricultural and Mechanical College came to a successful conclusion in 1908. The legislature which met early in that year adopted the desired measure, and the Governor approved it on March 16. According to the preamble, the act was passed because "The Agricultural and Mechanical College of Kentucky has out grown [*sic*] its original proportions and has for some years past maintained fourteen distinct courses of study, each extending over four years in the college proper and each leading to a degree, and . . . this diversity of education, theoretical and practical, requires that the name, title and designation of this institution, owned, managed and ministered by the State of Kentucky, should be commensurate with its character and work."[12]

The main feature of the law is found in section one, in

11 Hamlett, *History of Education in Kentucky,* 284-85; Lexington *Leader,* December 22, 28, 1907.

12 Kentucky *Acts,* 1908, p. 4.

which the General Assembly decreed "That the institution founded under the land grant of 1862, by the Congress of the United States, and known hitherto under the corporate designation and title of 'Agricultural and Mechanical College of Kentucky,' be hereafter known and designated as the 'State University, Lexington, Kentucky.' " The act further provided that the state should maintain the institution, that all federal and state laws relating to the Agricultural and Mechanical College should continue to apply to the university, that a revised system of appointing beneficiaries be put into operation, that the Board of Trustees be bipartisan, that the State Superintendent of Public Instruction be ex officio a member of the board, that the location of the school not be changed, and that students be permitted to take in Fayette County the examination for county teachers' certificates.

Section four demanded that the requirements of the Morrill Act be carried out "and that in addition to the other colleges of the said University, one of the colleges shall be denominated the Agricultural College, and another the College of Mechanical Arts of the State University." The next two paragraphs of the act provided for two new divisions of the school. "A department of law, or course of instruction in the science of law leading to the degree of Bachelor of Laws," was to be established and maintained on a basis equal in dignity and rank to that found in corresponding institutions elsewhere. Identical language was used in requiring the establishment of "a Department of Medicine and Surgery, or a course of instruction in the science of medicine and surgery," with an additional provision that diplomas from the Medical Department should be accepted throughout Kentucky on a basis of equality with diplomas issued from other medical schools. No other department or college was mentioned in the act, but it was not the intention of the lawmakers to restrict the university organization to the four divisions mentioned.

The necessary legislation regarding Kentucky University, to go into effect immediately upon its passage, was approved on March 20, 1908. Pointing out in the preamble that friends of the state school wished to change the name of that institution to "The State University, Lexington, Kentucky," and that such a change would result in confusion, the act changed the name of the denominational school to "Transylvania University." Control of the institution was to remain in the hands of the existing Board of Curators and its successors, which were also to own and control the property and funds of the school.

A third act, approved on March 16 of the same year, was of great value to the three state-controlled institutions of higher learning, the university and the two normal schools. In the first place the sum of $200,000 was appropriated for the use of the State University in paying debts owed for buildings and equipment, in erecting certain new buildings and in providing additions for others, and in purchasing additional lands if the Board of Trustees wished. Appropriations of $150,000 each, to be expended for the same general purposes, were made for the benefit of the Eastern Kentucky State Normal School and the Western Kentucky State Normal School. In order to meet the additional annual expenses of each of these three institutions, the legislature provided in this act for an annual appropriation of $20,000 for the university, the same amount for the Eastern, and $30,000 for the Western Kentucky State Normal School.

One portion of the act reflected the desires of the normal schools in regard to the curriculum of the university and carried out the agreement already reached by representatives of the three state-controlled schools late in the preceding year. The Normal Department of the university was abolished, and in its place the legislature provided for the creation of a "Department of Education . . . with collegiate rank leading to the usual degree in pedagogy as maintained in other similar state institutions." Power was given to the Board of Trustees, "subject to the approval of the State Superintendent of Public Instruction," to grant to students who completed one year's work in the department an elementary certificate which entitled the holder to teach two years in the public schools of Kentucky without further examination; upon the completion of two years' residence work the student was eligible to teach for four years; and upon finishing three years' work the student was authorized to teach for a period of three years, after which, if he presented evidence of good teaching and good morals, his certificate could be extended for life or for good behavior.

Those who successfully pursued a course in the department for the full four years and received either of the two degrees conferred, the Bachelor of Arts in Education or the Bachelor of Science in Education, were privileged to teach "in the common schools and high schools of the Commonwealth without further examination, during life or good behavior." As in the cases noted above, the privilege depended upon the prior approval of the State Superintendent of Public Instruction. Further provisions were added to enable the Board of Trustees or the State Superintendent to revoke a diploma or any certificate for cause. Because the appropriations were needed by the beneficiaries immediately, an emergency was declared to exist, permitting the act to go into effect as soon as the Governor approved it.

A new name could be adopted at one stroke, but the process of reorganization of old departments and the addition of new ones proceeded much more slowly. Tentative decisions were put into operation as soon as possible; some worked out satisfactorily, others had to be amended in time. Of the additions to the school provided by the act of 1908, the Law Department began operations in the next fall term, but a medical school has never been established.

Patterson and the Board of Trustees were eager to move as rapidly as possible in bringing about the desired changes. On April 14, 1908, approximately one month after the passage of the act converting the college into a university, a special meeting of the Board of Trustees was called to consider the appointment of a business agent and "all matters which may be necessary or proper in order to put in effect the recent acts of the General Assembly." The board approved the action of the Executive Committee, which had already selected Judge W. T. Lafferty, a member of the Board of Trustees, as the Dean of a projected law school. A five-man committee, including President Patterson and Judge Henry S. Barker, was set up to consider Judge Lafferty's plan for the organization of the new school and to select teachers and suggest the salaries which should be paid. Another committee of five was then established to investigate the possibility of establishing a medical school. A committee of the faculty, which had been considering changes in the curriculum necessitated by the new status of the institution, presented a plan for reorganizing the Classical and Scientific departments into a College of Arts and Science which should offer the following degrees: A. B., B. S., B. S. in Chemistry, and A. B. and B. S. in Education. A detailed schedule of courses accompanied this report, and the faculty pleaded for additions to the teaching staff as well as for enlarged laboratory facilities in order to put the schedule into effect by the beginning of the fall term.

President Patterson and Judge Lafferty had prepared recommendations concerning the title and duties of a new official whose manifold powers were to exceed those of the business agent and be second only to those of the President. The trustees agreed that the official should be known as the "comptroller," and they elected Judge Lafferty to fill that post as well as the deanship of the School of Law. The duties of the comptroller were extensive. He was charged with the supervision and care of buildings and grounds, the location of departments in the various buildings, the regulation of the dormitories, "the general oversight of the morals of the students," and the maintenance of discipline. He was authorized to audit and settle all accounts of the university, and to have general supervision over the collection and expenditure of all funds. He was supposed to keep check on all boardinghouses in Lexington which catered to students, to know where each student secured board and lodging, and to visit these places "at proper intervals" to "see to the welfare of the students." He was further to act as attorney for the school, and to visit classrooms and laboratories "in order to take note of the character and efficiency of the work done, the faithfulness and punctuality of instructors and students and by his presence stimulate and encourage the best results."[13]

By the time the regular June meeting of the Board of Trustees was held in 1908, Patterson was ready with some good advice regarding the reorganization of his school. In the first place, he pointed out that the income of the institution, now higher than it had ever been, would have been considered adequate for the operation of a good university thirty or forty years earlier. Times had changed, however, and this sum would no longer suffice for any of the older and better universities. Somewhat ruefully he faced reality: "Inasmuch, however, as the citizens of Kentucky had not yet been educated up to the degree of liberality which makes endowments five and ten-fold and twenty-fold that of ours possible, we must perforce for some years to come be content to operate as well as we can upon the somewhat meagre resources which have fallen to our lot."

Remarking that the available funds would "suffice for a beginning," he undertook to explain his ideas on universities in general and on the program which should be under-

[13] State University, Minutes of the Board of Trustees, April 14, 1908.

taken by the State University, Lexington, Kentucky. In his opinion the objective of a college was to impart to its students a body of knowledge which has "come down to the present generation," together with the discoveries within their own lifetime. The university should also impart such instruction, but it should go far beyond the work of the college. Its function is to "reach out by . . . original investigation and discovery into the unknown." After a clear and sage statement on the contribution of such investigation to the broadening scope of human understanding, Patterson concluded that "the first duty of the university of to-day, the State University of Kentucky, is to . . . make the most abundant provision which its resources will warrant for the endowment of research."

He insisted that regular college classes be provided for, as in the past, and that the next concern should be for research and original investigation. Ignoring the fact that he had on several occasions advocated the connection of professional schools with the Agricultural and Mechanical College, or perhaps having thought the matter through more thoroughly than before, he stated that he did "not regard a professional school as an essential and integral part of a university organism." He urged the board to provide for the higher functions of a university before attempting to found "so-called professional schools." In time Colleges of Law, Pharmacy, Medicine, and Dentistry might be added. His earnest advice was "consolidate what you have, make it as perfect and efficient as it is possible to be, and then consider the propriety of adding . . . annexes as opportunity may appear. . . . Upbuild and strengthen and consolidate all the essential features and characteristics of a University organism before we attempt to add any of the professional schools."

More specifically, he asked for a closer relationship between the Agricultural College and the Experiment Station. He suggested the organization of a School of Commerce which would go far beyond training in bookkeeping and would use the existing facilities of the university to turn out graduates well grounded in English, foreign languages, geography, mathematics, psychology, ethics and logic, physics, chemistry, botany, zoology, history, and banking. Thus trained, a young man could readily find employment "in any of the great mercantile establishments of the country" and possibly in the consular and diplomatic service. Deploring "the fact that American journalism is not up to the level which ought to be obtained in a country whose influence among the great world powers is second to none," he proposed the establishment at an early date of a School of Journalism on a broad basis, utilizing the existing facilities of the university.

The trustees applied themselves immediately to a consideration of Patterson's recommendations, which could not be followed completely. As Judge Barker pointed out, a plan for a Law School had already been approved, negotiations were under way for a Medical School, and the Schools of Commerce and Journalism would have to wait until some time in the future. A committee was set up to consider the question of closer co-operation between the Agricultural College and the Experiment Station, and after brief study, it recommended that the new Agricultural College in the university be composed of the Experiment Station and the Agricultural Department. It further suggested that the Director of the Experiment Station, since he was the senior in rank, become head of the college with the title of "Director of the Agricultural College." The committee proposed that it be authorized to continue trying to work out means for bringing closer co-operation between classroom instruction and the Experiment Station. The board agreed, and at the same time it added Patterson and Director Scovell of the Experiment Station to the group.

The committee which had been established earlier in the

year to organize the Law School recommended that the faculty of that division of the university be composed of Dean Lafferty, who had already been chosen to that post, Charles Kerr, a Lexington lawyer of high standing who had already had teaching experience in Kentucky University, and Thomas E. Moore, Jr., county attorney of Bourbon County, who was said to be "better versed in the law of real property than any person available for this position." Each of the two assistants was obligated to teach six hours a week during the school year. In addition to the regular staff, outstanding lawyers from over the state were to be invited to give special lectures at intervals during the year. A course of study covering only two years was outlined as filling the requirements for the degree of Bachelor of Law, but at the same time the committee recommended that the course be lengthened in a short time to cover three years' work. A postgraduate degree of Master of Law was set up, but no requirements were outlined at that time for it. The Board of Trustees accepted without argument the suggestions made by its committee, and the plan which it submitted was put into effect.[14]

While the details of the Law School were being worked out, a proposal was made that the Transylvania University Law School, which had been revived after long years of suspension, unite with the proposed State University College of Law. The combined departments would then be under the control of the state institution. By late July, 1908, according to the newspapers of Lexington, a general agreement had been reached concerning the merger, and it only remained for representatives of Transylvania and the State University to agree on details. A few days later, when the Board of Curators of Transylvania met, it was evident that opponents of the proposed union had been at work. Alumni and friends of the Transylvania Law School, as well as stu-

[14] *Ibid.*, June 2, 3, 1908.

dents, expressed their opposition to any arrangement which would cause the disappearance of their institution, and the curators rejected the proposed merger.

At its regular June meeting the Board of Trustees accepted an invitation to meet a few days later in Louisville with officers of the three medical colleges located in that city for the consideration of an offer made by these institutions to turn themselves and their property over to the university, which could then establish and operate a College of Medicine in the Falls City. The invitation and the offer were doubtless prompted by action taken by the American Medical Association and the State Medical Board of Missouri ordering the three Louisville schools to consolidate. When the meeting was held, on June 9, the Louisville and Hospital Medical College, which was the Medical Department of Central University, and the Kentucky School of Medicine agreed "to unite and discontinue said two schools, if the State University of Kentucky will make the two united schools the Medical Department of said University, and locate in the city of Louisville." Certain conditions were mentioned, of which the chief was that the owners of the two schools should receive $45,000 in five annual installments for giving up their institutions. The Board of Trustees of the University of Louisville was reluctant to give up its Medical School, but it invited the State University to work out some plan whereby both universities could operate the Medical School, which would remain in Louisville. In answer to these two proposals the trustees of the state institution resolved that they could not consider either, but that they would be willing to listen further to "a united proposition from all the medical schools of Louisville."[15]

Eight days later the board reassembled in Lexington once again to consider the proposals which had been made by the Louisville medical schools. Arguments were heard on both

[15] *Ibid.*, June 9, 1908.

sides of the question from doctors and others who cared to make statements, after which the board in executive session agreed to postpone a decision until the regular meeting in December. At that meeting a report on the question was received and filed, and no action was taken. On later occasions the subject was brought up, but the trustees never saw fit to approve any of the suggestions. Consequently, the provision of the legislative act of March, 1908, relating to the establishment of a Medical School in connection with the State University was never carried out.

During the summer of 1908 the framework of the university was reorganized to conform to its new status. Six major instructional divisions were established: the Colleges of Arts and Science, Agriculture, Civil Engineering, Mechanical and Electrical Engineering, Mining Engineering (soon to become the College of Mines and Metallurgy) , and Law. The Academy remained in operation, and President Patterson appeared to consider it as important as ever. A Graduate School was organized in 1912, after Patterson's resignation.

The conversion of the Agricultural and Mechanical College into a university brought no drastic changes in the faculty or in the old, established departments. The death of John Henry Neville in 1908 necessitated a slight rearrangement of personnel, which placed James G. White in the office of Vice-President of the university, Arthur M. Miller in the deanship of the College of Arts and Science, and T. T. Jones in the position of acting professor of Latin and Greek. A few newcomers in the College of Arts and Science, such as James Edward Tuthill, assistant professor of history and political economy, and Ezra L Gillis, assistant in education, served the university for approximately the next forty years.

The College of Agriculture, under Dean Mathews, was able to move into its new building, but few other changes were evident. The proposed consolidation of agriculture and the Experiment Station had not materialized by the time Patterson gave up control of the university. The three engineering departments were now three engineering colleges, each with its own Dean, and each pursuing its separate way. In every case personnel and courses were virtually the same as they had been before 1908. The College of Law, housed temporarily in the Education Building (now Frazee Hall), started with an enrollment of approximately thirty students. One session was enough to convince everyone concerned that a two-year law course was inadequate, and beginning in 1909 a three-year course was offered by the university. Another major division was added briefly to the university in 1909, when the Teachers College, under Dean Louis F. Snow, came into existence. In 1911 this college was abolished, and education became again a department in the College of Arts and Science.

Patterson found some causes for discontent in the condition of the university in 1908 and immediately afterward. He was disturbed, though he expressed confidence in ultimate victory, because a constitutional question, raised concerning the appropriation made by the legislature in 1908, had caused the state auditor to refuse to make payment of the additional funds to the institution until the Court of Appeals had ruled on the case. He was somewhat disgruntled because elimination of the Normal Department had caused a drop in the total enrollment of the university, a situation in which he could see the sinister influence of the normal schools at work. Finally, he was greatly dissatisfied with the new office of comptroller, as might have been expected. Patterson objected to the Dean of the Law School holding the powerful office of comptroller, stating that the duties of the two positions were "wholly incongruous." His request for the abolition of the office of comptroller probably stemmed from his distaste for any authority which might challenge his own. Speaking of the positions of comptroller and Dean of the Law College, he indulged in an ill-natured outburst: "They are wholly distinct and involve no necessary relationship, but in the discharge of the duties of Comptroller, opportunities for the exercise of an influence wholly incompatible with his obligations as a member of the faculty are afforded and the temptation is too strong to resist using them. I may add that the University has not yet reached the point where its wealth or its dignity require either the creation or the maintenance of supernumeraries and sinecures. Even in wealthy corporations these are regarded as excrescences and are indicative of disease rather than of a normal condition."[16]

On the whole, however, the President was well pleased with the course of events. In December, 1908, the Court of Appeals decided that the appropriation in question was constitutional, and the funds were made available to the university. New staff members were employed, long-needed salary adjustments were made, and plans for new buildings were considered and in some cases put into effect. The State University was a reality, and Patterson felt that perhaps the road might be easier to travel in the future.

[16] *Ibid.*, December 8, 1908.

Chapter Twelve

The Close of Patterson's Reign

THE TRANSFORMATION OF THE COLLEGE INTO THE State University constituted a fitting climax to James K. Patterson's long years of service to the institution; and having placed the new organization in operation, he began to think seriously of retirement. And yet, despite his advanced age, he was not willing to sever entirely his connection with the university, nor was he willing to rely on the Board of Trustees to choose unaided a successor or even to fix his own status for the future. So strong was his feeling of possessiveness toward the school that instead of submitting outright his resignation, he first outlined his own conditions of retirement, and not until they were accepted did he actually resign. One may well wonder what might have happened if the board had rejected his terms. Perhaps he could have held on doggedly until senility or death overtook him, or perhaps the trustees eventually would have come to the point of dismissing him. Fortunately, the problem failed to arise, for at the moment his grip was firm, the board agreeable, and his exit calm and peaceful.

A Frankfort newspaper stated in March, 1909, that Patterson had visited the Kentucky capital to consult with Governor Augustus E. Willson and Judge Barker, both members of the State University Board of Trustees, relative to his resignation from the post he had held for forty years. Since all parties to the conference refused to discuss the matter, the report could not be substantiated. Nevertheless, the rumor persisted and doubtless contributed to a decision on the part of Patterson's friends to stage in his honor during commencement week a grand celebration to mark the end of his fortieth year as President of the university. Judge James H. Mulligan presided over the exercises, which were held on June 1 in a large tent erected for the purpose in front of the Administration Building. The Governor, members of the Board of Trustees, faculty members, alumni, students, and friends joined to make it an impressive occasion as well as a warm tribute to the ancient warrior. As expressed in one written account of the affair, "The event was unique in the history of Kentucky, and was one of the greatest honors ever conferred upon any man in any walk of life in the State."[1]

The next day, at the regular meeting of the Board of Trustees, Patterson announced his intention to resign as soon as a competent successor could be chosen.[2] He suggested that a committee be established to search for a suitable person, who, he said, should be "abler than myself, well educated," and capable of developing all departments of the school without showing special favor to any. He expanded his ideas regarding the qualifications of his successor in words which seemed to suggest that the trustees seek a man as nearly like himself as possible:

> I should like my successor to be a man of proved executive and administrative ability, of good personal presence, prolific in thought and facile in expression, able to defend the institution from whatever point assailed and able to take aggressive measures in its behalf, without unnecessarily ruffling the susceptibilities of those who oppose. The President of the State University should be able, when occasion requires, to address and to interest educational associations, commercial clubs, and other bodies interested in the educational and material development of the Commonwealth in behalf of the University, asserting and maintaining its leadership in all matters relating to the intellectual uplift and culture of its citizens. He should, moreover, be a man of high moral character,

1 *Southern School Journal* (Louisville, 1889-1927), XX (July, 1909), 22-23.
2 State University, Minutes of the Board of Trustees, June 2, 1909.

> with a reverent attitude towards things sacred and divine, not necessarily a churchman, but in sympathy with the religious beliefs and aspirations of Christianity.

Realizing that the task of finding a person who answered these qualifications would require "time and patience and discretion and insight," Patterson urged the board to take no hasty action. He suggested that after he had presented his own resignation the school could be administered by "a good safe Vice-President," to whom Patterson would be glad to give aid and counsel.

The President expressed a wish to retain some connection with the school after his retirement, stating as his reason for this request his intention of making the university his heir. He took credit for obtaining from Andrew Carnegie the money used to erect the new library building, which, he said, "I am now ready to turn over to the institution." He then expressed his intention to leave to the university his own library, which he valued at nearly $10,000; a sum of money sufficient to erect on the campus "a commodious and handsome Chapel, capable of seating 1200 or 1500 persons," in memory of his only son; and an additional fund to be invested until the principal and accumulated interest would be adequate to "sustain certain professorships, fellowships and scholarships which shall bear my name in perpetuity." If allowed to retain an official connection with the school, he could be certain that his wishes would be "carried out in their integrity"; if the condition he requested should not be granted, he threatened that "as a matter of course" he would not make the school his heir but would "seek for a legatee elsewhere."

In regard to fixing his future relationship to the university, Patterson offered six conditions for the consideration of the board:

> 1. That the retiring President be allowed still to maintain a semi-official connection with the University,

through the honorary title of President Emeritus or some kindred designation.

2. That this carry with it the privilege of sitting with the Board of Trustees in their annual or semi-annual sessions and participating in their deliberations.

3. The privilege of sitting with the faculty and participating in their deliberations.

4. Recognition as adviser and auxiliary to the Vice-President and later to the incoming President, until he becomes familiar with the routine of business.

5. The privilege of representing the University at meetings of the National Associations, Kentucky Teachers Association, District Associations and county associations and high schools of the Commonwealth.

6. Generally, any service which might be of benefit to the University, but that these services be recognized as voluntarily given and that I be relieved concurrently therewith from personal obligation and responsibility. I may add that I should like the privilege of continued residence on the University grounds.

If any member of the board considered these proposals dangerous to the future of the university and unfair to Patterson's successor, he kept his own counsel. Apparently the only comment of any kind came from Judge Richard C. Stoll who, in the spirit of the previous day's celebration, delivered a brief eulogy on Patterson. Stating that the President had been the "benefactor and builder-up" of the institution, Stoll proclaimed flatly that "There is nothing that this University can do for President Patterson that President Patterson has not earned." Pointing out that the school owed to him its very existence, Stoll expressed his belief that Patterson had "earned a well deserved rest" and reiterated there was "nothing that this University ought not to do for him." Judge Barker then moved that the chair "appoint a Committee of five to recommend to this Board a successor to President Patterson, in case the President should tender his resignation . . . ; second, that they consider the conditions of retirement of President Patterson; third, that they consider and report on any other matters contained in the paper submitted by President Patterson." Upon passage of the motion the chairman appointed to the committee Judge Barker, Patterson, Stoll, Claude B. Terrell, and Tibbis Carpenter.

The board approved Patterson's recommendation that James G. White be made Vice-President of the university and that he be instructed to relieve the President of as much "of the drudgery of administration" as possible during the remainder of his tenure as head of the institution. An effort was made to keep at least a part of these proceedings secret, but a rumor that Patterson had resigned became "the talk of the city" of Lexington, where it was noted with surprise that Governor Willson was not a member of the committee to choose a new President. An air of secrecy surrounded subsequent negotiations; the next month, for example, after attending in Louisville a conference of the special committee, Patterson told a reporter that "the business under discussion . . . was not intended for publication," and he would give no hint of what had transpired.[3]

Two events of early summer of 1909 gave great satisfaction to Patterson and caused him finally to make up his mind to submit his formal resignation. In the first place he was gratified at the recognition granted to him in the form of a stipend by the Carnegie Foundation for the Advancement of Teaching, and his Scottish nature was doubtless pleased with the new source of income. Notice of the award came in a letter dated June 7, 1909, from Henry S. Pritchett, president of the foundation, informing Patterson that a "retiring allowance" of $2,940.00 a year had been voted to him in recognition of his long service as President of the Kentucky school. This allowance was to become available in the form of monthly checks when the recipient decided to discontinue active service. The second pleasing event was a decision of the special committee of the trustees, meeting in Louisville,

[3] Lexington *Leader,* June 4, July 2, 1909.

to grant Patterson's conditions of retirement. No doubt he was confident that the full Board of Trustees would accept the recommendations of its committee.

At the regular December meeting of the board[4] the committee report was adopted unanimously (Patterson not voting) and the university thereby agreed that upon the resignation of Patterson the following conditions would go into effect:

> First: To pay to President Patterson for and during the remainder of his natural life, sixty (60) per cent of the present salary which he now receives, which sixty (60) per cent amounts to Three Thousand ($3,000.00) Dollars per year; that this sum be payable in equal monthly installments.
>
> Second: That President Patterson be designated as President Emeritus of the University and shall continue a member of its faculty.
>
> Third: That he be permitted . . . to sit with the Board of Trustees in its annual and semi-annual sessions and that he be permitted to participate in the deliberations of the Board, but, without a vote.
>
> Fourth: That he be recognized as an adviser . . . to the Vice-President of the University until a new President is selected.
>
> Fifth: That he be given the privilege of representing the University at meetings of the National Associations, Kentucky Teachers Associations, District Associations, County Associations and High Schools of the Commonwealth and that when he does so represent the University, all of his expenses be paid but this privilege of representing the University shall not be exclusive and he shall not take precedence in such representation over the new President when he is elected should he be present at such Association.
>
> Sixth: That the University rent to President Patterson the house and premises which he now occupies for and during the remainder of his life for an annual rental of Two Hundred and Forty ($240.) Dollars per year.

[4] State University, Minutes of the Board of Trustees, December 14, 1909.

Having received the Carnegie grant, which with the stipend granted by the university gave him a larger annual income than he had ever had before, and having safely waited until the board committed itself, Patterson now submitted his resignation. In a prepared statement he reminded the trustees, as he had so often done in the later years of his administration, of the tribulations through which during the past forty years and more he had safely guided the school until it stood "an integral part of the Commonwealth, recognized by the constitution, head of the educational system of Kentucky, an honored member of the Association of American Colleges and Universities, and doing, according to its means, work equal to the best of them and superior to most of them." He requested that his resignation take effect at an opportune time between January 1 and July 1, 1910. He expressed gratitude for the conditions of his retirement, "conditions honorable and generous," and he invoked for the board the aid of the Almighty in selecting "a successor able, scholarly, skillful, wise in counsel, vigorous and tactful in administration, ruling with justice and with dignity, gentle, generous and manly, pure in morals and of incorruptible integrity."

In the discussion which followed Patterson's statement doubt was expressed that the resignation should be accepted at that time. The old gentleman insisted on action, however, and the board adopted Judge Barker's motion "that the Board accept the resignation of President Patterson under the terms and conditions as specified." Before adjourning the trustees resolved "that in the event there should be a vacancy in the office of President of this University . . . the Vice-President should assume the duties of President."

A special committee of the board, including Judge Barker, Cassius M. Clay, Jr., and John G. Crabbe, which had been appointed for the purpose, presented to Patterson a week later a response to his letter of resignation. The committee expressed regret that the time had come for the university to lose Patterson's "supervising oversight," gratitude for the work he had done for higher education, and warm personal affection "which originating in the intimacy of our official relations, has grown and deepened as the years have rolled on." Recalling the struggles which the school had experienced, the committee gave credit to the President for preserving it and causing it to grow in the face of adversity. Recognizing his learning, his patient toil, and his courage, the group expressed to him "the gratitude of the whole State for the noble work you have wrought." It is ironical, in the light of subsequent events, that Barker should have helped draft this communication which included this shortsighted statement: "We rejoice, however, that while we lose your services as President we will still have you with us as President Emeritus and as a member of the Board of Trustees, and that we may in the future still draw upon that fountain of wisdom and experience that has been so potent for good in the past." Years later, when reminded of his part in drawing up this statement, Barker replied, "Oh, yes, I was a big fool in those days."[5]

Early in January, 1910, Patterson wrote to Governor Willson, requesting that his resignation take effect on January 15. He then settled his accounts with the business agent of the university and arranged after January 15 to receive his retirement allowance rather than his usual salary. He informed the Executive Committee at its next meeting, March 12, 1910, of his action, which was "ratified" by that group, and he afterward considered the date of this meeting as the beginning of his retirement. Actually, however, Governor Willson did not accept his resignation until June 16, 1910, after Patterson had written to remind him of his failure to act. In a laudatory letter the Governor explained that his reluctance to accept the resignation caused him to procrasti-

[5] "Testimony Heard by the Special Investigating Committee," I, 225-26.

nate and that he finally acted "because it is your interest and because your life long service to the University entitles you to have any request in my power granted." Stating that "It has been given to few men to be as nobly useful as you have been in your work for the University," Willson assured Patterson that "you carry with you in leaving that work . . . the earnest interest, enduring affection and respect and very best wishes of all the Commonwealth." Meanwhile, Vice-President White had been carrying part of the administrative load during the previous year, and he became acting President of the institution upon Patterson's retirement.

Full of years, blessed with the knowledge that he had done a difficult task well, and basking in the warmth of the praises uttered by his friends and co-workers, Patterson stood on the threshold of a future which could have brought to him serenity and further honors. The only disturbing factor for him was the knowledge that the Board of Trustees was not following his advice in the choice of his successor. If he had recognized the right of the board to choose whom they pleased, if he had recognized the right of his successor to conduct his own administration without interference from the President Emeritus, and if he had removed himself physically from the scene where once he had been the dominant personality, he could have finished the remaining dozen years of his life in peace. Instead, he remained on the campus, occupying the building which had been erected as the President's home (while his successor occupied quarters in the girls' dormitory), unwilling to go into actual retirement. Friction developed, both the new President and the old considered themselves aggrieved, and the feeling between these two men, who once had been close personal friends, became charged with bitter dislike.

The special committee established by the Board of Trustees early in June, 1909, to recommend a successor to Patterson held its first meeting June 30 in Louisville. After agreeing upon conditions of retirement for Patterson, the committee decided to request the aid of Dr. Pritchett of the Carnegie Foundation in finding a likely candidate. Patterson himself undertook to get in touch with leaders in education who might be interested in the position, and when the committee met again on November 23 at the Phoenix Hotel in Lexington, several names were discussed. The group adjourned without reaching a decision, and Judge Barker retired to his room. Claude Terrell, another member of the committee, later said that not approving the suggestions which had been made, he "looked over the field, and it occurred to me that Judge Barker . . . would make a good man for the place." Tibbis Carpenter agreed, and the two men went to Barker's room to get his reaction to their idea. Years afterward Barker recalled that he had said on that occasion, "Claude, you are either drunk or crazy, go to bed, you will feel better for it in the morning, I don't want the office."

The next day Dr. Pritchett, who had attended the meeting, delivered the principal address at the dedication of the new Carnegie Library. Sometime during the morning, Judge Barker approached Patterson, according to the latter, and stated that certain friends had suggested that he become the next President of the university. Barker in 1916 protested that this account was not true, but Patterson swore that it was "true to the very letter—before my God it is true to the very letter." Patterson recalled that he did not take seriously the suggestion of Barker's candidacy because he believed that the Judge himself, who "did not think himself qualified for the position," did not take it seriously.[6]

During the next few weeks Barker's name was mentioned more and more often in connection with the presidency of the school. Somewhat disturbed by the turn of events, Pat-

[6] *Ibid.*, I, 198-99, 229-30, II, 77-78.

terson apparently expressed to Governor Willson a mild opposition to Barker's candidacy. The Governor replied that "When Judge Barker's name was first presented to me, I did not take to it because I did not wish to lose him from the Court of Appeals, and because I was thinking of a man of great learning." Further consideration convinced him, however, that Barker would be a fortunate choice. Willson characterized him as a "very fine and manly man," mistakenly called him a graduate of the university, stated that he was universally respected, and expressed confidence that he would make a good executive. He added that a President need not teach, but if he should "it might be some lecture in some branch that did not require the profound scholastic learning." Waxing eloquent in his effort to convince Patterson, he continued:

> He is a strong figure, a manly man, a man of very fine literary accomplishments. His opinions are among the most scholarly and perfect English in the whole history of the Court. He is a man of impressive appearance and a great hearted man, which I think is one of the most important needs in a President. I have been wholly converted to the suggestion of his name, and hope that the more you think of it, the more you will be inclined to it. Of course I understand that you are his warm friend, and that if you should hesitate it would be on the ground of expecting one who was more explicitly a learned scholar, and some grounds of that kind. I believe it is a good experiment to try. I am very warmly [*sic*] for this trial.[7]

Replying to a second letter from the Governor, Patterson wrote that he had "been greatly perplexed by the candidacy of Judge Barker for the Presidency of the State University. Excepting yourself, there is no man within the limits of the Commonwealth whom I love more. He has been my lifelong friend and the relations between us have been peculiarly intimate and affectionate." Still, he declared, Barker

7 Augustus E. Willson to Patterson, January 7, 1910, in Patterson Papers.

did "not measure up to my ideal of the requirements for the Presidency of the State University." He pointed out that the Judge was not a graduate of any college or university, that he had attended State College "thirty-five or forty years ago," when he went no further than would in 1910 entitle him to membership in the sophomore class. Patterson added that Barker had had no experience in teaching or in the administration of a college and that "men who aspire to high positions in educational institutions" were usually well educated and had served a long apprenticeship in college or university administration.[8]

News of Barker's candidacy reached the Carnegie Foundation, which was considering a grant to the university for establishing a retirement fund for professors. Late in January, 1910, President Pritchett of the foundation wrote to Barker urging him not to accept the presidency of the university. Stating that he was impelled to make his request because of his interest in education in Kentucky, Pritchett explained that the state, "educationally far behind its sisters," needed to develop a school system with the university at its head. Educational leadership in that institution was needed, and "no man can furnish this leadership who had not had touch with education and the educational methods of the last fifteen years." He further begged Barker to prevail on the Board of Trustees to find a man "equipped by training and educational knowledge to lead the educational forces of the state."[9] Apparently at about the same time Pritchett expressed the same or similar ideas to Governor Willson.

On January 13, 1910, Patterson, Stoll, and Terrell, constituting a quorum of the special committee of the Board of Trustees, met in Frankfort and decided to recommend the choice of Judge Barker as the next President of the university. On February 3, at a called meeting of the board,

[8] Patterson to Willson, February 1, 1910 (copy), *ibid.*
[9] Henry S. Pritchett to Barker, January 26, 1910 (copy), *ibid.*

which Barker did not attend, Stoll reported that the decision had been unanimous, but at the point Patterson took the floor to correct him. Patterson said that at the special meeting he expressed his views "pretty freely," but that he did not oppose the decision to recommend Barker. Instead, he "entertained a sort of negative acquiescence," rather than "raise any factious opposition." Now, in a prepared statement which he read to the Board of Trustees, he intimated his opposition to Barker by giving in detail his views concerning the qualifications which the successful candidate for the presidency should have. Again he stressed among these qualifications education and experience in educational work. Finishing his paper, Patterson added that he had heard from the president of the Carnegie Foundation that if the trustees chose a man without a university education and administrative experience, the foundation would not be likely to place the university on its list of beneficiaries.

At the end of Patterson's remarks, C. M. Clay moved that Barker's name be stricken from the committee report and that the name of "Professor [William Benjamin] Smith of the [Tulane] University of Louisiana" be substituted for it. The motion received no second, and the chairman ordered a roll-call vote on the question of the adoption of the committee report. With the exception of Patterson, who abstained, the board voted unanimous approval of the report. Without a dissenting vote the board then elected Judge Barker as the next President of the university, and a committee of four was appointed to notify him of the action of the trustees. Patterson was made a member of that committee.[10]

When approached by this committee, Barker requested that formal notification be postponed until June, which gave him several months in which to consider acceptance of the post. Immediately after the February meeting, Patterson

10 State University, Minutes of the Board of Trustees, February 3, 1910.

sent to the President-elect the statement which he had made to the board concerning the qualifications of a good university head. Barker expressed his thanks for the material and added that "As the trustees gave me until June to conclude whether I would accept the presidency of the University or not, I will have ample time to reflect upon your views before I determine what I will do in the premises."[11] The trustees knew the grounds upon which Patterson opposed his old friend, and Barker himself said "President Patterson did not think that I ought to be President, that is a fact, and he told me so, and I agreed with him and told him, and I told the Board so. He was opposed to me, and he told me so frankly, that the kind of man that ought to be a great educator, and he knew and the Board knew that I was not an educator or never had been one." Barker therefore made up his mind to reject the offer, according to testimony which he gave in 1916, and made arrangements to form a partnership for the practice of law.[12]

Sometime between February and June, Patterson's attitude changed. Hywel Davies, a member of the Board of Trustees, ventured one day to persuade Patterson to withdraw his objection to Barker. According to his own version of the interview, Davies said, "Dr. Patterson, if you have one friend on that Board it is Judge Barker, and I want to be perfectly frank with you and say to you that I consider him your real friend,—your fool friend,—what I mean by that is this, he is a friend that never questions, never investigates, never takes time to consider any proposition that you submit him; it is enough for him that you submit it to command his firm and greatest support." If elevated to the presidency, Barker would continue to rely on Patterson's advice and judgment, and Patterson could therefore continue to guide and protect the institution. The most convincing argument

11 Barker to Patterson, February 11, 1910, in Patterson Papers.

12 "Testimony Heard by the Special Investigating Committee," I, 201-202.

proposed by Davies was that if the Judge was not elected there was a distinct possibility that either F. Paul Anderson, Dean of the College of Mechanical Engineering, or M. A. Scovell, Director of the Experiment Station, might be chosen to fill the position.[13]

Patterson's account of the events of this period did not conform with that of Davies or Barker, but he admitted that he had advised the Judge to accept the presidency because he "was afraid that in the event he declined to do so, that some other man, or I might say men," might be chosen. He refused to identify these possible candidates, even after Barker supplied the names of Anderson and Scovell. Barker declared that "President Patterson hated those two men worse than the devil hates holy water." The Judge insisted that Patterson had come to see him in Frankfort and that he had visited Patterson at the university, and that on both occasions the old educator had told him that it was his duty to accept the presidency. With some show of feeling Barker testified in 1916 that "James K. Patterson is alone responsible for my acceptance of this office."[14]

As the months passed without an official announcement regarding the filling of the vacancy, contradictory rumors spread over the state. On February 21, a news report stated that Barker had accepted the post; six days later the story was retracted. In May a special dispatch from Paintsville, Kentucky, to the Cincinnati *Enquirer* asserted that the Judge had decided not to accept the offer and would "so inform the University Trustees at their meeting to be held in Lexington, May 31." Twelve days later Barker formally notified the board of his acceptance.

On June 1, during the meeting of the trustees, Patterson announced that Barker was ready to come before the board and receive formal notification of his election.[15] "Thereupon

[13] *Ibid.*, II, 37-39.

[14] *Ibid.*, I, 195, 202, 203.

[15] State University, Minutes of the Board of Trustees, June 1, 1910.

the Board stood upon one side of the room; Judge Barker came into the room, and standing on the other side," listened to Patterson read a prepared statement which seems to have been written by him alone, although he professed to speak for the special committee which had been appointed to inform the new President of his election. In his statement Patterson stressed the importance of the office to which Barker had been chosen, "an office second in dignity and in importance and in far-reaching consequences to none in the Commonwealth," and he declared that the university was well organized on foundations which had been securely laid. He discussed some of the problems and duties which the new administration would face and urged that "economy and efficiency and integrity . . . be the guiding principles of action." In general terms he gave some fine advice on the proper management of the school. He spoke in complimentary fashion of his successor's intellect, his judicial mind, his knowledge of men and affairs, his business capacity, his sound morality, his courtesy, and his integrity, all of which he called "important qualities in administration." Finally, he offered congratulations, pledged the support of the Board of Trustees, and expressed a hope and belief "that with the aid of the Divine Providence, you will make good and upon your retirement leave the University on a higher level than it has yet attained, loved at home and respected abroad."

Barker then read a formal letter of acceptance, in which he requested permission to postpone assumption of the duties of office until January 1, 1911, the date of expiration of his term as appellate judge. He said he recognized the difficulties which he would face, especially the difficulty that would result from being Patterson's successor, "of being contrasted unfavorably with one so splendidly endowed both by nature and accomplishment for the place he filled so long and so well." He justified his acceptance of the position in these words: "I have, however, put aside my own fear of a want of ability to discharge the duties of the office, and rely rather upon my confidence in your superior judgment. If the Board of Trustees, composed as it is of the ablest men of the State, having only the welfare of the University at heart, and well knowing what my qualifications are, have elected me to the position of President, I feel that I am justified in accepting the place without regard to my own apprehension for a want of qualification." He further declared that he was "much comforted in the knowledge that we have not entirely lost the services, nor in any wise the deep interest and solicitude of our loved Ex-President, who under the blessing of God, will be with us for many years as emeritus President, and his supervising care and advice will be at our service in every time of need and trouble."

The new President promised that he would devote his full time and energies to the university and do his utmost to cause it to grow and prosper. He pledged himself to maintain the highest possible educational standards, to deal justly with students and faculty, to promote harmony, "to prescribe and enforce a wholesome discipline for the students, allowing them every rational liberty commensurate with their own welfare and that of the University," and to insist on diligence in study and high standards of morality on the part of the students. He intended to advertise the institution and make it more popular over the state and to develop the interest of the alumni. He promised to aid in advancing the common school system of Kentucky and to cultivate better relations between the university and the high and normal schools. Finally, he stated that he would endeavor to increase the income of the institution in order that it might "go forward in its great and noble educational work, and take its place in the very fore-front of the educational Institutions of the country."

In accordance with his wishes President Barker began his administration of the State University early in January, 1911.

The date on which the institution reopened after the Christmas holidays, January 3, should probably be considered the beginning of his term, although he did not actually occupy his office until six days later. On Thursday night, January 5, more than a hundred prominent persons, from Lexington and elsewhere, gathered at an elaborate banquet at the Phoenix Hotel to welcome Barker to the city and to his new position. He formally began fulfilling the duties of the post on Monday morning, January 9, when acting President White turned the administration over to him. No inaugural ceremonies took place at that time since it was considered desirable to postpone them until commencement week in June. Available information does not show that a formal inauguration was ever held.

Chapter Thirteen

Patterson's Achievement: A Sound University

THE UNIVERSITY WHICH JAMES K. PATTERSON TURNED over to his successor in 1910 was vastly different from the college over which he had assumed control forty-one years earlier, and the development of the institution was one of his favorite topics of discourse. Even before he gave up the office of President, he frequently took occasion to trace the events in the history of the school, and in his later years, whether merely indulging in reminiscence or militantly defending his rights under the terms of his retirement, the old gentleman liked to remind his hearers of the difficulties, the struggles, and the successes that the college had known. Nor did he minimize the role which he himself had played, and in truth the university was to a large degree what Patterson had made it. Progress had come slowly, but on the eve of his resignation the President could contemplate with a sense of satisfaction the physical plant, the faculty, and the student body of the university which he had built.

The most obvious fruits of the efforts which had gone into the development of the school were the buildings and grounds, which gave no impression of grandeur but were for the most part attractively practical. To the three structures on the campus when the college moved to its present location in 1882, fifteen new buildings had been added. All of them, except the Experiment Station Building located south of the main campus, had somewhat similar architectures that fitted harmoniously together. Except for unnecessary towers on some of them and for decorative trims of stone or terra cotta, all were characterized by a lack of ornateness.

The fact that they had in every case been erected with as small an expenditure of scarce funds as possible was not visible to the casual observer, though it probably contributed to the trouble and expense of keeping them in repair in later years.

The nerve center of the campus was the Administration Building, which once had housed virtually all the college activities and which in 1910 was still used to full advantage. The offices of the President, registrar, and business agent were located there, as were the local branch of the United States Weather Bureau and the Chapel "in which, each day, the students and the Faculty meet for worship, and in which are held public gatherings and such other meetings as bring together the entire student body."[1] The remaining space was occupied by classrooms. In outward appearance the structure had changed little since it was erected, except that the upper half of the tower had been eliminated and that certain instruments of the Weather Bureau could be seen on the roof. A tree-lined driveway, sometimes referred to as the President's Walk, connected it with the other two buildings which had been built by 1882, the Old Dormitory for boys (now White Hall) and the President's home.

North of the Administration Building stood the Gymnasium, later known as Barker Hall. Constructed of pressed brick and Bedford stone, it housed a varied assortment of activities. The first floor of the central part of the building contained the armory, lockers for women, and certain offices; the second, the Trustees' Room, a literary society hall for women, the Y.M.C.A. Hall, and offices; and the third, two halls for men's literary societies and the Alumni Hall. The right wing was used during bad weather as a drill room, and the left, two stories high, contained a swimming pool, baths, lockers, and the gymnasium proper, which was said to be "equipped with the best apparatus that could be procured."

[1] State University, *Catalogue,* 1910, p. 4.

The Education Building (Frazee Hall) stood a few feet northeast of the Gymnasium. Constructed of brick and stone in "the most approved style of modern school architecture," this building provided space for two departments, Education and Domestic Science. Across Euclid Avenue from the rest of the campus, Patterson Hall stood in a location made attractive by forest trees and a spacious lawn. The women living there enjoyed the comforts of steam heat, electric lights, "a wardrobe in every bed room, and thirteen bathrooms." Tennis courts, croquet grounds, and walks on both the front and rear lawns offered the young ladies tempting opportunities for exercise.

Three buildings stood south of the Administration Building, facing Limestone Street. First, and only a few feet away, the Old Experiment Station Building provided classrooms and laboratories for advanced work in chemistry. Agricultural Hall, located farther south, was constructed as a wing to a much larger building which never was erected. About a quarter of a mile from the main part of the campus, the Experiment Station Building (now Scovell Hall), with its large portico and columns differing in style from the remainder of the university buildings, presented an impressive appearance. Its architecture was said to be "colonial, adhering mainly to classic proportion and combinations."

Several structures were loosely grouped behind the Administration Building and the Old Experiment Station. The New Dormitory for boys later became Neville Hall. Mechanical Hall housed the shops, classrooms, laboratories, drawing rooms, and apparatus of the College of Mechanical and Electrical Engineering, which undertook to "give comprehensive training in the science of dynamic engineering." Science Hall (now Miller Hall), erected for the use of the Department of Natural Science, included on its third floor the College of Law. The Library, whose existence was "due to the munificence of that prince of benefactors, Andrew

Carnegie," stood between the Administration Building and the President's home. Fifty-six feet square and including only two stories in addition to a basement, the building was more than adequate to house the university's books in 1910, though it did not provide room for future expansion.

Two Mining Engineering buildings stood at right angles to one another a few yards south of the President's home. One was used for classrooms, for the State Geological Museum, and for offices of the State Inspector of Mines and Director of the Geological Survey; the other was devoted exclusively to laboratories, including "one of the largest mining laboratories in the country" and the chemical laboratory of the State Geological Survey. A short distance away, on "the highest point on the university campus," the Civil Engineering and Physics Building (now Pence Hall) provided about 40,000 square feet for offices, lecture rooms, and laboratories. A new Chemistry Building, located south of the Civil Engineering Building, was almost ready for occupancy when Patterson retired. Intended mainly for the use of the large classes in general chemistry, this structure was a wing of the larger Kastle Hall constructed later. The Observatory, housing an eight-inch telescope, stood in front of the Chemistry Building.

Other buildings on the campus included a frame dwelling used by the Commandant and a greenhouse. The Director of the Experiment Station lived in a large brick house on the farm belonging to the university. Other farm buildings included a dairy barn, a storage barn for crops, "and the usual buildings for the care of tools, the protection of stock, and the like." Northeast of the President's home the athletic field, surrounded by a board fence, was an unattractive feature of the campus scene. The famous lake on the low ground north of the Gymnasium no longer existed, having been drained at the insistence of municipal authorities who considered it a health menace.

Acting President White in 1910 directed a co-operative effort to determine the value of property belonging to the University. According to figures which he considered trustworthy, the value of buildings owned by the school was $550,000; grounds, $225,000; apparatus and machinery, $67,000; furniture and miscellanies, $33,900; library, $34,700; and livestock, $10,000. As expressed by White, "These figures show that beginning with nothing in 1878 when the A. & M. College was by legislative act detached from Kentucky (now Transylvania) University, the material wealth accumulated by President Patterson's administration and bequeathed by it to President Barker's, is in round numbers nine hundred and twenty thousand dollars. Compared with the wealth of some of the larger Universities, ours is small, but when we consider the fierce struggle for existence that President Patterson found it necessary to maintain for many years, we should feel proud of his success."[2]

More important than the buildings and grounds was the faculty of the university which Patterson turned over to his successor in 1910. Most of the higher positions on the teaching staff were held by men who had been at the university for long periods of time and were known as careful, and in many cases methodical, instructors. Aside from Patterson, only six of the faculty of more than sixty members held the Ph. D. degree. Making up this group were three members of the Department of Chemistry, Franklin E. Tuttle, Ralph N. Maxson, and Lloyd C. Daniels; Louis F. Snow, Dean of the Department of Education; Glanville Terrell, professor of Greek; and James Edward Tuthill, assistant professor of history and political economy. Joseph W. Pryor, professor of anatomy and physiology, held the M. D. degree. Some of the younger instructors and assistants were working toward advanced degrees, which they eventually earned. In the Experiment Station only the Director, M. A. Scovell, held

[2] State University, Minutes of the Board of Trustees, December 13, 1910.

the Ph. D. and Walter R. Pinnell, inspector in the Food Division, the M. D. degrees.

The College of Arts and Sciences, presided over by Dean Arthur M. Miller, included the following departments and instructors: Anatomy and Physiology, Dr. Pryor; Botany, Professor C. W. Mathews and Assistant Professor Alfred H. Gilbert; Chemistry, Tuttle, Maxson, Daniels, and Assistant Harry Essex; Domestic Science, Miss Isabella Marshall; English and Logic, Professor Alexander St. Clair McKenzie, Assistant Professor Edward F. Farquhar, and Fellow Assistant Leonard DeLong Wallace; Entomology and Zoology, Dean Miller and First Assistant Miss Sue D. McCann; Geology, Dean Miller and Miss McCann; Latin and Greek, Professors T. T. Jones and Glanville Terrell; History, Political Economy, and Sociology, Assistant Professor Tuthill and Assistant Clarence R. Egelhoff; Mathematics and Astronomy, Professor James G. White, Associate Professor Joseph M. Davis, Assistants Elijah L. Rees and H. H. Downing; Modern Languages, Professor Alfred C. Zembrod and Associate Professor Columbus R. Melcher; and Physics, Professor Merry L. Pence, Assistant Professor William S. Webb, and Assistant Robert H. Spahr. The College of Agriculture, under Dean Mathews, was divided into the Departments of Agronomy, conducted by Professors J. J. Hooper and George Roberts; Animal Husbandry, Professor Hooper and Instructor William D. Nicholls; Horticulture, Dean Mathews and Assistant Professor Gilbert; Agricultural Chemistry, Professors Tuttle and Maxson; Botany, Mathews and Gilbert; Entomology, Miss McCann; and Rural Engineering, Professor Walter E. Rowe and Assistant Professor Daniel V. Terrell.

Dean Rowe, Associate Professor William J. Carrel, and Assistant Professor Terrell conducted classes in the College of Civil Engineering. F. Paul Anderson, Director of the College of Mechanical and Electrical Engineering, was assisted by Professors Alexander M. Wilson and Leon K.

Frankel. The staff of the College of Mining Engineering included Dean Charles J. Norwood, Assistant Professor Harry D. Easton, and Instructors Ralph D. Quickel and Thomas J. Barr. Classes in the College of Law were taught by Dean William T. Lafferty and Professors Charles Kerr and Thomas E. Moore, and guest lecturers were included in the instructional program. Dean Snow, Associate Professor Cotton Noe, and Assistant Professor Ezra L Gillis offered courses in the Teachers College. First Lieutenant P. W. Corbusier was head of the Department of Military Science; "She Pat" and six assistants conducted classes in the Academy; W. W. H. Mustaine was Director of the Department of Physical Education; and Miss Elizabeth Shelby Kinkead still delivered lectures in English Literature.

Few changes had taken place in the personnel of the Experiment Station since 1908, except that more employees had been added. M. A. Scovell was still the Director, and the heads of the various divisions were Alfred M. Peter, Chemical Division; Henry E. Curtis, Fertilizer Division; Harrison Garman, Division of Entomology and Botany; William H. Scherffius, Agricultural Division; Robert M. Allen, Food Division; Job D. Turner, Feed Division; and Edwin S. Good, Division of Animal Husbandry.

The university still had no Graduate School, although for years advanced degrees had been given. Two routes were open to anyone who wished to earn a master's degree. He might do one year's residence work beyond the bachelor's degree at the institution, select one major and two minor studies, pass written examinations in these subjects, and present an acceptable thesis. The alternative was to earn the degree *in absentia*. In engineering advanced degrees were conferred on graduates of the university who after three years of professional employment presented a satisfactory thesis on a subject which had previously been agreed upon by the candidate and the Committee on Degrees. In other fields the candidate *in absentia* had for three years to engage in advanced work which altogether would be the equivalent of the resident work required for the degree, to pass written examinations, and to present an acceptable thesis. Theoretically, the degree of Doctor of Philosophy was offered, but the faculty throughout the Patterson regime rejected all applications for it.

One of the barriers to graduate work, and one of the shortcomings of the whole educational program of the school, was the lack of a good library. During most of Patterson's administration the school had no central library of any kind, and the various departments had their own collections of periodicals and books. The United States government in 1905 made the university an official depository and so began to present it with a growing accumulation of public documents and a tremendous storage problem. In his building program President Patterson was never able to allot funds for a library, nor was he able to provide in any way for the construction of such a building until 1906, when he obtained from his fellow Scot, Andrew Carnegie, a gift of $26,500 to be used for that purpose. The building was occupied late in 1909. The collection of books was woefully small, though Patterson reported with some evidence of pride to the trustees that "There are upon the shelves more than three thousand well selected volumes, representing many departments in literature, and science, with a tolerably liberal collection of the best writers in fiction. The object has been to supply material for historical and literary research, illustrative of the sources of civilization and the growth and development thereof."[3] Taking into consideration the collections of the departments and the Experiment Station as well as of the new central building, library facilities at the school were not adequate for the work of a university.

The development of the school to 1910 and the success of

[3] *Ibid.*, December 14, 1909.

its President must be measured in more than material gains and enlarged faculty. Patterson's policies, conservative though they were, provided educational opportunities for many Kentucky boys and girls who could not otherwise have aspired to schooling beyond that available in their own communities. The training which they received, not as professionalized as some may have desired, was nevertheless sound, and the graduates of the institution were generally successful, at least in their own communities. These graduates were not numerous, nor did they play a dominant role in the economic and political life of Kentucky, but most of them became respected business and professional men and farmers. Many won local success in their vocations and in politics, a few performed more important roles on a broader stage, and one achieved international fame as the foremost personage in his field of endeavor.

It is impossible to list all the graduates of the institution during the Patterson era who have been successful, just as it is impossible to measure the degree of success which each attained. From the beginning nearly every graduating class included individuals who later made their marks in some respect. The first graduate, William B. Munson, became a railroad president, financier, and businessman in Texas; his brother, Thomas V. Munson, who graduated in 1870, operated in the same state a successful nursery business, published the results of some of his researches, and received from France in 1888 the "Diploma and Decorations of the Legion of Honor (Chevalier du Merite Agricole)." Alfred M. Peter, class of 1880, son of the famous Dr. Robert Peter, was for many years outstanding in the work of the Experiment Station. His researches in soils introduced new lines of investigation in soil analysis which were of assistance to other agricultural chemists. Also notable for his study of soils was George Roberts, B. Ped., 1899, and M. S., 1901, who rose from an assistant chemist in the Experiment Station to Assistant Dean of the College of Agriculture, a post he held from 1919 to his retirement.

Perhaps the most prominent chemist who received his training at the Agricultural and Mechanical College was Joseph H. Kastle, who received the B. S. degree in 1884. From Kentucky he went to Johns Hopkins University for graduate study and was awarded the Ph. D. degree in 1888. Returning to his alma mater, "Little Joe" served as professor of chemistry until 1905, when he became Chief of the Division of Chemistry in the Hygienic Laboratory of the United States Public Health and Marine Hospital Service, Washington, D. C., with the rank of major in the army. Four years later he resigned his commission to accept a position as professor of chemistry at the University of Virginia, and in 1911 he returned to the State University of Kentucky as research professor of chemistry, a post he held until he became Dean of the College of Agriculture and Director of the Experiment Station at Kentucky. He was an excellent teacher and a tireless researcher. His studies of milk and water at the nation's capital were of great value to the public welfare, but "Probably his most important work was done with his associates on the enzymes and especially the oxidases, and in discovering the reversibility of enzymic action which established a new phase of biological activity of immense importance."[4]

Among the alumni who achieved success outside Kentucky were Mattison B. Jones of the class of 1894, who went from Tuttle, Kentucky, to California, where he became an outstanding lawyer, a prominent member of the Democratic party, and an unsuccessful candidate for the governorship of his adopted state in 1922; James W. Carnahan, a graduate of 1896, who helped write several textbooks and who became president of a publishing company, Lyons and Carnahan, in

[4] G. Davis Buckner, "Joseph H. Kastle," in *Letters: A Quarterly Magazine Published by the University of Kentucky* (Lexington, 1927-1932), II (1929), 38-41.

Chicago; and Henry Clay Anderson of Seven Guns, Kentucky, a member of the class of 1897, who rose from an instructor in mechanical engineering at the University of Michigan to Dean of its College of Engineering.

The class of 1900 is notable in that it seems to have included more than a proportionate share of graduates who achieved some degree of prominence. Among this group were at least three men who are outstanding. William C. MacCarty, B. S., did graduate work at Johns Hopkins University and in Germany and became in 1907 consulting physician and surgical pathologist at the Mayo Clinic, Rochester, Minnesota, and professor of pathology in the University of Minnesota Graduate School. An authority on cancer, he has published a large number of articles in medical and scientific journals. A classmate, James Hiram Graham, engineer, author, and financier, earned the B. C. E. degree in 1900 and was awarded the C. E. degree three years later. During the first World War he rose to the rank of colonel, worked in various capacities in supervising railway, dock, and road construction and repair, and was decorated by the governments of both France and the United States. After the war he served briefly on the Liquidation Commission, later became president of the Indian Refining Company, and in 1935 returned to his alma mater to become Dean of the College of Engineering. Shortly after the outbreak of the second World War he was called upon to serve as a technical advisor to the War Department. James G. Scrugham (B. M. E., 1900, M. E., 1906), went to the University of Nevada in 1903 as a professor of mechanical engineering and was elevated to a deanship in 1914. His expanding interests led him to become a newspaper publisher, mine operator, and politician. He served as Governor of Nevada from 1923 to 1927 and was elected to Congress in 1932. After ten years as a member of the House of Representatives he was elected to the Senate, where he served until his death in 1945.

The most distinguished alumnus of the period to 1910 was Thomas Hunt Morgan, a native of Lexington, who entered the Preparatory Department in 1880, emerged with the B. S. degree in 1886, received the M. S. degree two years later, and was awarded the LL. D. in 1916. After leaving the Agricultural and Mechanical College he attended Johns Hopkins University, which awarded him the Ph. D. degree in 1890. He became professor of biology at Bryn Mawr College in 1891, was called in 1914 to fill a new chair of experimental zoology at Columbia University, and in 1928 became Director of the William G. Kerckhoff Laboratories of the Biological Sciences at the California Institute of Technology. He found time to work and study in Europe, and he wrote or contributed to fourteen books and over three hundred articles. He achieved international fame as an experimental zoologist before he began devoting full attention to heredity, the field in which he won his greatest recognition. According to his biographer, "The great contribution of Dr. Morgan was his clarification of the laws and mechanics of heredity, and of the mutation of species. He and his associates were the first definitely to locate the genes."[5]

Morgan belonged to a large number of learned societies, and he received many honorary degrees from universities in Europe, Canada, and his native land. His greatest honor came in 1933 when he was awarded the Nobel Prize in Medicine "for his investigations concerning the eugenic functions of chromosomes." It is noteworthy that this was the first time that this particular honor had been bestowed upon a nonmedical scientist. In 1941 Dr. Morgan retired, only four years before his death. A bronze plaque in Lexington marks the birthplace of this celebrated scientist.

[5] Wendell H. Stephenson, "Thomas Hunt Morgan: Kentucky's Gift to Biological Science," in *Filson Club History Quarterly* (Louisville, 1926-), XX (1946), 97-106.

Not all the former students of the college who later became prominent in various fields remained at the institution long enough to receive degrees. Outstanding in this category is A. O. Stanley, who attended the school in 1886-1887. Stanley served his state as Governor and United States senator, and subsequently he was appointed to chairmanship of the International Joint Commission. Patterson must have had a kindly feeling toward another member of this group, Alexander Bonnyman, who like the President was a native of Scotland. Bonnyman studied engineering at the college and used his training to advantage in his later connections with several railroads and mining companies. In 1927 all his mining properties were consolidated under the name "Blue Diamond Coal Company, Incorporated," and he became president of the corporation, located at Knoxville, Tennessee. Bonnyman had received no degree from the university until 1950, when he was awarded the honorary degree of Doctor of Laws.

Although the influence of the university through its students, alumni, and Experiment Station was by 1910 reaching into nearly all parts of Kentucky, most of its enrollment still came from Lexington and the central portion of the state. The presence of students from other sections indicated that it was more than a local institution, however, and the legislatures after 1908 were more generous in supporting it than ever before. At about the time Patterson chose to retire, Kentucky was beginning to awaken to the social and economic needs of the modern age. Her railroad system was extensive and she soon began building public highways where turnpikes and dirt roads had once existed. Natural resources were being exploited at an increasing rate, and burley tobacco had become the most important agricultural crop, although unrest among tobacco farmers still prevailed because of dissatisfaction with marketing practices. Kentucky was more aware than ever of educational needs, and the state not only gave added assistance to the university and state colleges but also reorganized the public school system and enacted a compulsory school law. An era was coming to a close for Kentucky, and perhaps it was fitting that the man who had guided the university through that era should step aside.

Patterson had been successful as the President of the institution, although judgment about the extent of his success depends on the point of view of those who consider the question. The history of the school to 1910 is largely the story of Patterson's efforts to build the foundations of a university in the face of indifference to the need of a state-supported college, of active opposition on the part of denominational colleges, and of unwillingness of legislatures to provide for the school appropriations comparable to those received by universities in neighboring states.

Considering the failure of the state to provide funds for Transylvania before the Civil War and the opposition faced by every effort made in the legislature to extend financial assistance to the Agricultural and Mechanical College after 1878, it is doubtful that anyone could have surpassed Patterson in his efforts for the State College, at least until 1900. A less-determined man might have become discouraged; a man more in tune with popular sentiment might have tried to develop the "practical" courses until they overshadowed the traditional features of a broad and sound program of education. Patterson talked about the training offered by his college in agriculture and the mechanic arts, but in reality he was more concerned about sound instruction in Latin, Greek, metaphysics, political economy, chemistry, zoology, and other classical and scientific courses. When speaking in general terms to the Board of Trustees, he could outline a program which would result in a well-rounded institution where a desirable balance existed among arts and sciences, agriculture, engineering, and perhaps other fields. His specific recommendations, however, failed to follow his plan, perhaps mainly because of lack of money to carry out his larger scheme.

Though he may have been too cautious in some respects, Patterson and those who worked with him had built well, and when the state should decide to create a great university it had a solid foundation on which to build. Perhaps the school had depended at one time upon Patterson for its very existence, but under his care it had grown until no individual was necessary to it. The old order faded into the background. The Agricultural and Mechanical College became the State University. James K. Patterson resigned the presidency, thereby unwittingly giving up more authority than he intended to, and Henry Stites Barker took up the reins of administration. An epoch in the life of the institution had come to an end, a new era began, and the brightest years lay ahead.

Index